Panzer Leader

Panzer Leader

The Memoirs of an Armoured Car Commander, 1944–1945

Otto Henning

Translated by Geoffrey Brooks
Foreword by Charles Messenger

Frontline Books, London

First published in German in 2008 as *Als Panzer- und Spähtruppenführer in der Panzer-Lehr-Division 1943-1945.*

This English edition first published in 2013 by Frontline Books

an imprint of Pen & Sword Books Ltd,
47 Church Street, Barnsley, S. Yorkshire, S70 2AS
www.frontline-books.com

Copyright © Verlagshaus Würzburg GmbH & Co. KG
Flechsig Verlag, Beethovenstrasse 5 B
D-97080 Würzburg, Germany
www.verlagshaus.com
Translation copyright © Frontline Books, 2013
Foreword copyright © Charles Messenger, 2013

ISBN: 978-1-84832-691-0

CIP data records for this title are available from the British Library
For more information on our books, please visit
www.frontline-books.com, email info@frontline-books.com
or write to us at the above address.

Printed and bound by CPI Group (UK) Ltd, Croydon, CR0 4YY

Typeset and designed by M.A.T.S. Leigh-on-Sea, Essex 12/14 point Palatino

Contents

Contents

List of Plates

The author and his three comrades.
Recruit training at Stahnsdorf on the Sd.KFz 233.
On the way to live-fire training.
The author aboard an armoured car.
The author having completed training, Christmas 1943.
The author on sentry duty, Bruck an der Leitha.
The author's panzer reconnaissance troop.
The radio panzer in snow and slush at Bruck an der Leitha, March
     1944.
Morning in the field in Hungary.
The radio panzer crew at Raab.
Hungarian civilians admiring German vehicles, April 1944.
General Fritz Bayerlin and Captain von Fallois.
Lieutenant Vogs.
The author in Normandy.
Map of the invasion of Normandy, June 1944.
Rommel inspecting a crashed glider.
Sketch map of the failed counter-offensive by Panzer Lehr.
Wrecked British tanks at Villers-Bocage.
A battered scout car of No 3 Company.
Cleaning the gun of a Puma armoured car.
Certificate awarding the Panzer Combat Badge in Bronze to the
     author.
Certificate awarding the Panzer Combat Badge 25 Class in Bronze to
     the author.
Family photo taken during the author's last home leave of the war.
German Panther tank.
German grenadiers in the Ardennes offensive.
A German motorcyclist attempting to start his machine.
American soldiers taken prisoner by the Germans.

German wounded passing a US convoy.
Warrant Officer Keichel.
A German Jagdtiger abandoned at the end of the war.
US troops passing ruined buildings on their way into the Reich.
German PoWs.
The author wearing the suit he escaped from the French in.

Foreword

As a former armoured reconnaissance soldier, this book is of particular interest to me. This is all the more so because accounts by Second World War German recce men are rare. As a result, Otto Henning does provide fresh insights on the 1944–5 campaign in North-West Europe as seen through the eyes of one who fought with the Panzer Lehr Division. He was clearly a good soldier, and an intelligent one, who rose to become a patrol commander and was twice about to do officer training, but events prevented it from happening.

Otto Henning himself was born in Mecklenburg in the eastern part in Germany in 1924. A furniture maker by trade, he volunteered for the German Army in summer 1941, enabling him to avoid the six months' compulsory labour service with the Reichsarbeitdienst (State Labour Service) and also allowing him to choose which branch of the army he wanted to serve in. He opted for the Panzer arm and did his training at the depot of the 3rd Reconnaissance Battalion, which belonged to 21st Panzer Division, then part of the Deutsches Afrika Korps. Qualifying as a tank gunner, he arrived in North Africa in early March 1942. He became a despatch rider, taking part in Rommel's summer offensive and winning the Iron Cross 2nd Class. In August 1942 he was made a gunner in an Sd.Kfz 231 eight-wheeled armoured car. As such, he fought at El Alamein and took part in the subsequent long retreat into Tunisia. Granted home leave in April 1943 as a reward for good service, he was flown to Sicily and thence back to Germany, avoiding the final Axis surrender in North Africa.

Thus, by the time Henning joined the Panzer Lehr Division in early 1944, he was already a veteran, even though he was just 20 years old. As for the Panzer Lehr Division itself, it was officially numbered 130th Panzer Lehr Division and was not formed until late

1943, drawing the core of its strength from demonstration units at the Panzer training schools. It was initially based in eastern France, but then moved briefly to Hungary, incorporating 901st Infantry Lehr Regiment while it was there. It returned to France in May 1944, just in time for D-Day. Thereafter it was in the forefront of the fighting, taking part in the defence of Caen and then being very badly battered during the American break-out from St Lô in late July. It took part in the counter-attack at Mortain in early August, but most of what then remained of it did manage to escape the Falaise Pocket. Thereafter it fought in the Saarland before being withdrawn to be re-equipped and brought back up to strength. The Division then took part in the Ardennes counter-offensive of December 1944 as part of Sixth Panzer Army. After the failure of this it was moved up to Holland to counter the British and Canadian advance to the Rhine before being sent south to attempt to eradicate the American bridgehead over the river at Remagen. Finally, the remnants of Panzer Lehr, Henning among them, were trapped in the Ruhr pocket and forced to surrender in mid-April 1945.

Apart from being a fascinating account of how the Germans handled their armoured reconnaissance at low level, Henning's book is revealing in other ways. Throughout the North-West Europe campaign the Germans operated in a situation of air inferiority and Henning makes plain how conscious he and his fellows were of this. Indeed, the recce soldier's maxim of 'See and not be seen' took on a new aspect and more than once he describes moving literally from tree to tree to ensure that his vehicle was hidden from the ever-watchful eyes of Allied fighter-bomber pilots. While the Normandy bocage certainly favoured the defender, the closeness of the country made it very difficult to establish exactly what was happening on the ground. Indeed, Henning admits that the best information was obtained from the Allied propaganda radio station 'Soldatensender Calais', to which he frequently listened, as did, apparently, many German staff officers. There is, too, an intriguing description of the destruction wreaked by Michael Wittmann and his Tiger company against the British 7th Armoured Division's attempt to advance from the village of Villers Bocage, although Henning clearly did not realise who had perpetrated the deed.

Otto Henning portrays well the German retreat across France –

the chaos and demoralisation. This reinforces what a remarkable achievement it was for the German Army to recover as quickly as it did. As for the Ardennes, he considers that it was doomed from the start, simply because the terrain was not suitable for the mass use of armour, but hindsight may be playing its part here. While he does not give any indication of what he thought of his American and British opponents as soldiers, the sheer weight of firepower that the Americans were able to put down the moment they made contact with German troops does impress him. This is especially since, as the war drew to a close, the Germans suffered increasing ammunition shortages.

Yet, this book is not just about the fighting. It is also a very personal story. Henning tells of his leaves at home, making the point that by his last, in autumn 1944, he found he was missing the comradeship (in the German sense) of his unit, something which also affected him when he was a PoW. There are the girls he meets, many of them very brief encounters in railway carriages and billets. There are also intriguing insights on what it was like to be in German-occupied Warsaw, where he went for a Panzer NCOs course, and how the German troops got on with the Hungarians. He repeatedly notes, too, the generosity of the rural German communities in the Rhineland and Mosel.

What will, however, come as a surprise to some is Henning's description of his treatment as a prisoner of the Americans and then of the French. Packed worse than cattle onto trucks and deposited in camps with no shelter and hardly any food, it was a shock to Henning, especially when compared with his experience of how captured Americans had been treated. When he was handed over to the French, their soldiers who were outside the camp and nothing to do with it were not averse to taking pot shots at the German inmates.

The subject of the ill-treatment of German PoWs at the end of the war in Europe was first tackled by a Canadian, James Bacque. His book *Other Losses: An Investigation into the Mass Deaths of German Prisoners at the hands of the French and Americans after World War II* (Stoddart, Toronto, 1989) claimed that some million German PoWs died through ill treatment and neglect. Some have even gone so far as to assert that President Truman's administration purposely planned the deaths as part of the Morgenthau Plan, although the latter was actually designed to so emasculate Germany's industry that the country could never wage war again. It is certainly true that a significant number of German prisoners did die, but not because it was official policy. Rather it was that in mid-April 1945, with the advance into Germany continuing, the Allies had simply not got the logistical infrastructure in place to cope with the 325,000 prisoners from the Ruhr pocket and the many other thousands falling into their hands each day. There was, too, the horror resulting from the much publicised liberation of concentration camps such as Dachau. This undoubtedly caused many Americans to take the view that all Germans were bad Germans. Consequently, some of them, at least, took it out on their prisoners. As for the French, their attitude was coloured by the humiliation of four years of German occupation. None of these reasons are sufficient to remove what was a black mark on the part of the Western Allies, however.

Charles Messenger, 2013

Translator's Note

Whereas in British military practice the only rank below that of an NCO is 'Private' or 'Trooper' etc. depending on the branch, in German Army usage there were two levels equivalent to a trained soldier: Gefreiter (Private Soldier) and Obergefreiter (Private Soldier, senior grade, usually after two years' service). Whereas the holder of the latter rank could be given occasional power and duties which might resemble those of a British lance-corporal, the Obergefreiter was not an NCO.

The German Army had no lance-corporal rank. The lowest ranking NCO was an Unteroffizier (full Corporal). It should be noted that Unteroffizier is also the generic term for 'NCO' in German, i.e. any rank from Corporal to Warrant Officer I. The ascending ranks were Sergeant (Sergeant), Warrant Officer (WOII) up to Senior Warrant Officer (WOI). The latter rank would be held by the company sergeant-major and the holder was always known as the 'Spiess', this term being retained in the book wherever the author uses it.

The author abbreviates the term Aufklärungsabteilung (reconnaissance battalion) to 'AA' in the text and refers often to units such as AA3, AA33 and AA580 with which he was familiar in North Africa. 'Pz ALA' with which he served is 'Panzer Aufklärungslehrabteilung' (Panzer reconnaissance training battalion).

Otto Henning

Otto Henning was born on 4 February 1925 at Grevesmühlen/Mecklenburg. Following the death of his mother in September 1929, he and his sister were fostered out to a good family. He began school in April 1930. He entered the Jungvolk in 1934, and though enlisted into the Hitler Youth in 1939 was not active in it because all the local leaders had been called up.

On 1 April 1938 Henning had been apprenticed to a furniture maker in his home town, and qualified as a carpenter/joiner on 22 March 1941. In July 1941 he volunteered for a twelve-year enlistment with the Wehrmacht. This enabled him to avoid the compulsory six-month labour service (RAD) and also choose the branch in which he wished to serve, in his case the panzers.

In August 1941 he began his recruit training at Stahnsdorf/ Teltow. This depot was the home of AA3 (Aufklärungsabteilung 3, a reconnaissance battalion)/12th Panzer Division which was supplying troops for North Africa. At the end of his training Henning qualified as a panzer-gunner with this unit. His batch of trained soldiers went to Sicily with the battalion vehicles by train and from there he flew out to Tripoli by Ju 52 on 1 March 1942.

At the front, by virtue of having obtained a Class 3 driving licence he was made a VW Despatch Driver. On 19 July 1942 he was awarded the Iron Cross, 2nd Class. In August 1942 he applied for duty as a panzer-gunner and was crewed aboard an eight-wheel heavy armoured reconnaissance vehicle (Sd.Kfz 231) attached to AA580(mot)/21st Panzer Division.

On 7 April 1943, after a brief talk with his commanding officer on his devotion to duty and bravery, Henning was one of very few men at that time to be sent on home leave from Africa, and was promised a promotion from panzer-gunner to panzer-driver on his return. On 11 April 1943 he was flown out from Tunis by Ju 52 to Trapani in Sicily, from where he returned to Germany by train.

Author's Acknowledgements

When the German Reich capitulated in early May 1945, the guns fell silent. Though there was no more fighting nor bombing of German cities, desperate need and misery dictated for years the lives of the German people in the two zones into which Germany was divided.

When the guns fell silent I was living rough in a field with neither shelter nor facilities, known as the American PoW camp at Andernach on the Rhine. My wife-to-be was sixteen years old and fleeing from Falkenburg, Pomerania with her mother from the Red Army.

In the former DDR I had no contact with former comrades in arms or soldiers' organisations, and not until the political change in 1989 did I have the opportunity of establishing links with former colleagues in the Verband Deutsches Afrika Korps e.V. Above all my grandchildren encouraged me to write my war memoirs based on contemporary notes and photographs from my period in the military. These appeared initially in the magazine *Die Oase* ('The Oasis') periodically between 1999 and 2004 and subsequently in 2006 appeared in book form published by the Verlagshaus Würzburg GmbH & Co in two volumes:

Als Panzerschütze beim deutschen Afrika Korps 1941-1943
(A 17-year-old volunteer in 580 (Motorised) Reconnaissance Company)

Als Panzer- und Spähtruppführer in der Panzer-Lehr-Division 1943-1945
(With Panzer Reconnaissance Battalion (ALA) 130 in Hungary, Normandy and the Ardennes)

I would like to thank my sister Thea who developed all my many negatives for my memoirs. My thanks also go to my former comrades with Pz ALA 130 especially Heinz Helms of Rostock, Karl Witzorky, Albert Schwarz and Ernst Westerkamp. I would like to thank the publisher of the magazine *Die Oase*, Hans-Günther Stark, my comrades of the Panzer-Lehr-Division e.V. Karl Hoffmann, Maximilian Ziemke and Kurt Doscholel: the chairman of Panzer-Lehr- Battalion 94 e.V. Herrn Bernd Hillmann: Herrn Albrecht Homeyer for allowing publication of personal photos and documents of my former Company Commander, Friedrich von Homeyer. I give heartfelt thanks to Herrn Peter Hulansky who arranged for the contact to Verlagshaus Würzburg and supported me in the production of both volumes. Hearty thanks also go to Franz Kurowski who made available photographs and helped with details of the various movements of the Panzer Lehr Division. A very special word of thanks is due to my wife who kept things off my back during the compilation of the manuscripts.

Otto Henning
Rostock, April 2006.

Author's Foreword

Never once in his country's darkest hours did British Prime Minister Winston Churchill give up the idea of Britain's return to the European continent. After the defeat of France in 1940, Britain stood alone against the powerful war machine of the Axis Powers. Gradually, through determined resistance, Britain's position improved: the Battle of Britain was won, and with the help of the United States North Africa regained and the U-boats defeated in the North Atlantic. In the summer of 1941 Germany invaded the Soviet Union and in December that year the Japanese attack on Pearl Harbor brought the United States into the war. Thus did a Central European conflict develop into the Second World War before 1941 was out. The Allied headquarters in England had long planned the reconquest of France as a prelude to the ultimate defeat of Germany. This would require the cross-channel transportation of an army approaching four million men, 2.5 million tons of material and half a million vehicles of all kinds. The preparation forged ahead in an unparalleled scientific, technical and military effort. The requirement in ammunition, fuel and provisions for such an enormous invasion army, strong enough to fight its way deep into France once it arrived, could only be met with daily deliveries calculated in thousands of tons, and there was no prospect of capturing intact a port with the necessary capacity.

The shortest route was the Pas de Calais, but the ports of Calais, Dover and Folkestone were all too small. To the south-west lay the enticing Cotentin Peninsula, whose eastern shores offered a certain protection against the prevailing westerly winds, and was far less well defended than the area around Calais. It was also close enough to enable Allied aircraft to fly several missions daily.

Operation 'Overlord' was the greatest military deception in history. Everything, from captured carrier pigeons to espionage and the newest electronic equipment were so arranged as to convince Hitler that the landings in Normandy were a mere diversionary measure to cover the real invasion in the Pas de Calais. The Allies went to enormous lengths to point the Germans to the Pas de Calais. A phantom fleet of landing craft mock-ups lay at Dover, military camps were erected, the Calais area given more attention from their bombers than any other stretch of the coast. They also had a major advantage in having the German espionage network in Britain under their own control. The Pas de Calais ruse protected the real invasion theatre of Normandy perfectly. Hitler still suspected it was a diversion to cover the main thrust farther east when the struggle to hold Normandy was as good as lost.

The final talks about 'Overlord' took place at the SHAEF head-quarters on 8 February 1944. It was decided that the most important measure was a bridgehead between the rivers Vire and Orne. The directive, composed four days earlier, envisaged landings on the European continent in May and then, after securing suitable harbours along the Channel coast, the Allied force would advance along a broad front into the German Reich and totally destroy the Wehrmacht.

On the Allied side, US General Eisenhower was nominated supreme commander of the invasion forces while Rommel's opposite number in North Africa, Montgomery, would command the landings in the first phase and the combined British-American land forces consolidating the bridgeheads. There was no love lost between Eisenhower and Montgomery but the demarcation lines of command were clearly drawn and absolute agreement existed as to the joint intentions in the first ninety days.

On 15 May 1944 the historic conference was held at St Paul's School in London attended by King George VI, Churchill, Eisen-hower and all senior commanders. Eisenhower opened the session. Montgomery explained that his opposite number, Field Marshal Rommel, would attempt to prevent any incursion by Allied troops. He would attempt to frustrate the landings of Allied armour on the beaches by positioning his panzers well forward in order to meet the invasion force as it came ashore. That would be the military necessity.

On the night of 20 April 1944, 1,000 RAF bombers attacked railway installations in France and Belgium. That towns and villages would sustain serious losses in civilian casualties was accepted as collateral damage. In a US raid on Rouen on 24 April, 400 French civilians were killed and 700 injured.

Not until the end of 1943 was the man who matched the Allied commanders in imagination and understanding for the technical side of the war sent to France: at Hitler's request, Rommel inspected the 'Atlantic Wall' and was appalled at what he found. Rommel threw himself into the job of securing the coast. Six months later the number of mines laid had trebled, refined obstacles of his own design armed with explosive devices stood in the surf to repel seaborne invaders and sturdy stakes, known as 'Rommel's asparagus', had been planted on all flat surfaces along the coast and in the rearward area to hinder the landings of enemy troop gliders.

Field Marshal von Rundstedt, aristocrat and General Staff officer of the old school, viewed the 'Propaganda Wall' with disdain because he did not believe that a defensive battle on the beaches could be won. His idea was to let the Allied armies come ashore unopposed and then repeat his Blitzkrieg triumphs in Poland, France and Russia. He had not, of course, done all this against an enemy with supremacy in the air.

Rommel knew from bitter experience in Africa and Italy that the chances of success using classic, fast panzer thrusts were limited if the enemy controlled the skies. He therefore demanded that the panzer divisions should be stationed immediately behind the coast. Out of all this came a compromise. In Normandy, 21st Panzer Division occupied the region around Caen, but 12th SS Panzer Division Hitler Jugend and the powerful Panzer Lehr Division lay well back as far as Orléans and were, moreover, in the role of the OKW reserve, commanded from Führer HQ, a catastrophic error based on the especially strong belief 'it would be Calais'.

Looking farther back to 13 September 1937, on that day the French Army had begun its major autumn manoeuvres. Through the morning mists enveloping the Orne Estuary, landing craft appeared. Warships far offshore opened fire and bombers thundered overhead. The disembarked troops headed for Caen despite determined resistance. In the presence of the French and British War Ministers, the Chief of the French General Staff, senior military officers of both countries and accredited military attachés, 'the enemy' landed on the coast of Calvados which was, in the opinion of the French strategists, the most suitable section of the French coast for such an invasion. The German military planners do not seem to have taken this lesson to heart, for five years later in 1942, when Berlin gave some thought to where major Allied landings might take place, the Calvados coast attracted little attention.

The most important people of either side at the critical time in 1944 were the meteorologists. The Allies naturally desired clear summer weather with unlimited visibility for their aviators, and as little wind as possible. This was the hoped-for 5, 6 and 7 June when there would be a full moon for the airborne invasion and the tide would set at first light. At the beginning of June, however, an extensive low pressure system with showers, low cloud, rain and wind from the Atlantic covered Western Europe. The operation planned for 5 June was therefore called off, but on the morning of the same day Eisenhower was informed by his meteorologists that between the low pressure systems arriving from the west there was a small period of high pressure providing some improvement in the weather situation for 6 June. As a result, Eisenhower gave the order setting the gigantic machinery in unstoppable motion.

The senior German commanders in the West knew that in June there were only two periods when the moon, daybreak and the tides coincided to meet the requirement for an Allied invasion: between 5 and 7 June, and the 12 and 14. Without allowing this critical period to pass, they relied on the assurance of their meteorologists that 'this bad weather will last some days' to absent themselves from the headquarters or command posts.

- Field Marshal von Rundstedt, Commander-in-Chief West, prepared to make an inspection of the Normandy coastal defences with his son Lieutenant von Rundstedt on 5 June.
- Field Marshal Rommel, Commander-in-Chief Army Group B, left early on Sunday 4 June 1944 for Herrlingen near Ulm to celebrate his wife's birthday on 6 June, and planned to be in Berchtesgaden on the 7th in order to discuss with Hitler the operational guidelines for the panzer divisions.
- Admiral Krancke, Naval Commander-in-Chief West, travelled

to Bordeaux on Monday 5 June to begin a tour of inspection having advised von Rundstedt before leaving that 'patrol vessels cannot leave their bases because of rough seas'.

- Colonel General von Salmuth, Commander-in-Chief Fifteenth Army (Pas de Calais) was on a hunting trip in the Ardennes.
- Colonel General Dollmann, Commander-in-Chief Seventh Army (Normandy) was preparing for the following day's war games at Rennes (Brittany) on 5 June to which he had summoned all his divisional commanders.
- Lieutenant General Hellmich (243th Infantry Division/Cotentin Peninsula) and Lieutenant General Falley (91st Airlanding Division/Cotentin Peninsula) left on the evening of 5 June 1944 for the war games at Rennes.
- Lieutenant General Feuchtinger (Commanding-General 21st Panzer Division) left on 5 June 1944 for a pleasure trip to Paris with his chief of staff.

For years, historians, senior military men involved and researchers on both sides have reported the apparent impotence of the German meteorologists resulting from the lack of weather reports from distant areas. The German High Command therefore had no prior warning that the weather would change on the night of 6 June 1944. The German meteorologists themselves do not bear blame for this: they had nothing like the forecasting opportunities open to their Allied counterparts and so it is all the more astounding that they did eventually predict the change in the weather for the night of 5 June 1944.

The invasion of Normandy began at 00.15 hrs on Tuesday 6 June 1944 with the Allied landings codenamed Operation 'Neptune', when the first airborne troops parachuted down behind the coastal defences on the Cotentin Peninsula. At 03.30 hrs three divisions of paratroopers and heavy gliders landed in the dark to the rear of the coastal defences. At daybreak amphibious shipping put ashore eight regiments and 6,500 vehicles under the covering fire of five battleships, twenty-three cruisers and 105 destroyers.

The first casualties occurred in the heavy seas when landing craft overturned. Their occupants were abandoned because of the embargo on rescue operations. Amphibious tanks were not meant for use in the open sea. The idea was that they should swim ashore with a waterproof canvas superstructure but many Shermans sank. Countless tragedies occurred: gliders disappeared with all aboard in the swamps of the flood plains, numerous paratroopers were dragged under water by their heavy equipment and drowned. Finally, many small groups with men wounded, soaked or still distraught gathered together and set out to fulfil their objectives.

Eisenhower and Montgomery were agreed that each army should establish its own bridgehead in order to reduce as much as possible the inevitable confusion in the organisational area. Therefore the 'Neptune' invasion area was divided into:

- Utah Beach: eastern shore of the Cotentin Peninsula, 4th US Infantry Division.
- Omaha Beach: in the bay between Vierville and Colleville: 1st US Infantry Division.
- Gold, Juno and Sword Beaches from Bessin to the Orne Estuary: 50th British, 3rd Canadian and 3rd British, and 2nd Canadian Divisions respectively.

Along these sectors of beach all hell broke loose for the German defenders at daybreak. Carpet bombing flattened bunkers and gun emplacements. Wave after wave droned overhead, with four-engined heavy bombers above the cloud base and nimble two-engined Marauders cruising at low level. In between this the guns of the heavy naval units were ploughing up the earth.

The German defensive measures against the British troops in the Gold, Juno and Sword landings zones were ineffective. Towards evening the bridgehead extended up to six kilometres inland. 1st US Army had major problems because their landing beaches Omaha and Utah were not adjacent and Omaha beach could not be secured until mid-afternoon.

The Germans had only one and a half divisions in position to oppose eight Allied divisions with fourteen armoured battalions. At least one army Staff was working on the evening of 5 June, however. In the command bunker of LXXXIV Corps, part of Seventh Army at St Lô, and controlling the five divisions in the coastal reaches from the Cotentin Peninsula to the Orne Estuary,

General Erich Marcks had wanted to attend the war games at Rennes but his Staff was unhappy at the high level of enemy activity in the air after darkness fell.

At 01.11 hrs on 6 June the first telephone reports were received from the divisions regarding enemy airborne landings. Information was quickly obtained from prisoners of war that seventy-five per cent of the Anglo-American airborne units in southern England were involved, according to the information of corps intelligence officer. Marcks raised the alarm immediately with the Seventh Army Chief of Staff who informed Army Group B, Rommel's head-quarters. A short while later he added the alarming rider that the naval radar stations at Cherbourg were reporting a large number of unidentified ships in the Bay of Seine.

The lassitude which had long prevailed amongst the staff officers at Army Group B was now confirmed when they dismissed the reports of 'enemy paratroops' as 'only dummies fitted with pyro-technic devices'. The prisoners captured by 716th and 719th Infantry Divisions later supplied information voluntarily about their units, but this knowledge was not passed back forward and Army Group B decided not to rouse Rommel from slumber in Germany.

When the Allied landings began on 6 June, the German military commanders forgot all the instructions they had been given for the eventuality. The main aim had been to force the invaders back into the sea with strong panzer forces while the landings were actually going on. For this purpose, three panzer divisions were being held in readiness as OKW reserve. Towards midday at Führer HQ, the most pressing question was decided by Hitler: the three panzer divisions standing west of the Seine could now proceed to the Calvados coast. Because the conviction remained entrenched that the real invasion would fall in the Pas de Calais, the other panzer divisions remained in reserve.

At 02.01 hrs, 21st Panzer Division stood south of Caen with ninety-eight Mk IV panzers, motors running, awaiting the order to engage the enemy. At 08.00 hrs it received the order to destroy the enemy forces ashore east of the Orne. Once on the way, Panzer Regiment 22 was ordered instead to attack the main enemy force which had come ashore west of the river. This change of direction meant passing through Caen, which had been heavily bombed and was burning. Colonel von Oppeln had given the order to attack at 14.30 hrs. The panzers came up against a cordon of anti-tank guns which had been set up an hour before. The leading panzers were destroyed and the advance ground to a halt.

At the time the invasion began, 12th SS Panzer Division Hitler Jugend had completed training and was fully operational. It stood at Lisieux, about 30 kilometres from the coast. General of Panzer Troops Geyr von Schweppenburg moved it 50 kilometres farther back.

During the movement towards the front, Panzer Lehr Division received the order to join 21st Panzer Division at midday on 7 June for a joint attack to the north whose purpose was to throw the enemy back into the sea. Panzer Lehr Division lay in the Nougent-le-Retrou area between Le Mans and Chartres. It was commanded by Lieutenant General Bayerlein, Rommel's Chief of Staff in North Africa. It was the only 100 per cent armoured panzer division and was equipped with 260 panzers and 800 tracked and half-tracked vehicles. The Panzer Lehr Division alone was strong enough to have driven the invasion force into the sea, as General Guderian had told the divisional commander on a visit: 'Bayerlein, your goal is not the coast! Your goal is the sea!'

After waiting fifteen hours, at 17.00 hrs Panzer Lehr Division received orders to move forward. It had to cover 150 kilometres. Enemy bombers roamed the five routes of advance attacking crossroads, villages and towns while low level aircraft strafed vehicle columns. By 7 June, without having fought the enemy on the ground, Panzer Lehr Division had already lost 10 per cent of its vehicles.

III Flak Corps under General Pickert, whose role was to proceed immediately to the invasion front with his motorised forces as soon as the invasion began, was not informed that it had begun. Pickert went to Paris to personally obtain his orders from von Rundstedt. Meanwhile three flak regiments with numerous 8.8cm batteries waited inert at the Somme instead of being on the invasion coast where they were desperately needed. Not until the night of 8 June did they reach the front area. On the way the Corps lost 200 men dead to air attacks.

It is simply impossible to disabuse oneself of the impression that instructions were deliberately ignored, forces held back, and decisive orders never given. On the evening of 6 June 1944, von Rundstedt still held the view that this could not be the main invasion. Despite every pointer to the contrary, he remained convinced that the real invasion had to be somewhere else. Even Hitler thought that a second invasion had to follow to the north-east. He also blocked the withdrawal of 319 Infantry Division from the Channel Islands and prevented the flak brigade and panzer regiment there from being recalled.

On 7 June a Cossack patrol from 439 East Battalion on the Vire Estuary at Gefosse-Fontenay found a stranded US landing craft. In the papers discovered on the body of a dead US officer were detailed plans for the US V. and VII, and the British XXX Corps, with the listing of all daily objectives for the coming weeks. On 8 June 1944 at 01.00 hrs the Commanding-General, LXXXIV Corps was informed accordingly.

On 10 June the command post of Panzer Group West (General of Panzer Troops Geyr von Schweppenburg), who commanded the panzer divisions in Normandy, was attacked and destroyed by fighter-bombers. The panzer signals centre was totally destroyed, and the counter attack by all panzer units set for 11 June, and which had been promised would repel the Allies, did not take place.

On 13 June 1944 the aerial bombardment of southern England with the V-1 flying bomb began. This was an unmanned aircraft for indiscriminate attacks. It was 7.35 metres long and armed with a one-tonne warhead. Propulsion was by ramjet giving a speed of 640kms/hr. [Author states incorrectly it was a rocket. Tr.] Of the first ten fired, five blew up immediately after launch. Once the technical defects were overcome, fifty-five left the ramps on 15 June.

After the enemy attacks across the Cotentin Peninsula converged on Cherbourg as the decisive phase, on 17 June Hitler occupied the advanced Führer-HQ at Margival near Soissons and summoned von Rundstedt and Rommel with their Staffs to render detailed situation reports. While doing so, Rommel requested that the V-1 offensive be directed against the Allied armada, the Mulberry harbours and the southern English coast. Hitler rejected this idea as being 'alien to the purpose for which the V-weapons were built', the V-1 being intended to bomb Britain until it was 'ready for peace'.

General Eisenhower indicated Cherbourg as the goal and centre for the invasion in Normandy. 'If we do not capture Cherbourg quickly and the enemy brings us to a halt beforehand, it may then be that our invasion operation collapses.' Cherbourg fell on 28 June because unknown commanders at Führer-HQ succeeded in preventing Seventh Army on the peninsula being reinforced from elsewhere. An entire Army Group with two armies, including twenty-four divisions and five Luftwaffe field divisions, and a Panzer group with six panzer divisions, stood ready but idle in northern France, Belgium and Holland while the remnants of Seventh Army on Cotentin and at Tilly-Caen bled to death.

After Hitler turned down Rommel's suggestion that Seventh Army should fight its way through to Paris, Rommel concluded that defeat in Normandy, and as a corollary in all France, was near. By 1 July 1944 the Allies had shipped 920,000 men across the Channel to Normandy. These had been supplied with 586,000 tons of war material and 177,000 vehicles. With a total of thirty-one divisions, the Allies were far superior in numbers to the Germans on both sectors of the front.

On 1 July Field Marshal Keitel telephoned von Rundstedt to tell him that the Führer had forbidden him to yield an inch of territory. 'With that,' von Rundstedt replied, 'I am deprived of all my own initiative. I request to be relieved of command.'

'So what should we do?' Keitel asked.

'Sue for peace, you idiot!' Rundstedt told him.

Next morning Lieutenant Colonel Borgmann appeared at Rundstedt's HQ, gave him the Oak Leaves to his Knight's Cross and informed him that the Führer had granted his request. His successor would be Field Marshal von Kluge. The same day, the Commander-in-Chief, Panzer Troops West, General Geyr von Schweppenburg, was dismissed and replaced by the seasoned panzer strategist, General of Panzer Troops Heinrich Eberbach. 'I am next in line to go,' Rommel predicted. He was, but in another sense. On 15 July 1944 Rommel wrote to Hitler that he had lost 97,000 men, in a short while the enemy would strike across France, '. . . the unequal struggle is now inching towards its end. I must request that you draw the conclusions from the situation at once'.

Two days later, on 17 July 1944, Rommel's staff car was attacked by two enemy fighters near Vimoutiers. The driver, Warrant Officer Daniels, was hit in the shoulder, Rommel struck his head against the windshield and was thrown from the car. He landed on the roadway and sustained a fractured skull. His escorts, Captain Lang, Major Niehaus and Sergeant Holke were unharmed. They brought Rommel to the nearest village which by a strange coincidence was called St. Foy de Montgommery. The surgeons at the Luftwaffe field hospital at Bernay found numerous splinter wounds, a serious skull fracture and broken bones in the temple and cheek. These ruled him out of further operations in the western theatre of war.

By 30 July the Allies in Normandy had thirty fighting-strength infantry and thirteen armoured divisions together with special formations of artillery, anti-tank guns and engineers. To face these in the invasion zone the Germans had twenty infantry and eight panzer divisions: the greater part of the remainder had been destroyed in previous heavy fighting. Two German armies stood at readiness to the north-east of Normandy. They could have turned the tide long before. Whichever way one looks at it, this military decision to do nothing, together with the many other absurdities, remains the great mystery of the Western Front.

In connection with the attempt on the life of Adolf Hitler and the incomprehensible events on the invasion front, it is known that the conspirators and resistance were to be found predominantly in the highest positions in the staffs of Army Group B at La Guyon and the headquarters of the Commander-in-Chief West at St. Germain. Days previously they had received their sealed orders on how to react after the successful coup and receiving the codeword 'Valkyrie'. The Allies let the Germans know after 20 July that the murder of Hitler and the seizure of power by men ready to negotiate peace would have changed nothing whatever with regard to the Allied demand for 'unconditional surrender'.

On 25 July 1944, 2,500 medium and heavy bombers dropped 4,200 tons of bombs on the positions of the Panzer Lehr Division. The areas affected extended into the territory controlled by the neighbouring 13th and 15th Paratroop Regiments. The front line was reduced to a barren landscape over seven kilometres in length and three kilometres in depth, a sheer moonscape, and the forty panzer and artillery units in the immediate readiness positions were destroyed. This bombing spilled beyond the German targets to engulf spearhead units of the 9th and 30th US Infantry Divisions, and particularly the US 129th Infantry and 12th Artillery Regiments. Lieutenant-General McNair, inspector of US land forces and a personal friend of Eisenhower, was killed by a bomb which fell short. After this softening-up, 1,000 guns opened up on the German lines. Some 140,000 shells were fired while 400 fighter-bombers attacked anything which moved in the rear areas. When darkness fell the assault divisions of US VII Corps streamed through the wrecked Panzer Lehr Division positions into the open country beyond.

Rommel's prophecy came true at the end of July. At Avranches, at the western end of the front, the Americans broke through and General Patton's armour were into open country as Rommel had done four years earlier. Now the Germans were on the receiving end as the French had been before them. A materially-superior enemy, certain of victory and equipped with the best there was technically, and working in combination with his air force, hunted across the land and struck out ruthlessly wherever he found any organised defence being prepared. Everything on the Allied side was motorised and mechanised, while the Germans were short of petrol for their few remaining panzers.

On 28 July 1944 von Kluge passed to OKW a report from Lieutenant General Bayerlein that the Panzer Lehr Division had been wiped out and the enemy was pushing southwards from St. Gilles. Hitler now approved the transfer of troops from Fifteenth Army into the worst endangered spots in Normandy. The penny had finally dropped and now the action was taken which should have been done at the latest by 12 June when it became obvious that this was the invasion. In the meantime, Seventh Army had paid dearly for the enforced inactivity of Fifteenth Army.

Far from the battlefields Hitler played on his maps with divisions many of which existed only on paper. He decided to strike a powerful blow at the base of the Cotentin Peninsula and cut off the US troops streaming into France. Rocket-equipped RAF Hawker Typhoon fighter bombers made short work of the German panzers and the attack came to a bloody end.

At Falaise the encirclement caused a catastrophe for the Army in the West. Forty-five thousand men went into captivity or were killed. Hitler shuffled his field-marshals: Model relieved von Kluge, who in a parting letter appealed to his Führer to end the hopeless struggle, and then took his own life by poison on the journey to Germany. Hitler raged and ordered the defence of Paris, but a stand on the Seine never came about. Model finally succeeded in erecting a defensive line from the estuary of the Scheldt to the West Wall through Luxemburg and Alsace-Lorraine to the Swiss border. France, occupied by German troops since the summer of 1940, was back in the hands of the Allies, who now prepared for the assault on the German Reich itself.

The Führer and Supreme Commander of the Wehrmacht, Adolf Hitler, now faced the choice of accepting the Allied demand for unconditional surrender or keeping on fighting a desperate battle against hopeless odds. Despite the impending catastrophe, Hitler was not prepared to throw in his cards. Trusting in his intuition he decided to gamble everything on a final throw of the dice by making a surprise counter-attack in the West. On his orders OKW made preparations for an offensive in the Ardennes involving the remaining reserves. For this purpose important panzer divisions were withdrawn from the Eastern Front where later they would be sorely missed.

The Ardennes had only five US divisions along a 140-kilometre front. Hitler's plan had German troops advancing the 80 kilometres from the German front line to the Meuse river, crossing it, and after setting up bridgeheads, going a further 120 kilometres in order to capture the Belgian port of Antwerp, indispensable for Allied supplies. When Chief of the General Staff Heinz Guderian warned of the unjustifiable weakening of the Eastern Front, Hitler forbade any more such lectures. On 16 December 1944 the Germans embarked on their last great offensive of the Second World War. Some 240,000 troops and 500 panzers moved westwards through the wooded uplands of the Ardennes. The initial success of Operation 'Wacht am Rhein' appeared to justify Hitler's self-confidence. Many US units fled before the enormous enemy force. By 18 December German panzers had won back 30 kilometres of territory but after these initial successes the weather changed, the skies cleared and the Ardennes offensive collapsed under heavy US bomber raids and a counter-offensive. On 8 January 1945 Hitler approved the retreat of his troops, some of which were almost at the Meuse. This signalled the failure of the offensive.

On 28 January 1945 the Ardennes offensive was officially terminated. Although the offensive delayed the Allied invasion of the Reich by about five weeks, the use of the last reserves and the transfer of German divisions from the Eastern to the Western Front made possible an unexpectedly rapid and energetic advance by the Russian Army into the Reich.[1] One may therefore say with some justification that Hitler's surprise attack in the Ardennes was a causative factor in the erection of the 'Iron Curtain' on German soil.

At the centre of my memoir are the operations of the Panzer reconnaissance battalion of the Panzer-Lehr-Division as I experienced it. The fate of the battalion can be taken as an example for all German units opposing the Allied invasion and later in the Ardennes. The remnants of Panzer Lehr Division laid down their weapons on 15 April 1945 in the Ruhr around Altena-Iserlohn and accepted captivity.

---

1. From mid-January 1945 when the extent of the Soviet winter offensive on the Eastern Front became clear, large numbers of German troops were switched from the Western Front to the Eastern Front: the entire Sixth SS Panzer Army, ten panzer divisions, six infantry divisions, ten artillery corps, eight mortar brigades and significant parts of the Luftwaffe. Despite this watering down in the West, the exhausted remnants 'held the Western Allies at bay' at the German western border until early March. For this reason some Russian historians question whether this was just 'good soldiering' or more underhand dealings were involved. See Valenin Fallin: *Die Zweite Front – Die Interessenkonflikte der Anti-Hitler Koalition* (Knaur, 1997), pp 459–60. Tr.

Chapter One

Back to Stahnsdorf

After my return from North Africa, the second part of my military career began at my old Schlieffen training barracks, Stahnsdorf. Tired and at a low ebb after the long journey from Naples, we Afrikaners had now to report at once to the Company Office. It was mid-May 1943, the best time of year in Berlin. We were all veterans of the front, many of us recovered from wounds. NCOs could no longer give us the run-around as they had in our time as recruits there, and so we stood around grumbling and complaining in the office. The Spiess was not sure what he should do with us and decided that anybody who could prove he had an address to go to in Berlin would be given leave to check out of the barracks with the necessary ration coupons. The remainder were given quarters in the barracks. Thus peace and quiet was restored to the Company Office.

I went to the Götze family on the Alexander Platz. Their son with whom I had served as a recruit, had been taken PoW by the Americans in North Africa. Frau Götze had a small shop which sold nick-nacks and there was everywhere a peculiar clean, pleasant aroma. Next day back we went to the Company Office where the commander had had the great idea sending all Afrika Korps returnees on fourteen days' leave. This solved his Afrikaner problem and we set off hotfoot for the Stahnsdorf suburban train terminal. With leave pass in hand, one had to take the shortest route possible to remove oneself from the sight of Company despots, particularly in times of crisis.

Finally I stood on the doormat at my parents' house in Afrika Korps uniform. It was Whitsun and I had a wonderful leave in Mecklenburg rambling the Iserberg with four friends in the most fantastic spring weather. We quenched our thirst with cold beer in the Dorst tavern at Hamberge and were generally happy and

1

contented. Two days before our leave was up my father awoke me in bed with a telegram. 'You have to get up right away, you've been recalled!' I turned over and told him, 'I shall have a nice long lay-in before I go!'

'Don't you want to read it?'

'No, leave it on the bedside table, the war won't go away.' My father insisted I read it. Caramba, what was this? I read it twice over – ten days extension of leave, right there in black and white. This was certainly unexpected. I got dressed in uniform – I missed wearing the military belt at the waist, it gave you the feeling that it held the man together. My mother told me: 'Better you go. The neighbourhood women are already worked up that a young soldier like you has so much leave while fathers of families have been stuck in Russia for over a year with none.' Thus I was soon back at Schlieffen barracks.

The Stahnsdorf permanent staff did not know what they should do with us Afrika Korps men and so we were given leave from the barracks at the request of the Berliners. The leave pass always ran from seven in the morning to seven at night, and it was best not to be seen on the streets between these hours, for by day Berlin swarmed with field-gendarmes.

We lodged with Gerhard Rusch's parents, and in a flat in the Wedding district. The occupants had gone off to Oranienburg to escape the bombing and so we spent the night squatting in their flat, and lodging by day with the Rusch family. We four were Heinz Brünje from Wesermünde, Erwin Sigle from Stuttgart, Gerhard Rusch from Berlin and myself from Mecklenburg.

Every Saturday I went to Stahnsdorf to check that the barracks was still standing after the week's bombing. Should it not be we would have to find something useful to do with ourselves if we wanted ration coupons and pay. On my return one Saturday I found a girl talking to Frau Rusch in the kitchen. I introduced myself and then went into the living room where Gerhard greeted me with: 'That surprised you, didn't it?' It dawned on me only slowly that the girl had come to the Rusch house from Oranienburg on my account.

In the workshop at Sfax in Tunisia a colleague of the AA3 [3rd Panzer Reconnaissance Battalion] had given me the address of his female cousin in Oranienburg. She and I exchanged a couple of letters through the field post and now I had met her at the Rusch house. By coincidence the owners of the flat in which we were squatting were related to the girl and that was how she suddenly turned up in Frau Rusch's kitchen. It was some time before I pieced it all together and saw the connection. My God, how puzzled I was beforehand. Now I had to show willing and escort her back to Oranienburg on the suburban train. On the platform I saw a large number of very young SS men who wanted to get to Berlin. My leave pass was actually not valid for Oranienburg, only Greater Berlin, but I did not notice that until I was reading it more closely later.

We agreed to meet the following Sunday morning at the Oranienburg train station and now she headed purposefully to her parents' house with myself in tow. I realised this only when we got to her garden gate and it was too late, and I had no choice but to go in, where I was invited to dine. In the afternoon we all took a stroll through Oranienburg. On the way we passed a concentration camp. There were houses on one side of the street and a fence with watchtowers, manned by SS, on the other.

The girl's father told me that some Russian prisoners had broken out and raped women and even pregnant girls in the houses. When cornered the Russians put up no fight and were taken away for 'severe punishment'. The camp resounded to very loud music on Sundays. Through the fence I could see barrack huts and prisoners washing clothes. At the camp gate we saw a group of inmates in prison clothing being led out. They were in the charge of a civilian who carried a sort of elephant gun longer than he was. The terrible things that went on in that camp could not be seen through the fence, and I only heard about them after the war.

Principally because of my age and being a member of our quartet, relationships with a girl and her family were not really desirable at that time, and so the Oranienburg affair died a natural death. Not even the home-baked cakes the girl made, which tasted wonderful, could change my mind.

One day we were just about to enter the suburban train station when the door opened and there stood Lieutenant Kettler. Overjoyed and astonished we greeted our old company commander from North Africa. He was the last person we had expected to run across in Berlin. After the usual greetings what we wanted to know most of all was how our company had fared in the death struggle of the Afrika Korps in the final days in Tunisia. Unfortunately he alighted after a few stations, having only managed to describe how he had been brought out by an assault boat.

We laughed amongst ourselves about his fighting speech delivered to the Company on New Year's morning 1943. We would be receiving new weapons, he had proclaimed; the Tiger tank, already in Tunisia, was practically invulnerable and its 8.8cm gun made it far superior to all British and American tanks! We would destroy the enemy on all fronts in North Africa and arrive one day at the gates of Cairo and the banks of the Suez Canal – victorious, trusting in our leaders and the new weapons! That had been just six months ago and now here he was surfacing on the Berlin suburban railway.

My three companions were all aged twenty-one and thus three years older than I was. When we went to an inn at the weekends, dressed in our impressive Afrika Korps uniforms, we would march to the washroom in step one behind the other and return to our table the same way. We were now the last members of the Afrika Korps in Berlin, or at least that is how it seemed to us, and we got a kick from the way the girls looked at us. Now and again we would visit a tavern with a table telephone. Heinz always got the most calls because he was a blond Nordic youth. I was not in demand because I looked young and the women who frequented these taverns tended to be older than I. Otherwise there was not much else for us to do in Berlin, there were no dance halls but many air raid warnings. Once we found a tavern we really liked but upon our second visit all we found was a heap of rubble.

One day from our Berlin squat they sent me off to see if the barracks was still standing after an air raid. I usually looked it over from a distance but this particular day I showed my off-barracks permit to the gate sentry and wandered over to the swimming pool with a diving board to see if it was full – I was a certificated lifeguard with the DLRG (German Lifeguards Society) and a far superior swimmer to my colleagues. On the way back I ran into the Spiess who asked me where I had come from. I explained and he said,

'That's all over now, report at once to the Permanent Company Office!' and wrote my name in his little report book. I cursed, for now that he had my name the game was up, our dissolute life in Berlin was over, I had to report next day at 08.00 hrs.

Rather crestfallen and morose I went back to Wedding and informed my colleagues of our misfortune, but they were not too upset and agreed we should all report together and put an end to the loafing. Actually there had been some friction amongst us, for endless leave and doing nothing is ultimately intolerable.

At the Permanent Company Office we had to hand in our tropical uniforms and receive black panzer gear again. At the barracks I came across many old faces from Pz.AA 580 [580 Panzer Reconnaissance Battalion], Pz.AA 3 and Pz.AA 33 [33rd Panzer Reconnaissance Battalion] in North Africa who had come from the convalescent companies at Kleinmachnov [just outside Berlin]. A small troop of 'Old Afrikaners', including myself, was formed for convalescent leave to Fontainebleau near Paris under the leadership of a lieutenant of the former AA 33. Once we were all sitting excitedly in the Paris train a messenger came running up to recall all Pz.AA 580 men to barracks. In great annoyance we de-trained. Later I met some comrades from the Panzer Lehr Division in Paris who spoke of how wonderful they had found Fontainebleau.

About a fortnight later came notice of our posting as infantry to the Russian Front. In the Infantry Company office while waiting for orders a runner shouted out my name: I was to report at once to the company commander of the Permanent Company. The captain had my documents before him on the table. I had been selected as an auxiliary training instructor: would I like to be one? The Russian Front or training instructor in Germany – what choice did I have to make? I took my leave of my close friends, who would now head for Russia. I never saw any of them again. I heard from Gerhard Rusch's parents that he fell during the Ardennes campaign in late 1944.

I was to train recruits in weapons handling and the panzer. At the conclusion of the course we took an eight-wheeler Sd.Kfz 233 to Zielenzig military training grounds for live ammunition practice with the 7.5cm tank gun. The vehicle was loaded on a goods train at the Potsdam marshalling yard: the driver and I travelled for three days in a goods wagon to Zielenzig. The firing practice went off without complications and afterwards the training staff had Sunday leave. On the Friday afternoon, 23 July 1943, our senior instructor asked me, 'What is your problem, Henning? Don't you want home leave?'

'I would love it, Herr Leutnant, but my home is in Mecklenburg.'

'All I want is that you're back here Monday for duty.'

'Very good, Herr Leutnant, I shall check the railway connections to see if I can manage it.'

I got my leave pass and worked out my travel route. I took the Reichsbahn from Zielenzig to Frankfurt/Oder and then a train to Berlin for men on leave from the front. Saturday morning leaving Berlin Lehrter station for Schwerin found me sitting comfortably between two men from the front. The conductress opened the sliding door and asked, 'Any Sunday leave men here?' We all shook our heads and she went on her way. A thought struck me and I looked closely at my leave pass. The small print said, 'Only valid for 100 kilometres.'

'Oh shit,' I told the infantrymen in the compartment, 'I've just noticed that my weekend leave pass only lets me go a short distance.' This started up a conversation about where I was coming from and my destination.

'Main thing is not to get caught by the railway police,' they advised. I went hot and cold. After a while one of the infantrymen came back into the compartment and said, 'There's a patrol in the rear coach checking all soldiers.' Mama mia, this was bad news.

'Keep my place,' I said to the infantrymen, 'I'll make myself scarce in the corridors.' In the corridor I could see the patrol, three men with steel helmets and the blank shield on the chest. They looked frightening. The captain stood at the corridor door carefully looking at the documents. His two assistants, senior sergeants, let nobody pass unchecked. I turned away and climbed over all the luggage strewn through the corridor. The train slowed to make an unscheduled stop at a small station. I alighted, wandered slowly along the platform beside the train and reboarded at the rear. I went directly to my compartment where the infantrymen told me, 'Come in, they've already been.' Around midday Saturday I arrived at my home station.

I had to leave home for my unit at Zielenzig the following afternoon to get there for Monday morning. At midday on Sunday my mother said, 'Come out into the yard, there's a total eclipse of the sun.' It was a cloudless day but the sun was only a bright disc. Our poultry thought it was evening and were already roosting in the stables. The eclipse went on and on and finally we realised that smoke was darkening the sun and getting ever worse. We did wonder what the source of the fire could be but there had been no air raid alert and the fire brigade had not been called out.

About 16.00 hrs on Sunday 25 July 1943 my mother and sister accompanied me to the station. A railway official told me there would not be a train until perhaps 18.00 hrs. I obtained a docket to the effect from the station superintendent and returned home for a couple of hours. Finally at about 19.00 hrs a train came up from Hamburg-Lübeck bound for Bad Kleinen. It was full of refugees from Hamburg including a female cousin who had survived the big bombing raids there. She was a total mess, her hair matted, face and clothing sooty. Now we knew the cause. The eclipse of the sun was the smoke from the oil tanks in the port of Hamburg.

I went to Bad Kleinen but from there no scheduled connection to Berlin was running. I got another docket. Finally I arrived in Berlin on Monday morning. The Reichsbahn in the capital was total chaos. I got a third docket, for one never knew who would demand to see the evidence for my absence. Late that evening I got back to my unit. My lieutenant was overjoyed to see me. The Reichsbahn chaos caused by the big air raid on Hamburg was by now common knowledge and he waved away my three dockets.

We spent about another week at the training grounds practising with live ammunition. For our return to Potsdam the driver and I loaded the eight-wheeler on a Reichsbahn low-loader at Zielenzig, chocked the wheels and anchored the car with wire. The previous commodity carried in the goods truck allotted to us had been fertiliser, of which a thick layer remained. Lacking a broom we improvised seating by putting blankets on top of petrol drums. The two wagons were then coupled to a goods train and off we trundled.

In the night at Rummelsburg the train was rearranged by shunting. There was no advance notice of this procedure. A fierce jolt rolled us around the goods truck, the petrol drums worked loose and we finished up in the fertiliser dust with our belongings and blankets. Our eight-wheel scout car, hand-brake applied and chocked, tore free from its anchorage and came to rest with the leading wheels overhanging the buffers. Our furious complaint to the managers of the marshalling yard met with shrugs since they were all foreigners and alleged they spoke no German. They had deliberately shunted us so fast that damage was inevitable. Luckily the eight-wheeler had eight-wheel drive and was restored aboard the low loader without problem, but now we had to do the whole lashing down business again in the pale light of the marshalling yard. At Potsdam we unloaded the vehicle and began panzer training with new recruits. Slowly I found pleasure in the barracks yard in the midst of war.

I was sent to the Field NCOs' Training School for Panzer Troops at Rembertov near Warsaw from 1 September to 16 December 1943. Our platoon consisted of panzer reconnaissance men from the most diverse panzer divisions, principally from the Russian Front and also SS men. The barracks was a former Polish Army war academy. Our instructors were aged veterans of the front, some of whom had been in the 100,000-man Weimar Army and taught the corre-sponding military drill. Daily we would be divided alternately as group or platoon leaders and given responsibility for the scheduled activity that day. Practice alternated with theory. The exercises were preceded by sand-table tactical instruction and always used live ammunition. Panzer attacks were practised with panzer grenadiers riding on the vehicle and with flame throwers. In the school we were taught about the newest German and Soviet tanks. We had to wear a gas mask for three whole days, even sleep wearing it, only being allowed to remove it at mealtimes. The training staff kept a constant check on the filter to make sure it was not being tampered with to make breathing easier. Night shooting exercises and sleeping in a bivouac on frosty terrain were intended to accustom us to the winter conditions in Russia. It was an extremely tough training routine but I gained a lot of military knowledge from it.

Rembertov lies east of the Vistula river and behind the Praga district of Warsaw. It had a large military training ground. Sunday was generally a free day for us and we could go into Warsaw using the suburban railway. Warsaw was not a healthy place to be for

German soldiers, many were murdered there. The Polish Resistance was keen on German weapons. Officers and men carrying a holstered pistol would be assaulted from behind, the belt cut through, at which their weapons would fall to the ground, and then they would be shot or stabbed in the back. If the soldier lived through this he was very, very lucky. Accordingly we had to go around in fours and carry our service pistols in our trouser pockets secured by the lanyard.

One Sunday afternoon at the soldiers' hostel with three colleagues we decided to wander the city. Some Blitzmädchen [female signals staff] joined us, which resulted in a lot of teasing and fooling around. At a crossroads we came across two Polish heavies wrestling. In a flash a large number of spectators assembled. The wrestlers worked their way towards us. At that the Blitzmädchen girls saw the danger and cried, 'Get your backs to the house wall and draw your pistols, this is an attack!' We panzer men had failed to understand the purpose of the charade but the girls' urging convinced us and we did as they said. When the wrestlers saw that they were going to be shot everything calmed down and the crowd dispersed. Then the girls explained to us how the Polish Resistance worked. They had been in Warsaw for some time and knew the dangers.

At the panzer school each course had a well-organised 'comrades evening' with good food, beer from the keg and entertainment by a female dance troupe. The Wehrmacht food source in Poland were the German collection centres for agricultural products in Polish villages. Trainees at the NCO's school were detached to the local Polish villages to protect German employees at the collection centres against Polish partisans. One day it was the turn of our platoon to enjoy this special assignment.

Eight of us armed with machine-pistols, handguns and two British-type hand grenades went to a large village on motorcycles. I was found quarters with a colleague in a Polish farmhouse, a room with two beds. We did nothing all day but show ourselves in the filthy village and get our boots muddy. The partisans hid out in the great forests. If they got active and robbed the collection centres or beat up the local mayor, a German police unit would arrive in a lorry. They were armed only with carbines, and so if they came under heavy partisan fire they would usually have to cut and run for it. Following talks they invited us to accompany them as reinforcements. To have veteran panzer men come along armed with machine-pistols was an important increase in their fighting strength. Personally I had no experience of fighting partisans, and as far as I know there had been none in North Africa, only commando raids by the British jeep-borne Long Range Desert Group which attacked German provisions stores, supply routes and airfields. We were sent out in our heavy scout cars to look for them, but these searches were always fruitless, and with the police unit in the Polish villages we were equally unsuccessful. The police never entered the forest with or without us. At night we could always hear enemy aircraft circling, probably dropping arms and equipment.

After a fortnight our relief arrived and we returned to barracks at Rembertov. I bought fifty eggs cheaply from the German collection centre to supplement the miserable fare in the barracks canteen. A lot of Polish girls worked there and in the kitchen and at midday at the serving counter several had been appointed to collect the rations coupons. I came to an arrangement with one of these girls called Paula. At midday I would go to her counter and when she received my coupons she would tell the girl dishing out the food, 'Twice!' and so I got a double helping. Polish girls went no further than friendly words, they were too scared of reprisals from their own people if the war ended in their favour. On the walls of the houses we found many slogans in Polish which were apparently aimed at us.

On 15 December 1943 our course ended with a well-organised revenge against our instructors for the hard time they had given us. We used training ammunition we had stolen. That night we placed explosive devices on their doorsteps and window ledges. Some of the ammunition misappropriated during field exercises was stowed in the ventilation duct in the ceiling above my bed. In previous such parting ceremonies the pyrotechnics had provoked a severe reaction from the instructors. Now they cracked, spattered and whizzed all night long in every corner of the barracks while the staff searched for the devices in every nook and cranny.

On Thursday 16 December 1943 I set off on leave carrying with me my 98k carbine, 9mm pistol and my entire wardrobe – panzer uniform, field grey combinations, fatigues, boots and shoes, rucksack, trunk and goods bought in the canteen. I had to report to the Schlieffen barracks on 28 December. That evening I arrived in Berlin. Because of a heavy air raid on the city, the train did not go into the Berlin-Warsaw terminal and I had to change to the suburban line and then walk with all my belongings to the Berlin-Lehrter station. The place was a shambles and a railway official told me that 'nothing at all will be leaving from here' and I should try at the Berlin-Stettin terminal. I trudged with my great pack through the night and found that there was an early departure to Stettin. The train had some broken windows which caused a terrible draught during the journey. The main thing was to get one stage closer to home, and by a roundabout route in bitterly cold December weather I got to my home town via Stettin, Rostock and Bad Kleinen.

For the first time since 1940 I was able to spend Christmas with my family, but spirits in this fifth Christmas of the war were low. The setbacks in Russia, at Stalingrad, the loss of North Africa and above all the many obituaries in the newspapers – 'Fallen for Führer, Folk and Fatherland' – were difficult to bear. Additionally we now had the increasingly heavy bombing raids on the so-called Home Front. I spent my furlough mostly with friends and acquaintances on convalescent leave, loafing during the day and boozing in some tavern in the evening. I liked being with my family, but such was the wretched atmosphere in my home town that when I left to rejoin my unit it was without much pain in the parting.

On Tuesday 28 December 1943 I reported my success at the NCOs course to my company commander at Stahnsdorf barracks. The last days of 1943 passed quietly. I celebrated New Year with colleagues and at midnight the streets were crowded. 'Comrades, drink up and enjoy the war – the peace will be ghastly!' was the watchword. I do not remember much after that, I learned afterwards that I had been helped back into barracks and next morning had a dreadful hangover.

Recruit training continued. I was attached to the panzer training section. Many of the recruits came from the Napolas [elite SS-run secondary schools]. One day a major wearing the Knight's Cross and his wife attended shooting practice. When I reported he waved the formalities aside immediately and told me that he had only come to take leave of his son before returning to the Eastern Front. Then he wished each one of us soldiers good luck.

I had experienced the first air raids on Berlin in 1941, but they were mere pinpricks to what we were seeing now. The British had begun what they called the Battle of Berlin in the autumn of 1943, and the American bomber squadrons came by day to turn Berlin into a lunar landscape. From Stahnsdorf we could still see the smoke a whole day after an attack. One day during an air raid alarm I was detailed to take some recruits to the loft of the barracks building for fire watch duty. It was a sunny day and through the roof hatches we could see the American bombers. Suddenly the whole squadron lost altitude and I ran with the recruits to the steps where we squeezed under the upper stairway. Happily their business was not with us that day. Once we went back to the parade ground a Ju 88 came in over the training grounds very low, probably intending to land at Gatow airfield. Suddenly the flak opened up and the aircraft fired off emergency flares and disappeared from our sight. The Berlin flak was now manned by veteran soldiers, schoolboy 'flak aides', works staff, German girls and Russian PoWs, and they fired at anything that flew.

What the German people had to endure with these bombing raids! The morale of Berliners, who stood up in the most remarkable way to these terrible raids, became ever more firmly consolidated. The Berliners gave free rein to their ironic humour, and as the heaps of rubble grew ever higher they said: 'Only one more year and Berlin will be a city of hills and dales!' Most people accepted it and got on with their daily lives as best they could, even accepting their sufferings from the endless raids as a 'fact of life'. Those bombed-out found means and ways to return to their ruined city. The German armaments industry proved equally as capable of resistance as the people.

I was with a colleague and two girls in Berlin when the preliminary air raid warning started up. We sprinted to the suburban railway station so as to get away from the centre of Berlin. At the Zoo station service was suspended for now it was a full alert and everybody had to get out and seek shelter in the big Zoo bunker. It was night and a great throng blocked the narrow entrance. The 10.5cm flak on the bunker roof began firing, and this caused panic. Women and girls screamed, and men were angry because people were smoking and they said that the enemy pilots could see it.

Our two girlfriends clung tightly to our arms and almost fell to their knees entering the bunker while above us the flak barked fiercely. Inside the bunker soldiers were separated from civilians and our girls were very distressed to be parted from us. After the All-clear we searched for each other in the darkness outside the bunker, and once reunited brought the girls to the suburban railway where we left them, since we had to return to barracks. In the train we got another surprise for the girls had been wearing angora wool pullovers and our black uniforms were covered with fluff. It took half the morning to get it off. We never came in close contact with the pullovers again.

About mid-January 1944 the company commander told me that all soldiers who had been in the Reich for some time had to be reassigned to the front. I could choose where I wanted to go, either France, Denmark, Italy, the Balkans or Russia. I had 24 hours to think it over and I should report to him next day. I had read in the newspapers that the Hermann Göring Panzer Division was being formed and wondered if I could get on the training staff there as well and so avoid the fighting front. Next day the company commander crushed my hopes by telling me that no more applications for the Hermann Göring were being considered. Instead he made an interesting suggestion. A new reconnaissance group was being set up at Nedlitz near Potsdam and he was being transferred there as company commander. I could go there with him. 'Well, Henning, what do you think of that?'

'Agreed, Herr Captain, I shall go with you to Nedlitz!'

Two days later it was all arranged and he handed me my transfer to No.2 Panzer Reconnaissance Company of Panzer Lehr Reconnaissance Battalion at Nedlitz. When I arrived, I should convey his best wishes to No. 2 Company's Spiess, Senior Warrant Officer Rudi Petschner.

I took a suburban train from Stahnsdorf to Potsdam with my pack. I also had a sealed A-4 sized envelope with my military documentation. Curious as to how I had been assessed at the NCO School and the training company at Stahnsdorf, I was keen on seeing the paperwork before being relieved of it at the new barracks. I bought some glue, found a seat with a good view over the room, ordered a beer and then carefully opened the envelope. My entire military

13

career was laid bare before me on the table, and I rummaged through the material. In my service record book I found many of those battles listed, from El Alamein to Tunisia, in which I had taken part and was impressed at what a veteran warrior I was. In itself this record would normally be enough, I imagined, for a soldier to spend the rest of his life in some quiet backwater resting on his laurels, but in Joseph Goebbels' total war that could not be allowed. I made a good job of gluing the envelope, and there was no trace of my unauthorised perusal of the contents. Then I took the bus to Hohenlohe barracks at Nedlitz.

In the snappy military manner I had been taught at NCO School I reported to Senior Warrant Officer Petschner in the No. 2 Company office and conveyed to him the salutations I had been asked to repeat. Petschner was pleased to have an Afrikaner before him, and mentioned that I would meet many men of my former Africa unit in my new Company. Petschner wore the German Cross in Gold and the Iron Cross 1st Class, and had led a reconnaissance troop in North Africa with AA3. He introduced me at once to the Company commander, Lieutenant Weinstein, and I was installed as commander of the radio panzer of Lieutenant Vogs' reconnaissance troop.

No. 2 Company consisted predominantly of Afrikaners and I ran across many old faces from my former company. In our troop of nine, five were Afrikaners. The remnants of the three reconnaissance battalions AA3, AA33 and AA 580 who had escaped capture in North Africa either by being on leave or wounded now formed the core of the new Panzer Lehr Reconnaissance battalion described below.

Lieutenant von Borris, who brought eighty men out of North Africa in a ferry boat in the final days on that continent, was adjutant to the commander, and Lieutenant Exner leader of 2. Company reconnaissance troop. My captain at Stahnsdorf who got me the transfer never made it to Nedlitz. He was drafted to the Russian Front at short notice and fell in action fourteen days later. Unfortunately I do not remember his name.

The battalion commander was Captain Gerd von Born-Fallois, a former Afrika Korps man, and the battalion consisted of the following companies:

Headquarters Company.

No. 1 Panzer Reconnaissance Company (eight-wheeled Puma armoured scout vehicles).

No. 2 Panzer Reconnaissance Company (half-track heavy armoured scout vehicles).

Nos. 3 and 4 Panzer Reconnaissance Companies (panzer grenadiers in light scout cars).

No. 5 (Heavy) Company (7.5cm gun platoon, light infantry gun platoon, anti-tank platoon and engineer platoon).

Supply Company.

The battalion was particularly suitable for reconnaissance and security work by virtue of its armoured vehicles and great fire power. In January 1944 it joined the Panzer Lehr Division and was given the number 130. The divisional commander was Lieutenant General Fritz Bayerlein, formerly Rommel's Chief of Staff and also a former Afrikaner.

No. 1 Company was equipped with the Sd.Kfz 234/2 Puma heavy armoured scout car armed with a 5cm KwK tank gun. In all, eight patrols each of two cars. No. 2 Company consisted of eight patrols with three half-track heavy armoured scout cars each. Each patrol had two Sd.Kfz 250/9 half-track armoured vehicles armed with a 2cm KwK-38 tank gun and an MG 42 machine gun in the turret, and an Sd.Kfz 250/3 half-track radio car fitted with an MG 42 and MG 34 machine guns plus a 100-Watt transmitter with a range of up to 200 kilometres. Each vehicle had a 'car to car' radio with throat microphone and a range of up to 10 kilometres. The company commander also had his own radio vehicle.

A patrol was made up of nine men, three to each vehicle. After losses to vehicles in action later operations were carried out with one Sd.Kfz 250/9 and one Sd.Kfz 250/3. The front armour was 14.5mm and the side armour 8mm. A speed of 60 kms/hr was available with the Maybach HL42417 motor giving 100 hp; with a full tank of 140 litres and depending on the terrain a radius of action of between 175 and 300 kilometres was possible. The vehicles had a complicated differential gear unit linked in to the steering and brakes. If the steering angle exceeded 15° the tracks that side braked as in a panzer. An intensive theoretical and practical training on the

15

military exercise grounds around Potsdam now began using the armoured vehicles and frequently involving the panzer grenadier companies.

On Friday 4 February 1944 in the battalion exercises I had my hands full as a novice commanding a radio vehicle. It was my birthday and I was twenty that day but there was naturally no thought of a celebration for once the exercise terminated the radio equipment had to be removed and the weapons and ancillary gear checked over. As the training approached its end I could see in the near future a train transport going somewhere.

On Tuesday 7 March 1944 Nos. 2 and 3 Companies were loaded up and the train left the goods yard towards 13.00 hrs. Nobody knew our destination but from the railway routing it looked like either Italy or Russia. The journey took us via Jüterbog, Dresden, Tetschen, Brünn and Vienna to Bruck an der Leitha. Two days later we unloaded the vehicles and proceeded to a camp with barrack huts. We spent a few quiet days at Bruck and exercised only with the scout cars. Our patrol went to the Neusiedler See. On one of these outings an old lady shouted at us in a scarcely comprehensible dialect: 'You're only here to invade Hungary!' Nobody could think of a suitable reply to this for Hungary was Germany's Axis ally and so why should we want to invade? Being very young and not much interested in politics, we turned our attention to the pretty girls in Bruck, among them many refugees who had been bombed out of the Rhineland. Some of my colleagues even went in small groups to Vienna, but unfortunately I was not amongst them.

On 18 March 1944 all leave was suddenly cancelled and we had to prepare our vehicles for an operation. We were going into Hungary. That night our two companies drove to the border at Nickeldorf not knowing whether Hungary would resist. Before daybreak next morning we crossed the frontier. During the night panzer grenadiers had occupied the border post without incident and now we pressed on for Budapest. Every half hour we had to report our position by radio. Around dawn numerous high-altitude bomber aircraft flew along our route of advance and then turned back. Later they came in lower but finding no opposition returned to their airfield.

A short distance past Raab we came to an Hungarian barracks. Two horses, unsettled by the rattle and clank of our tracks, appeared suddenly and galloped ahead of our vehicles. The two riders came running along the avenue at the rear in pursuit. Lieutenant Vogs, our patrol leader, had orders to reach Budapest as soon as possible and could not stop for the horses. At a crossroads they veered away and were lost to sight. Our column passed through Raab, Kamarom, Sütto and Darog to the north-west of Budapest. We were billeted in a village where the friendly reception of the inhabitants surprised us. In the evening young girls sang German songs. Next day to our regret we had to continue and the battalion arrived at the Valence Lake, forty-five kilometres south-west of Budapest.

On 28 March 1944, No. 2 Company occupied a school in the village of Nagytarcsa. Early next morning I went to a farmhouse and begged for water for washing. At once I was invited inside and served an abundant breakfast. The whole time I was there the friendly Hungarians provided me with this addition to my basic rations. Our only problem was language. One morning the farmer was absent and I asked in sign language where he was. The wife took me into the bedroom where the farmer was in bed wearing a large bandage around his head for toothache.

From Kistarcsa, a half-hour walk away, we took a suburban train to Budapest and spent our time either in a thermal spa or wandering the city. I was pleasantly surprised by its peaceful nature and beauty. We took the vehicles into Budapest frequently and so I got to know it well. I went on the Gellertberg, to the fish quays and crossed the Elizabeth and Chain bridges. It did one good to look down on the city from the heights, and on the Danube with its slender bridges which joined the river banks of the Pest and Buda. It was a moving experience to know this city with its friendly people in the grey routine of war.

On one of my strolls I got to know a young man and his fiancée. He spoke very good German and asked if he could show me their Parliament. The building impressed me as did the interior setting and the monuments near the Parliament and city, but I had to admit ignorance of Hungarian culture. Hardly had we arrived in Hungary than the Allied bombers came. The young man met up with a friend whose house had been bomb-damaged and I was left alone on the street with the fiancée who could speak a little German. She took me to her parents' house for lunch. Both spoke excellent German. The

Rath family were musicians who had played in Berlin and other German cities. The mother made me a hot and tasty meal. Upon my departure I was assured I should be welcome to visit again should I return to Buda. I was their guest a couple of times more but the war destroyed the contact between us.

On 12 and 13 April 1944 the entire battalion exercised with the panzers. At the end of a practice attack our young company commander led us over a large wet meadow. His radio car then sank down to its belly and he transferred into my radio panzer. The column leaders were warning urgently over the vehicle radios that the whole unit was liable to get stuck soon, but our Lieutenant Vogs ignored the advice and kept going. Watching over the side I could see our tracks sinking in ever deeper and pointed out this fact to him. We had gone hardly another ten metres when we also sank down to our belly with the tracks bogged down.

More than half of our vehicles were now stuck fast and so the whole exercise had to be called off. This incompetent and blasé manner of going into mock battle boded ill for the real thing. In the exchange of radio messages depraved voices complained about the shit that was being dished out here. Now began the laborious toil of getting the heavy armoured cars afloat again. Each one had to be dragged free by long tow-ropes.

On 29 April 1944 Lieutenant Vogs' patrol went for a week's convalescence at Balaton. The drive there was to be a radio training exercise. At Gödöllo on the first day I was made acting quarter-master and had to arrange billets for us all for the night. This was not difficult with the friendly Hungarians. I got myself quarters with a young mother who had a small daughter. Her husband was also a soldier and serving on the Russian Front, as she informed me in broken German. Next day very early we received a radio message to return to battalion at once. Our sojourn in Hungary had come to an end.

Chapter Two

May 1944: Normandy

On Friday 1 May 1944 we loaded our vehicles aboard trains at Gödöllo for the journey to France. I ran to my billet and took my leave of my hostess. With a few words and gestures she wished me all the best and waved me off. The wonderful time in Hungary with its likeable and cooperative people was over.

Wherever we went the talk now was of the Allied invasion of France. We Afrikaners knew in advance from bitter experience what we were to expect. Our Sd.Kfz 250/9 vehicles with the 2cm KwK cannon and MG 42 were spaced out along the train as anti-aircraft defence. The transporter train trundled out of Gödöllo and covered the last kilometres to the frontier. We took our wistful leave of a beautiful country and headed for an uncertain future. Those days in Hungary would linger long in our memories.

Via Bruck an der Leitha, our last stopping place before we had entered Hungary, the train passed through Austria into southern Germany and from there westwards to Nogent le Rotrou, about 150 kilometres south of Paris, where we detrained on 5 May 1944 and occupied a neighbouring village. All vehicles were hidden in barns and any movement by day forbidden. The powerful Panzer Lehr Division was transferred aboard seventy railway waggons to Le Mans and Chartes with negligible losses and dispersed in small numbers in woods and villages.

In mid-May Nos. 1 and 2 Company commanders toured the Normandy highways. Individual patrols remained in their barns, all exercises and troop movements were strictly prohibited. Each Company had a standby patrol, changed daily, at instant readiness to move on receipt of the codeword Blücher. On Whit Sunday 28 May 1944 our patrol celebrated Whitsun in a small abandoned farmhouse. In the afternoon in glorious May weather we set up table and chairs in the garden, spread a white table cloth and put the coffee service on it. Jochen Kobs and Günter Fleischer played lively melodies on the accordion. Our patrol leader Lieutenant Vogs was made an active officer. On 4 June 1944 General of Panzer Troops Cramer, last Commander-in-Chief of the German Afrika Korps, released from British captivity on the grounds of poor health, gave a speech to Nos 1. and 2. Companies.

Almost daily when the skies were clear we saw enormous enemy bomber formations heading inland to unload their cargo of death on some German city. We despaired, despondent and helpless, thinking of the women and children who had to endure it or die under it.

That 6 June 1944, Lieutenant Vogs' reconnaissance patrol was the No.2 Company standby. Towards 04.15 hrs we set out along a predetermined road to the Channel coast where enemy paratroopers had been reported. Accurate information about the enemy and his dropping zones was not supplied. At high speed Lieutenant Vogs' three half-tracks headed north. I occupied the second car, the radio panzer, and Corporal Kobs brought up the rear. Passing through a village my driver took a bend too quickly and we finished up in a ditch. This was a dangerous position, close to a house. It was almost daybreak and the other two vehicles would have to drag us clear. Vogs was irate at the delay and urged everybody to get on with it. We stepped up the pace and the tracks began to thud against the track cover causing the first rubber pads to fly off. Recovery work had to go slower, or wreck the vehicle.

The morning mist dispersed to reveal a day cloudy and cool. Back on the road we were now held up by a convoy of lorries. Lieutenant Vogs tried to pass it but the infantrymen were stubborn and we had to pull back repeatedly. Suddenly enemy aircraft appeared and attacked at a right angle to the road. They fired too high and only managed to hole the canvas covers of a few lorries. These pilots looked like beginners, probably their first time out. The convoy set off again. On the second attack the lorry drivers dived into bushes and the convoy sustained moderate damage. On the third attack the convoy was peppered and we received a hit. An AP round went through our cooking pot which was hanging on the outside of the vehicle. Otherwise our patrol escaped harm. These attacks cleared the road of German supply convoys and now we proceeded more easily. On the way we saw more and more wrecked or burnt-out vehicles. In the middle of the road at Caumont l'Evente a large panzer was burning with a thick cloud of smoke. Because its ammunition could go up at any moment, it was only safe for armoured vehicles to pass by it.

The nearer we got to the coast the more enemy aircraft were about. We stopped in a wood and camouflaged our half-tracks with bushes and branches. We had to spend long periods amongst the trees pinned down by enemy aircraft. We soon identified which were flying protection and would not become involved in ground fighting, but we had to be very wary of fighter-bombers and only moved from cover to cover. Our timetable was discarded and we were forced to maintain radio silence unless attacked. At Tilly sur Seulles we positioned ourselves at a farm as a standing patrol on security duty. Until then we still had had no contact with the enemy on the ground. All night long heavy artillery was firing ahead of us but we had no idea which side was shooting and at what.

Because of our initial fast speed, the dust and constantly watching the skies, my eyes had become inflamed so badly that I could not read a map nor make out aircraft types. Lieutenant Vogs stopped a passing ambulance and a doctor gave me some eye drops and ointment. Next morning I had my sight back. Scarcely had 7 June 1944 dawned than we resumed our reconnaissance. On the road south of Bayeux we passed the first wrecked American jeeps. We also met a No. 1 Company patrol with the eight-wheeler Pumas and the two commanders exchanged news. Cruising between Bayeux and Caen we had little idea which was ours and what was theirs. Ahead were bases, villages and hilltops occupied by the enemy and looking backwards we could not determine how the German front line ran. It was a paradox: only rarely did we see a German soldier. There was no German force around which could have done anything to impede the enemy advance. We had established that the Tommies were ahead of us. If they now set off smartly they could walk in and overrun half of France. Additionally the skies were full of enemy aircraft and we said that if anyone looked up and could not see an Allied aircraft anywhere he should shout Hurrah! There were few Hurrahs. Enemy shells howled overhead and ploughed the earth behind us with a deafening explosion. There were no

German troops there, the other side seemed to be aiming at deserted crossroads. During the day more and more Panzer Lehr Division forces arrived to assume security duty south-east of Bayeux. On 8 June we scouted towards Caen and met units of 12th SS Panzer Division Hitler Jugend which were fighting the Canadians. Lieutenant Vogs gave their position and details by radio to battalion and division. As reconnaissance liaison we accompanied a tank attack by 2nd Battalion of the Panzer Lehr Regiment for spot height 103 near Tilly. The attack had no depth and only succeeded in halting the Allied advance.

In the darkness of the late evening, several Ju 88s flew over us, I recognised them from my African service by the sound of their engines. At the coast there rose up immediately anti-aircraft fire such as I had never seen before in my life. A sheer impenetrable wall of tracer screened the invasion front, and apparently our pilots were not prepared to fly through it for they circled above our position and finally released their bombs on us. We dived for cover: naturally we were not overjoyed at this greeting from the Luftwaffe. For three days we had never seen a German aircraft, and now they do this!

During the night a number of coastal artillery men reported an uncountable number of ships and landing craft near the coast. Days before they had had to hand over some of their ammunition and had only a single issue for their guns. As the result of this depressing statement, slowly I began to doubt that the enemy could be forced back into the sea.

We returned from the mission and were co-opted into defence of the base that evening. With our vehicles we were to reinforce the infantry trenches in the meadows behind the high earth walls with their protective hedges that characterise the Normandy bocage. The farmers use them to fence off their agricultural land, pasture and orchards. The earth walls are topped with prickly whitethorn and blackberry bushes and have deep ditches at the sides. The strong, deeply splayed roots consolidate the ground into a dam almost as hard as stone. The banks protect the fruit harvest and cattle against Atlantic storms and supply the firewood which we could always find bundled up in the farmyards. The farmers and their herds could only access their fields through narrow openings. Numerous sunken paths led to the pastureland below arches formed by the tops of the individual hedgerows. These provided good cover against aircraft. From a tactical point of view the bocage formed a natural defensive network but made the operation of panzers extremely difficult.

To reinforce our security line in No. 2 Company's defence zone we positioned our vehicles behind the earth walls. The nightmare of every panzer reconnaissance man was to lose manoeuvrability and be forced to function as protection for the infantry with its light weapons. Now we found ourselves behind the earth walls in range of enemy artillery and mortar fire which went on day and night.

Each crew had to dig a large hole behind the earth wall and park the vehicle over it. When the enemy opened fire we crawled into this protected trench. To give ourselves a field of fire we had to cut away some of the prickly hedgerows. Daily we could see how the green meadows grew ever more grey under the welter of enemy shelling. During the day we often set off on patrol and if it was decided to adopt a new location then we had to dig a new hole. If enemy aircraft activity was scarce over our sector, our three-man crew would stretch out on the armour plating over the motor forward to avoid lying in the dirt. One early morning there began a fearsome howling and screeching. Half asleep we were rolled up near our panzer and wondered what this new racket could be. It was a battery of six-tube 15cm rocket launchers firing at the enemy positions. This must certainly have woken the Tommies up, for shortly afterwards their answer came back ten times as powerful. The German battery had already moved on, but the reply fell around our ears and we were forced to drop swiftly into the trench below our vehicles.

Sometimes the cattle had been abandoned in the fields leaving the cows in distress because they needed to be milked and their udders were inflamed. We would happily have done the job for the milk, but the cows objected to our approaching them. One evening I saw a young bull, a magnificent creature, within a small herd in the succulent grasses of a neighbouring field. Next morning his legs had been torn open by shell splinters and the stumps of them spread wide. He looked at me with sad, glistening eyes.

On 9 June 1944 our patrol headed towards Balleroy to link up with the infantry supposed to be holding the front line there. Strangely there were hardly any enemy aircraft about, perhaps it was foggy in England, and so we made good progress. The patrol had an Sd.Kfz 250/9 at front and rear with my radio panzer in between. We went northwards along a country lane to find the German troops, but there were none about. On our left hand was a high wall enclosing a large spread of terrain with a tower. At the end of the wall was a tree-lined road, and the wall ran off to the left of it. We looked at each other baffled, for neither in the avenue nor anywhere in sight was there an interception point, nor any German soldier to be seen. Lieutenant Vogs reported back by radio that a breach in the front line existed which had to be repaired immediately. We had no defensive system in depth, and since the coastal line had been penetrated, German control had apparently been lost.

Lieutenant Vogs decided to continue north along the country road and brought up the other Sd.Kfz.250/9 from third to second position in the column. Suddenly fighter-bombers arrived overhead and we had to shelter amongst the trees, making little progress, moving only from tree to tree. Because of this precaution, the crew of the command vehicle discovered the enemy moving unmolested through the area with tanks and armoured vehicles.

Warily our patrol returned to the crossroads. After sending a radio message about the situation, and to avoid duplication of resources, Lieutenant Vogs had decided to defend the crossroads. He ordered me to take my radio operator Günter Fleischer and the MG 42, and set up in a ditch. I thought he was joking. My immediate objection, 'It is pure nonsense to try to stop an enemy armoured column with one machine gun' annoyed him and he stood on his order. 'Take out your MG and set it up in the ditch in the avenue facing north!'

Muttering and shaking my head I did as ordered. The radio operator brought up two cases of ammunition, we hurled everything on the parapet of the ditch and I cried, 'Order carried out, Herr Leutnant!' Satisfied, he shouted, 'Attention! Proceed!' and the three vehicles of the patrol set off down the country lane following the high wall. Fleischer and I found it incomprehensible that he should have gone off without a radio operator. Because of this ludicrous decision, the column had no radio contact with Battalion and so no tactical value in the area.

On my earlier reconnaissance outings in North Africa and in training at NCO school, a good radio operator was the most important man in the patrol. Now he crouched with me in a ditch with the ridiculous job of defending a crossroads against enemy tanks with an MG.

We were sitting on the parapet watching the patrol reach the far end of the high wall when there came a roar. Lightning fast we threw ourselves into the ditch and lay on the bottom. A salvo of heavy shells straddled the crossroads with a deafening explosion. When I stood up and peered over the parapet of the ditch I saw an enormous gaping hole in the wall large enough to drive a car through. The enemy fired again and we threw ourselves down. This salvo fell near the patrol. 'Well, that's that,' I said to Fleischer, 'We're sitting here served up on a plate being watched nearby by an artillery spotter.' We surveyed the surroundings but could see nothing suspicious. Our patrol was not to be seen and we guessed it had received the full weight of the salvo. Damn, damn, with this lieutenant our days are numbered, we raged inwardly. Map-reading was one of his weaker points, as we had discovered not only in France but also in Hungary: and he could not have had any training in reconnaissance, for this defending the crossroads with a machine-gun lark proved it.

After having seen nothing of our vehicles for about an hour I decided to find out where they were and if they had survived the shelling. 'Pack up your ammunition boxes, we are now following the patrol on foot' I told Fleischer, and shouldering the MG I led the way. Using the high wall as cover we followed it to its end where it bore right. At last we saw the patrol in the distance, and just as it disappeared behind a tree nursery a salvo landed just where it had been before. 'There's definitely something fishy about that,' I told Fleischer, 'No friend or foe as far as the eye can see and the enemy artillery keeps up accurate fire on our vehicles!'

After a while Fleischer said, 'Look back, I bet the artillery spotter is in that tower.' Sure enough, now we saw the houses with the tall tower behind the high wall.

'There will be French artillery officers with the French Resistance up there passing the coordinates to the enemy battery,' I told him, and added in indignation, 'it is simply incredible that the patrol went off and just dumped us at that crossroads.'

'Lieutenant Vogs went for reinforcements and left us there as an insuperable bulwark of the Atlantic Wall,' Fleischer replied.

The artillery fire ceased and we trotted with our equipment in the direction we had last seen the patrol. Behind the tree nursery we spotted our vehicles and went straight to our radio panzer, tore open the rear door and tossed everything inside. The driver called from his seat, 'Thank God you're back, I spent half the time blindly following the other two cars and with all this damned banging and crashing had no clue what was going on.' We climbed in and took our seats.

'Well, Henning', I told myself, 'now our lieutenant will probably have you court-martialled for having deserted your MG post at the crossroads without having first brought the Allied invasion to a halt.' I had not reported myself back to him, but without anybody ever mentioning it we set off back to battalion. Probably he was glad I had acted on my own initiative and the patrol was fully staffed again. In the evening we occupied our trough behind an earth bank. By its colour I could tell that the meadow had been shelled again.

Our patrol now received orders to scout to the west in order to ascertain the whereabouts of the enemy and our own defences. Lieutenant Vogs secured an important crossroads with houses, placing one Sd.Kfz 250/9 gun wagon facing north and the other west. I took my radio panzer to a farmhouse yard for cover against aircraft and Lieutenant Vogs radioed his position to battalion.

A reconnaissance patrol from 2.Panzer Division came up from the south. The force was two eight-wheel Pumas commanded by a sergeant. They reported no contact with the enemy so far and Lieutenant Vogs brought the sergeant up to date about the enemy situation. Shortly afterwards an enemy reconnaissance unit was reported to the north. Lieutenant Vogs felt he was justified in assuming overall command of the crossroads and decided to destroy the two enemy vehicles with the 5cm KwK of the leading Puma which he then shuffled hurriedly into a shooting position.

I was keen to see this action and from the stables I had a wonderful view of the two British scout cars through some ventilation slits in the rear wall. Coming from the left the road had a bend to the right and along this highway with fruit trees either side came the two enemy vehicles slowly and directly towards our position. At about two kilometres they were still coming up quite slowly when the Puma fired a 5cm shell. This range was too great and the round missed. Both British scout cars pulled back immediately. There was no second shot, why not I have no idea.

Lieutenant Vogs radioed at once: 'Enemy armoured cars driven back from crossroads X successfully', to which he received the immediate reply, 'Reconnoitre along highway Y, report enemy situation.' This was what he should have been doing from the outset, he had overstayed his welcome at the crossroads. Now he persuaded the sergeant commanding the two Pumas to join him in a strong five-vehicle reconnaissance with us to the west. The entire column formed up like this: first the Sd.Kfz 250/9 gun wagon commanded by Lieutenant Vogs, then the two Pumas, fourth my radio panzer and at the rear our other gun wagon to guard against attack from behind. This was a powerful column with good fire power, but no match for enemy tanks. The experience of the commander was of great importance. He had to anticipate enemy armour and anti-tank guns, and know when to dismount and scout the bends in the road on foot, or we were mincemeat. Enemy fighter-bombers left us in peace and we advanced unhindered.

We were passing some houses on the left-hand side of the road when suddenly the leading gun wagon opened fire with the cannon and MG 42. There was no answering fire. After a gentle right bend, Lieutenant Vogs' vehicle had seen British soldiers appear on the highway and opened fire at once. His driver Hans Suse pulled off the road to the right through a gap in the bocage leading into a meadow, leaving the first Puma to cover the bend facing forward. My radio panzer and our other gun wagon pulled off the road to find cover against aircraft, leaving the second Puma to protect the rear. All remained quiet. Nowhere was there a German infantryman to be seen, nor any kind of makeshift front line. Lieutenant Vogs decided that the patrol should hold out here come what may.

About an hour later an enemy reconnaissance aircraft (a high-winged machine like a Fieseler Storch) flew ever decreasing circles above us, always losing height. We could see the heads of the crew, who were able to observe all our vehicles wonderfully. Lieutenant Vogs organised our anti-aircraft defence. At his word of command we had to fire at the intruder with the two 5cm KwKs and all the machine-guns. The pilot banked quickly and climbed to 1,500 metres to continue circling out of range.

I began to have an uneasy feeling that we were in a trap here if we did not move on quickly. Because nothing was happening on the ground, I tried to convince Lieutenant Vogs that Tommy would certainly be planning to bag us. The officer dismissed my fears with a vague gesture of the hand. He felt very strong with the two Pumas and was determined to stop the enemy at this spot.

I had been on many scouting operations in North Africa but never had I seen anything as stupid as this. Our job was to reconnoitre, see much and be seen little. That had been drummed into us in training over and over again. Our present assignment was to run along this sector of the front and find out the present location of the enemy armour spearheads for the information of our military commanders. If possible we had to determine how strong the enemy was and with what forces he would eventually attack, but most importantly establish where our own front-line forces were, and what units they consisted of.

I discussed the worsening situation with the commander of the second Puma and we both thought this was going to end in a fiasco. The Puma crews were also nervous and talking the situation over heatedly with each other. My radio panzer was standing in a country lane and for the sake of caution I set out to discover where it led. I could not get a good view and it looked like it ended at a field. Caution is the mother of the porcelain cabinet as they say, and the reconnaissance patrol commander should always have a line of retreat in the back of his mind.

The enemy reconnaissance aircraft had departed, leaving us with the feeling that over there they had worked out how to bag us. A young Frenchman then arrived from up ahead on a bicycle. The first vehicle let him pass. Lieutenant Vogs stopped him and called for me to interpret with my schoolboy French. The Frenchman, in his early twenties, came up with the old story of his mother having been killed in an Allied air raid and he cursed the Allies. This impressed our gullible lieutenant and he escorted the Frenchman up and down the road to give him an accurate picture of our strength. I was dubious about this Frenchman who looked to me like a Fifi (Forces francaises de l'Interieur – FFI).

Lieutenant Vogs' idea was to send the Frenchman back the way he had come, spy out what troops and tanks were ahead, and then come back and tell him. This seemed a tall order. As gently as possible I tried to persuade the lieutenant against this course of action. 'Herr Leutnant, for heaven's sake do not believe anything the Frenchman says. The Allies have come to France as liberators, and are being received as such. He has seen everything we have and knows each of our vehicles. Do not let him go.'

In the radio panzer we were always well supplied with enemy intelligence reports by courtesy of Soldatensender Calais, and the reports from the front were mostly correct so far as we could judge in our sector. As a final rejoinder I added, 'All France is in rebellion and the Maquis [the Free French Resistance] has introduced illegal mobilisation in all France!' At that Lieutenant Vogs had a great new idea. He removed his uniform tunic and cap and replaced them with the Frenchman's jacket. He would cycle ahead himself to reconnoitre disguised as a civilian. Shaking my head I told him, 'If the Tommies pick you up, a Prussian lieutenant disguised as a civilian, you will be shot on the spot as a spy.' All argument was futile, he swung a leg over the bicycle and pedalled to the first vehicle where he told the sergeant he was 'off on a war patrol'. We watched him go in disbelief. Fifty metres beyond the eight-wheeler he had second thoughts and came back, put on his uniform again and sent the Frenchman instead to determine the enemy strength and report back.

Renewed efforts to talk this nitwit of a lieutenant out of it failed and the Frenchman cycled away, never to be seen again. This gave us reconnaissance veterans the definite feeling that the noose was closing in on us. The crews were now quite loud in their criticism. The lieutenant did not like it and wanted to show us who was boss here. 'Henning and Kobs,' came the order for us two veteran Afrikaners, 'prepare for foot patrol!'. Both panzer commanders had to accompany him and this meant that if anything befell us all three vehicles of our patrol would have no commander. We carried machine-pistols, Vogs just a pistol in a belt holster. He reported our departure to the sergeant in the first Puma and then we crossed the meadow behind the earth wall with a tangled hedge.

Just at that moment, the driver and gunner of the rearguard gun wagon saw enemy soldiers scampering across the road to occupy the houses on the right. This cut off our only line of retreat. The crew was undecided whether or not to fire because their commander was on foot patrol. To be on the safe side they did nothing and just watched as ever more Tommies dashed across the road.

The foot patrol meanwhile had no knowledge of what was brewing behind the fifth vehicle and we forged slowly ahead, Lieutenant Vogs leading, then myself and last Corporal Kobs. We crept through two hedges following the road. Suddenly the lieutenant stopped short having glimpsed a Tommy standing on the bend taking a bearing on our leading Puma. Lieutenant Vogs took my machine-pistol and shot the man down from a range of two metres through the hedge. He returned my machine-pistol and as he did so we saw some hectic activity on the woodland path running at an angle to our line of advance, and also a long convoy of vehicles.

Now the Tommies returned fire. I threw myself to the ground and lay like a flounder in the grass. Machine-pistol and MG rounds chirped in the hedgerow while explosive bullets amputated branches. I told myself not to move an inch. We were wearing our field-grey combinations which provided some camouflage protection but foot patrols never wore steel helmets. The Tommy fire was unabated and they obviously had endless ammunition. It seemed probable that they had not seen us, only heard our machine-pistol shoot. As if demented they emptied their magazines into the earth wall and hedgerow. I had never seen such a demonstration with infantry weapons before in the war.

After what seemed an eternity the firing ebbed and I raised my head to locate Vogs and Kobs. I could not see the lieutenant but Kobs was lying with his head near my boot. Using the lull, Kobs and I crawled backwards through the tangled undergrowth and nettles for our lives. Now we showed what we had learned at infantry school. We got across the first bocage enclosure, placed ourselves out of sight of the Tommies, and then made a run for it bent double.

As we got to the meadow near the leading Puma, it opened fire with its 5cm gun. The commander shouted 'Tank ahead!' and reversed. At his shout there was uproar on the road; this was the worst emergency for a reconnaissance column which was hopelessly inferior to a tank. Exhausted from our escape, I arrived gasping at my radio panzer, which the driver had put on the road and rolled back. I had no idea where Lieutenant Vogs was, and apart from the two men in the rear gun wagon, nobody knew that the enemy had sealed off the road behind us.

In the chaotic situation on the road the second eight-wheeler passed us and I ordered my driver to follow. The Puma then roared off so fast we could not keep up. Suddenly, firing from the houses caused the Puma to stop abruptly. On the road arose a wall of exploding shells; the Puma was hit and began to burn at once. Muddled and shocked, my driver braked to avoid the bazooka fire. Staring death in the face if we stayed here, I sprang forward behind the driver and pushed the hand accelerator down to 'full'. Drumming with my fists on his shoulders I shouted, 'Go left, go left, full gas, full gas!' Thus we passed the burning eight-wheeler in the middle of the road and after a short while finally got away from the fireworks.

None of our vehicles was following us out and I feared the worst. At walking pace we reversed along the ruler-straight road and saw black smoke rising steeply skywards from the burning Puma. The shooting went on endlessly and we could hear distinctly our gun wagons firing their 2cm guns and long bursts from the MG 42. As long as they had weapons and ammunition to defend themselves there was still hope that the fight was not lost. Surely we were not the only vehicle to have escaped this predictable shambles? The firing tailed off and soon our two gun wagons and the other Puma came towards us leaving the other eight-wheeler burning. Our lieutenant was with them, safe and well. The convoy drove on a little and stopped in a light depression. Lieutenant Vogs quickly dismissed the 2nd SS Panzer Division sergeant without leaving his vehicle. Nothing was said about the wrecked and burning eight-wheeler nor its crew, who had probably been burnt to death since nobody had seen them since their vehicle was hit. The crews of our patrol had thought we were done for they had seen a huge wall of fire near our radio panzer and therefore held back and engaged the enemy in the houses from where they received fire from infantry weapons, hand grenades and bazookas in an attempt to close down the road.

We noticed that a track link on the right side of our vehicle was half broken through. A round from a bazooka must have hit the track and exploded. Amongst all the bangs and crashes in the radio panzer we were not aware of it. The driver replaced three damaged track links immediately. It was a miracle that the track had held together at all, otherwise we should have shared the fate of the other Puma crew. Lieutenant Vogs sent his report to Battalion. As far as he was concerned the incident was closed, with no word of regret for the useless sacrifice of lives!

Our patrol stood west of Tilly and Lieutenant Vogs was in the command seat of another vehicle. It was a cloudless June day. To the east of us, enemy warships shelling from offshore always hit in the same place. We watched with interest as three great points of fire flared up about 100 metres high followed by three black clouds as large as a railway truck. These drifted on the southerly winds and merged slowly into a single cloud. Every minute, scarcely had the last three clouds been wafted aside by the wind than three more appeared at the same spot. We thought of our poor comrades upon whom a rain of metal splinters would be falling with each salvo. I had once experienced a bombardment by naval guns in North Africa. The heavy shells roared overhead and crashed into the desert sand to our rear where there were neither German nor Italian forces. Salvo after salvo ploughed the desert to no purpose. The aim was high: a bit shorter and it would have been curtains for us.

Radio operator Fleischer decoded a new message. 'Go to position XY' we read. We were horrified to see on the map that XY was Tilly, the precise spot where we had been observing the shelling. The enemy had probably triangulated the many radio transmissions and was bombarding the suspected centre. Our Sd.Kfz 250 half-tracks were open-topped and the shell splinters could enter the vehicles and kill the crews. Lieutenant Vogs ordered us to set off for Tilly. Approaching the locality we put on our steel helmets as a precaution but the splinter effect was not as bad as first feared. The splinters were probably hurled far and wide by the enormous force of the explosions. I thought that a bombardment of a village would have had a much more devastating effect, but for safety's sake we crept into the houses very quickly.

Returning from a mission on the road, we were given quarters in a large village with a church. The village had been abandoned by the population and our radio panzer occupied a farmyard inside a surrounding wall. In the yard the farmer had dug a splinter trench and camouflaged it with faggots. We made ourselves comfortable in the farmhouse and made dinner in the large kitchen. There were beds on the first floor lacking bed clothing but we had our own blankets. As befitted his rank and status, Lieutenant Vogs took over a large property two houses down for his quarters.

Because of losses in the company, some patrols were made up of only two vehicles, a gun wagon and a radio panzer. This relieved us of having to help out the grenadiers in their trenches. That evening when we were seated companionably in the kitchen the Tommies began to shell the village. We noticed quickly that they were aiming initially at the north end of the village then dropping the range towards the south end, our own location, then starting again to the north. The shells falling near us caused the plaster to flake from the ceiling, and so we crouched under the large kitchen table. At midnight there came a fearsome crash filling the whole kitchen with dust so that we could hardly breathe. We sprinted for the splinter trench. The shelling went on all night bar the occasional pause, so we got no sleep at all and spent the whole time in the shitty trench. At daybreak we surveyed the damage to the farmhouse. A shell had hit the upper floor. The roof and bedroom had disappeared leaving only the chimney. Luckily the great oak table had protected us, our eating and cooking utensils were still on it but buried under a thick layer of muck. I ran to the quarters of Lieutenant Vogs to check that all was well. I found him quietly at breakfast with Hans Suse and Lambert Fleskes in a shell-and-splinter proof cellar. After an exchange of pleasantries I returned comforted to my own crew, but the lieutenant should have paid this call on us, not the other way around.

The deafening racket of mortar and infantry fire around the village went on all morning, together with occasional rounds from anti-tank weapons and enemy tanks. Now it sounded as though house-to-house fighting had begun. Where was Lieutenant Vogs? Still in his cellar? I ran to the farmyard gate to assess the situation in the street. At that moment some panzer grenadiers came running past carrying their weapons calling out 'Get out quick, there are Tommy tanks at the church!' At full tilt I ran back to rouse my crew from the trench, we got aboard the radio panzer and headed down the road, two grenadiers hanging on the trailer coupling for dear life. I did not have time to warn the other crew or probably I would not have been able to give the Tommies the slip myself. I saw Lieutenant Vogs' vehicle farther back behind the interception line set up by our panzers and anti-tank weapons. The swine had simply driven past our farmyard. We were very disappointed in our lieutenant, and in due course Suse and Fleskes both received my boot up their arses!

Our column had returned to Battalion from a liaison assignment with the paratroopers of 3rd Parachute Division. On the evening of 13 June Lieutenant Vogs, who had just come back from head-quarters, announced that the Panzer Lehr Division was sur-rounded. The enemy had avoided the Division in the west, broken through at Villers Bocage and was now advancing on Caen. We were to leave in the early hours to ascertain the location of the enemy armour spearheads.

To be surrounded affects the morale of every soldier immediately. With a powerful Division such as Panzer Lehr Division, there would always exist a hope of breaking out, however. To be on the safe side, we had literally put all our eggs in the pan in case they went to waste on the morrow. What is already in the stomach cannot be taken away and one never knew if we would get anything to eat next day. About fifty metres from us was a large infantry carrier for the panzer grenadiers and in the darkness we could see a fire through its open door. We assumed they were having a fry-up as we had done. Suddenly the vehicle burst into flames and burned until totally gutted, bestowing a ghostly illumination over our dark location. The cause of this fire was a mystery. So much goes up in smoke in wartime that nobody cares why.

Before daybreak we broke camp and headed for the area to be reconnoitred. Coming from the north, over Monts en Bessin, we felt our way cautiously towards the main Villers Bocage-Caen highway N175. About a kilometre short of it Lieutenant Vogs took me on foot patrol with him. The road was hemmed in either side with walls and hedgerows and so we made good progress. Just before reaching the N175 we saw three British tanks ahead. Inching our way closer we observed no movement either in the tanks or around them. This was a very remarkable situation. Were they all having a nap?

We crept forward and determined that the tanks were undamaged and unmanned. In disbelief we searched for something to explain it.

A couple of houses lined the N175 and here stood a British armoured column, all wrecked, but no German soldiers around of whom one could enquire the facts of the matter. The houses seemed to be the property of an agency running holiday tours of the region, and on their lawn lay a row of dead British soldiers. We signalled our vehicles to come up the approach road, but they stopped near the three tanks and Lieutenant Vogs went to dictate his radio message for Battalion. He asked me to fetch my camera and photograph the British vehicles. I took two snaps with Fleskes, one of a British Sherman tank, and another with the lieutenant in front of it.

I had just glanced up to see where the sun was when to my horror I saw aircraft diving towards us from its glare. I sprinted across the main road shouting 'Fighter-bombers from the sun!' and then threw myself in a shallow roadside ditch. All hell broke loose. The aircraft raked our position with MGs, dropped some bombs, I placed my hands to protect my eardrums, the earth shook and I thought my last hour had come. As suddenly as it had started it fell quiet. It stank of cordite. Dazed and filthy I looked up and counted nine Lightnings, quiet American Lockheed P-38 single-seaters, which had circled to gain altitude and were now diving towards the highway from the east. With a hop, skip and jump I landed in a large bomb crater and curled up. They followed the road firing their MGs, concentrating on the wrecked British vehicles, and then disappeared to the west.

My thoughts went to my radio crew and our three-vehicle patrol. I scrambled out of the bomb crater and saw the now-ruined houses and the wrecked British military vehicles. The bodies of the British soldiers had been raked by MG fire and were a ghastly sight. There was no sign of life anywhere and I wondered if I were the only survivor. Still dazed I made for our vehicles on the approach road and was overjoyed to see they were undamaged. And where were Lieutenant Vogs and Fleskes? When the aircraft attacked they climbed into one of the British tanks, shut all hatches tightly and thus came through unscathed. Nobody had been hurt although I looked as though I appeared to have been 'through a desert sandstorm!' My photography had been the root cause of the trouble, for the Lightnings had spotted the activity on the open highway and attacked. I put the camera back in my trunk and swore never to take photos again in action.

Lieutenant Vogs ordered us to mount up and head for Villers Bocage. On both sides of the road were these enclosed meadows and fields, that made up the so-called bocage. Now and again a rifle bullet would come whistling by, and the sporadic fire continued, occasionally with explosive rounds. What we did not know was who was firing at whom. Lieutenant Vogs had brought us right into a sheltered meadow because he had had another bright idea. I was sent out alone to scour through the tangled undergrowth and find out who was doing the shooting. I left my crew with a grumble, for in an armoured reconnaissance patrol it was not the practice to send a lone man forward to scout.

I set off with my machine-pistol, crept over the first wall and thus disappeared from Lieutenant Vogs' sight. I removed my cap and carried the machine-pistol on my back with the safety catch off so that if necessary I could shoot from the hip. My idea was to look like a civilian crossing the meadow to the next hedgerow rather than a well-armed soldier. I took my bearings and set off again for the next hedgerow. Having quietly crossed more pasture I tired of it and settled down at the corner of a wall after assuring myself that I was completely alone.

On foot patrol we never wore a steel helmet. Every soldier of whatever nationality will fire quickly at an opponent wearing a helmet and equipment. The patrol commander always went himself with two men in order to give covering fire in an emergency unless his name was Lieutenant Vogs. After resting at the corner of the wall for thirty minutes and finding no origin of the firing and explosive bullets in the hedgerows I thought that enough time would have passed to satisfy the lieutenant that I should be turning back. Behind the last wall I heard footsteps approaching. I adopted the firing position with my machine-pistol in the belief that this could be an enemy foot patrol, but it was only a civilian, probably a farmer from the district. I crept after him through the hedge and took him back with me, reporting to Lieutenant Vogs that I had returned, no special occurrences to report and 'this farmer walked in front of my musket'.

Lieutenant Vogs said at once, 'That is a spy, a partisan and you come back with him as though you had both been out walking? Have you searched the man for weapons?'

'What for? It's obvious he's just a poor farmer.'

'Search him for weapons!'

Reluctantly I made the farmer empty his pockets. All he had was a dirty handkerchief, a few francs, a piece of string and an old pocket knife.

'Well, there you have it,' Lieutenant Vogs said, 'The spy is armed with a knife and you will shoot him immediately.'

'Who? Me? I am not shooting any civilians.'

'I give you an order to shoot that spy,' Lieutenant Vogs shouted.

'If you think he is a spy do it yourself.'

'I shall court-martial you for refusing to obey an order in the face of the enemy,' he threatened.

The whole affair had now escalated into a duel between the lieutenant and a panzer commander. He had to show who was boss and that his orders had to be obeyed. When I think back on this incident, I feel that the attack by Lightnings while he sought shelter in the British tank, and the disquieting shooting in the hedgerows, had disturbed the balance of his judgment.

He tried a new tack. 'Mount up and prepare MG to fire!' When I had obeyed this order, he pushed the Frenchman into the field of fire with a gesture suggesting he was free to go and ordered me 'Open fire at the target!' I ignored the order and now he called the Frenchman back. I was ordered to dismount.

'You have refused to obey my order and that is a crystal-clear case of disobeying an order in the face of the enemy!'

'I have not refused your order, you did not order me to release the safety catch on the weapon and so I could not fire it, Herr Leutnant. Why don't you do it yourself if you are so keen to shoot this man. I will not do it!'

'Listen. I'm fed up with this. A soldier who refuses an order does not have the right in the Wehrmacht of Greater Germany to make demands. Now you be very careful,' – and at this he rose to his full height and placed emphasis on every word – 'I shall now give you an order and if you refuse to obey it, I shall report you for court-martial!'

'Mount up – MG – make ready to fire – MG – remove safety catch!' Now he tried to push the Frenchman in front of the radio panzer, but this time the old farmer baulked and fell to his knees.

From all the goings-on and gesticulations the penny had now finally dropped that he was the problem. He clung to the lieutenant and pleaded with me that he was not a fifth-columnist and just wanted to go home.

Lieutenant Vogs thrust him away and the Frenchman then gave me an imploring look before shuffling off in the direction ordered. The lieutenant shouted 'Fire at that man!' but again I ignored him. Lieutenant Vogs gave up and let the Frenchman go home.

The crews of our patrol stood to one side watching this fiasco appalled, but did not intervene. For those of us who had served in North Africa and had been in action under Rommel the shooting of civilians could never be justified. (This incident occurred on Wednesday 14 June 1944 on the highway about two to three kilometres from Villers Bocage. Hans Suse, the lieutenant's driver described the incident to my wife in Berlin after the war.)

Boiling with rage the lieutenant ordered 'Mount up!' and, forgetting all about enemy fighter-bombers and the firing in the bocage, rushed us to the first houses at Villers Bocage. He knew that he had been unable to enforce his order before the men of the patrol and was now attempting to regain respect by a fast dash disregarding any danger. He pulled us up at the first houses, and on the left of the road we saw a panzer Mk IV apparently undamaged and no sign of the crew. Our lieutenant now developed a lively interest in this panzer. It had been abandoned in the left lane of a right-hand bend and was stuck with its tracks resting on some thick logs. The gun barrel was inclined forward pointing down the road leading into the village centre. We removed our vehicles to a position among the houses where they were shielded from the air and now Lieutenant Vogs had a closer look at the Mk IV.

Suddenly some shells came howling over from a German 10.5cm howitzer battery to our rear. The observation post had probably spotted us driving around and mistaken us for the enemy. We were now being plastered by our own artillery, and the salvoes seemed to arrive at a faster tempo and impact with greater violence than the Tommy ones, but perhaps that was just an impression one got by being under fire from one's own side. Luckily we had gone directly to the houses for cover and suffered no harm. Our radio operator sent an immediate message: 'Own artillery shooting at us', but after three more salvoes they stopped of their own accord, probably for shortage of munitions.

Lieutenant Vogs was very taken with commanding the Panzer Mk IV because it would provide a quite different dimension to our patrols than standard-issue lightly-armoured cars, which had to make themselves scarce whenever an enemy tank appeared. Here was an opportunity to make his mark. We made a careful examination of the machine and ascertained that a shell had jammed in the barrel and the breech could not be opened. I tried to get the shell out but could not, and then everybody had a go with equal lack of success. This was possibly the reason why the original crew had given up on it.

At Lieutenant Vogs' side I stood on the panzer behind the turret and we looked down the incline of the road into the village. The business with the refusal to obey an order and the court-martial had already been overtaken by events and were as good as forgotten. Suddenly there was an explosion. We both sprang from the rear hull of the panzer and sought cover believing that we were under fire again. The shell had hit the centre of the carriageway about fifty metres off – fortunately nobody was about – and then one of the men appeared in the turret hatch beaming with joy to announce: 'The shell's free!'

Our lieutenant now got busy and we had to drag the tank off the logs with our vehicles. My driver was a qualified panzer driver and the lieutenant now swung himself into the commander's hatch. He was totally fired up and sent a radio message: 'I hold Villers Bocages with my own forces.' For weeks after we were mocked in the Company: 'Lieutenant Vogs' patrol held out and held out where there was nothing to hold!'

It was a difficult situation nevertheless, for each half-track now had only a two-man crew and was therefore not operational. We came across no enemy on the ground apart for a couple of dead Tommies in a front garden: a few fighter-bombers strafed us with MG fire but missed. I was nearly caught out in a meadow but managed to dive under a small bridge across a stream.

After this air attack Lieutenant Vogs decided to pull out, and I had to drive the radio panzer. Proudly he led our convoy from the turret of the panzer as if at a parade. We drove back to somewhere around

Mondrainville where we arrived at a command post which was new to me. What went on inside I never found out but he came out with his tail between his legs. Whatever else, they made him leave his pride and joy, the Panzer Mk IV, where he had parked it. If he had returned to Battalion instead of making this detour he might have earned a few words of recognition or at least a bit of praise for having salvaged the panzer.

Nothing was said at Battalion about my refusal to obey an order although it was an incident still discussed by the men long after it had happened. For Lieutenant Vogs the matter was closed, he had probably realised in any case that he had threatened what he could not carry out. We heard at Battalion that a Waffen-SS battalion with Tiger tanks had destroyed the spearhead of a British armoured unit, forcing Tommy back to Livry.

The Panzer Mk IV caper did at least give us something to laugh about. Hans Suse, the lieutenant's driver, had found a batch of letters which belonged to a corporal in the Mk IV crew. The latter had a French girlfriend who wrote to him in German. When we had the time and inclination Hans Suse used to read out bits of these letters. One in particular was requested over and over and always had us laughing. One sentence read: 'You are the big rogue, you go Puff! and not come to me again.' In sweet and amusing style she emptied her heart to her grand amour. It was the best reading matter we had with us, and went the rounds of the Company.

We were issued the Panzerfaust anti-tank rocket, and our lieutenant was very keen for successes with it. We had a short course in aiming it, and were warned to stay clear of the exhaust gasses when the weapon was discharged. We had already made our acquaintance with the American bazooka and knew more or less how it must work. The Panzerfaust was carried on the exterior of the vehicle which we did not like much because nobody knew what would happen if we came under fire and one of these things was set off, particularly what effect the exhaust gases might have.

On a patrol we spotted a line of British tanks stopped close together on a road through woodland. Lieutenant Vogs was immediately desperate to destroy his first enemy tank with the Panzerfaust. I was selected as his assistant, which meant I had to carry the thing. In the bocage we crept up to within 20 to 30 metres of the tanks through hedges. The lieutenant found himself a clear shooting position behind the earth wall and had me pass him the Panzerfaust. I could see at once that as soon as the first missile hit a tank all hell would break loose, and I positioned myself five metres behind him ready to run for it.

I watched impatiently as he fiddled about with it but no fiery tail announced a successful discharge. After some time he laid the Panzerfaust on the edge of the ditch cursing and we crawled back. Despite having every advantage, our lieutenant had no success to report.

Because of very heavy and constant mortar and artillery fire, and the Tommy attacks which followed, our No. 4 Company under Lieutenant Exner had to pull back. I had been in his company in 580 Panzer Reconnaissance Battalion in North Africa. He wore three badges on his sleeve to denote three enemy tanks destroyed in Russia. An officer highly esteemed by everybody, unfortunately he fell on 25 July 1944.

An SS unit was assigned to recapture the position. We were to take part as liaison reconnaissance and report successes by radio immediately. With dash and shouts of Hurrah! the young SS men entered the small wood and soon achieved their objective. A number of Tommies were captured. After the attack several SS came to our radio panzer and said, 'See how they creep back into their old MG position which they ran from!' We avoided mentioning that those people were from our own battalion. Lieutenant Vogs was at a command post. We were to one side of the attack spearhead and saw the enemy in a small wood regrouping for a counter-attack. With some SS we dispersed the enemy force which retired at once.

Next day on the road we saw two German self-propelled (SP) guns enter a wood and disappear from sight. Suddenly there came an enormous explosion and we saw a column of smoke rise above the trees. There were no aircraft about, nor had we heard naval gunnery to explain it. A second explosion soon followed accompanied by a second spire of smoke, upright as a candle. Shortly afterwards we received a radio message ordering us back to Battalion. We discovered that engineers had laid two barriers of T-mines and the SP-guns had run onto them. The vehicles had been totally destroyed. A crew member was hanging half-out of one of the vehicles, arms and legs twitching convulsively as he lay dying. Nobody could explain why the engineers, who had been at one end of the mine barrier, had made no attempt to give a warning.

On Friday 30 June 1944 we arrived back from patrol in the late afternoon. Our company was dug in at the edge of a wood on meadowland. A cursory glance at the brown patches told me at once that this meadow had received a lot of mortar fire. This meant that if we had to stay here we would, like our company commander Lieutenant Weinstein, have to camp in a hole under our radio panzer.

Our vehicles were parked on the road. We heard unspecific engine noises. Many infantry were on the road which led north through the wood. A number of large aircraft suddenly approached at low level. The assumption was that these would be German bombers returning from a reprisal raid on the invasion front. Their bombs fell directly along the line of the road. I turned back, using the edge of the wood for cover and crouched in a depression. The Allied bombers roared overhead and I tensed for the explosions, but instead there were merely a number of dull thuds and the earth trembled. The force looked to be over 100 four-engined bombers with strong fighter escort.

I rejoined our patrol cautiously because of the gigantic bomb craters in the road. A great hole gaped before my radio panzer, and the leading gun wagon was covered in debris from a near miss. My driver was spitting sand and brushing dirt from his uniform, he had been pulled out from under a landslide by my radio operator and an infantryman. Otherwise we had nothing to report. The large craters covering the length of the road were now thought to have been caused by delayed-action bombs dropped with the intention of disrupting our supply lines. We had to work all evening to clear the dirt from the interior of the radio panzer. Since we heard no mortar fire all night, it was assumed that Tommy must have abandoned his trenches before the bombing as a precaution against these delayed-action bombs falling off target.

On 1 July 1944 a British ambulance from Hottot came through our lines towards the enemy, intent on not stopping for some reason. It was halted short of the enemy lines by MG fire. In the attempt to capture the ambulance some panzer grenadiers were wounded. The

British then attempted to get the vehicle home and in the effort ran over a German minefield. Undeterred they tried again, and a large group of Tommies lost their lives when a shell from an SP-gun exploded amongst them.

On 2 July 1944 an American radio unit sent a message in clear text offering to release eight German female nurses they were holding. The Battalion radio officer agreed the transfer with Division and next day the girls came to us during a local truce, an act of chivalry.

The enemy was using heavy artillery and mortar fire with armoured support allied to aerial superiority to force us slowly but surely back from the coast. He had already crossed the Balleroy-Tilly and Caumont-Juvigny highways. Our losses in personnel and fighting vehicles were taking on alarming proportions. All our reconnaissance patrols were now being run with only two vehicles, and so our radio panzer was on the road almost daily maintaining contact with neighbouring units and reporting changes in the situation at the front by radio to Battalion and Division. Led by Lieutenant Vogs we found ourselves continually in ambushes or in situations from which we often escaped by the motto *sauve qui peut*.

The jungly bocage very often saved our lives when under fire from enemy tanks. By immediate avoiding action and going to ground as the last hope we succeeded in returning to our company singly. I brought my radio panzer back on three occasions in advance of our lieutenant. At Company we had the reputation of being a suicide squad because it was always our misfortune to become entangled in complications which should have been avoided with caution and experience.

One such incident occurred on a reconnaissance towards Caen. We had reported our presence to German security who were holding a road with two Panthers either side of it. The lieutenant's gun wagon and my radio panzer were diverted along a ruler-straight road with bocage either side. This was north of Odon and led directly to Caen. Shortly before the city two Waffen-SS reconnaissance vehicles came towards us, their commanders shouting in passing 'Tanks coming from ahead!' The eight-wheelers had flat tyres and disappeared down a side road. Lieutenant Vogs ignored the warning and proceeded at slow speed. I let the distance between his vehicle and mine increase and made a mental note of the escape possibilities down those side roads we passed.

Caen was a ruin, destroyed by enemy bombing, and now outlined against the destruction I saw a British tank about to join the highway. Lieutenant Vogs' vehicle raced ahead, disappearing to the right along a country lane, this being done purely on the initiative of the driver, Hans Suse, as he told me later. On my road I was hemmed in by the earth walls to either side and could not follow Lieutenant Vogs down his country lane because the tank was coming up. I fired smoke grenades ahead, and under cover of the fog turned back to the side road where I found the two SS Pumas changing their tyres. Their commander, a Sturmführer (lieutenant) asked me at once why we had not reacted to their shout 'tanks coming from ahead'. He thought the British tanks should have destroyed us on the highway. I could only answer that our lieutenant always accepted danger up to the last moment before embarking on mad flight. We exchanged experiences and I told them that I had been a gunner in an eight-wheeler in North Africa. Having received no information as to the whereabouts of Lieutenant Vogs, my radio panzer went down various by-roads back to the security line to await his return. After a reasonable time waiting I reported back to Company and Battalion.

Lieutenant Vogs had an experienced crew who had prevented a number of his worst fiascos turning into disasters. I had been with gunner Lambert Fleskes in a panzer reconnaissance company, and with Hans Suse as a panzer driver in North Africa with AA 3. Hans Suse was reckless and thick-skinned. If we came under artillery fire in a town or village everybody would find a cellar or other cover, but Suse would stay up until the windows shattered. On patrol he always wore gym shoes, even in winter.

At the beginning of July 1944, Panzer Lehr Division moved to the area west of St Lô in an attempt to stall the advance of the US divisions. Our patrol was sent out immediately as an advance unit to scout the new sector. Because of a breakdown in his usual gun wagon, Lieutenant Vogs took another vehicle with a different crew.

It is always difficult for a reconnaissance patrol to get its bearings along a new sector of front. After two or three days have passed one generally knows how best to prepare for enemy attacks: where he is aiming his naval guns, field artillery and mortars, the location of his armour spearheads and the favourite operating areas for his fighter-bombers. Until now we had had contact mainly with the Tommies and Canadians, but this time we faced the Americans. Shortly before reaching our scheduled area, nine fighter-bombers flew along our line of approach as we passed through a village. I saw at once that they posed no threat, for they were heading for home. Lieutenant Vogs opened up on them with cannon and MG 42s and bawled me out for not firing. I considered it a pointless waste of ammunition to shoot at aircraft as they were flying off. After the lieutenant finally quietened down I said to Günter Fleischer my machine-gunner, 'I really must see if it is possible with the MG 42 theoretical rate of fire of 1,200 to 1,300 rounds per minute to saw a chimney in half!'. Aiming towards the departing aircraft I pointed the MG at the chimney of a house and sprayed it slowly from left to right. The attempt was not successful but I had satisfied my curiosity. The lieutenant heard my gun firing and peace was restored to the patrol.

Near Le Glinel Hommet we left the highway and followed a country lane through woodland to a meadow surrounded by bocage about 200 metres down the lane. About two kilometres to the north, enemy artillery was firing shells of large calibre into a nearby region of which we knew nothing. We had just settled down for a meal when Lieutenant Vogs ordered me to reconnoitre and find out at whom and what the Americans were shooting.

I set out, machine-pistol slung at my back and without a cap. At the edge of a large meadow I saw the Americans in the bocage on the far side, their shells churning up the grassland. Searching with binoculars I saw no vehicles or German soldiers. I decided to seek a higher vantage point from where to better observe the terrain. The meadow was very wet, not suitable for vehicles, and so I was quite safe this side. I lay on my stomach in the sun and imagined myself back on the training ground, watching how columns of smoke rose at a certain distance. Next I imagined being with the American battery, and went over their routine. The gunners, sweating in the sun, dragging the shells to their howitzers. Load – fire – the shells roar over, explode with terrific force and after three seconds the thunder hits my eardrums. This means the impact occurred one kilometre away. I was the only audience to this gunnery and the numerous moles in the meadow had to bear the brunt. How do they react to it? Do they dig in deeper as we do? Overhead at great altitude was some Allied fighter activity, not interested in us. We rarely saw German aircraft. In clear weather we would see the condensation trails of German reconnaissance aircraft, or guessed they were. Apart from that the Luftwaffe was a washout.

Nine fighter-bombers came cruising towards me at low-level, forcing me into the hedgerows. We camouflaged our vehicles with branches against aircraft, but we never forsook cover and always advanced from tree to tree when these aircraft were about. Going down a woodland road they would be suddenly above us, for we could not hear them on account of the rattle of our caterpillar tracks. Seeking cover in the woods was often difficult because of ditches. The fighter-bombers would then line up over the empty road and fire into the woods in the hope of hitting something. Others seemed to drop their bombs on a hunch. We liked those pilots best who decided to transfer their attentions elsewhere.

At Tilly, the Allied pilots' claims of panzers destroyed must have gone through the roof. Either side of noon daily a disabled German Panther was strafed again and again by Allied aircraft. We often drove past this Panther with a wary eye to the skies. It stood on an open stretch of road and we could follow the process of dismantling it at a glance. At night German workshop teams would remove this and that from it: the guns, wheels and tracks had all been taken off, but for the fighter-bombers it remained a target they could not resist.

I lay dreaming in the July sun on the American artillery meadow thinking about damned fighter-bombers for an hour and then decided I ought to head back. Lieutenant Vogs would probably be anxious for my report, having sent me out alone to reconnoitre. All this dreaming in the sun business could be dangerous, for the French Resistance organisation, the Maquis, were not squeamish with captured German soldiers, and one would not have wanted to fall into their hands.

Lieutenant Vogs was thirsting for my news when I showed up. After my report about the American artillery practice in the middle of nowhere he told me that he would hold this position overnight with our two armoured vehicles. 'What?' I asked in disbelief, 'In this mousetrap, all earth walls and hedgerows and only one exit to the highway? If the Americans come and shut that door the war is over for us!'

In all my patrols in North Africa the patrol commander always had a mental escape route at the back of his mind. The need for this precaution was not obvious to Lieutenant Vogs. If at least he secured the path into the woods I could see some intelligent thinking behind it, but sitting in pastureland surrounded by hedges made no sense. My radio operator told me that Lieutenant Vogs had already signalled Battalion that he intended to hold this position with his own force. This would give them something to grin about, and at Company they would come out with the sly old jokes about holding where there was nothing to hold. After that Fleischer tuned the set in to the enemy Calais radio station and we listened to the latest enemy bulletins.

When darkness fell an SS company came down the highway to secure the low ground into the woods. One group set up on the road to the north and thus we were no longer totally isolated. The night passed quietly and the enemy artillery was silent. Next morning in the woods to the east of us we heard increasingly loud infantry fire which indicated fighting. Lieutenant Vogs decided to scout the situation alone with his own vehicle and I was told to remain behind with the radio panzer. The operator tuned in to Calais, which at this hour broadcast good music. Lala Andersen's *Lili Marlene*, Rudi Schurike's *Hörst Du mein heimliches Rufen?*, Zarah Leander's *Ich weiss, es wird einmal ein Wunder geschehen* and *Kann denn Liebe Sünde sein?* were the hits of the time. Occasionally they played German military marches, *Badenweiler Marsch* or *Preussens Gloria*. The purpose of all this musical fare was to get German soldiers to listen to enemy propaganda. 'Calais' was always well informed about the current situation at the front and I think that many German staff officers also used to listen in to bring themselves up to date. At Company nobody cared if the radiomen listened to enemy broadcasts although in Germany it was a very serious offence to do so.

Around midday I began to feel some disquiet because Lieutenant Vogs had failed to return and the shooting in the woods seemed to be coming closer. I told my crew: 'I am going to find out what is keeping the lieutenant and why he has left us idle here for so long!' From the road I went up to the main highway. In a meadow this side of the woods the SS were digging in and also checking the bocage. In another enclosed meadow they had set up a dressing station identified by Red Cross flags.

I was about ten metres from the main highway and crossing the meadow heading for the woods when a fighter-bomber sneaked around the corner of the trees very low down and banked towards me. I dropped at once, assumed the foetal position and covered my face with long grass as camouflage. The fat Thunderbolt wobbled as it passed overhead and I saw the pilot's head clearly. No sooner had it passed than the next one appeared around the same block of trees and once overhead his MGs rattled. I had not moved from my huddled position, which was horribly exposed in the meadow. Fortunately I was wearing my field-grey combinations.

A wing of nine Thunderbolts circled the wood at low level, occasionally machine-gunning the bushes. On the German side it was deadly quiet, nobody fired. It seemed to me to last an age and my only hope was that all this circling would exhaust their fuel. The centre of their orbit was about 250 metres wide between the hedgerows and the woods. Their relief turned up. These aircraft joined the carousel and the first nine flew off. After a while they decided to circle somewhere else and I was able to make a dash for safety into the woods.

The chatter of small-arms went on amongst the trees without a break and I edged slowly in the direction of the highway. At the first bend I stopped and considered if I should go on. Overcoming my doubts I proceeded to the next bend where I heard so much shooting that I decided to halt. I had only my pistol with me, for my original intention had been merely to discover the whereabouts of Lieutenant Vogs. Beyond the bend, a good distance away I spotted the lieutenant's gun wagon. The gun barrel was pointing obliquely upwards. I sprinted for the vehicle keeping my head down while shells and ricochets howled and pinged over the highway. I found the driver and gunner cowering in a roadside ditch.

'What happened here and where is the lieutenant?' I asked.

'He went off to the SS command post in the woods and is late coming back,' they told me. They asked what they should do, but I could only advise them that if they came under direct fire they should make for the nearest bend and, depending on where the enemy was, return to Company with the radio panzer even without the lieutenant. For the time being they were not happy about moving off without him. They were a replacement crew and not keen to act on their own initiative. I ordered them to sit in their vehicle and leave immediately should the enemy approach.

I had an uneasy feeling as I took my leave of them and proceeded along the highway at a trot, distancing myself from the impenetrable wood with its weapons fire from all corners. I had no problem in crossing the meadow for the fighter-bombers, though visible, were far off. I met up with my crew to learn that in the meantime Battalion had sent two radio messages asking us to report our position and situation. Not knowing what had happened to Lieutenant Vogs, I told the radio operator to maintain radio silence. I was very annoyed with the lieutenant for splitting up the patrol, which consisted of only two vehicles, to make another of his side trips, leaving us without orders. Having nothing else to do, we listened to the German hits on the Calais station feeling secure against surprise because the SS were guarding the roads, and thus the hours passed unworried.

Suddenly in the afternoon wild shooting started in the immediate vicinity. We drove the radio panzer at once to the gateway out of the enclosure where we received infantry fire from the road. The driver halted the vehicle in shock, and at the roadside we saw our first Americans, who opened fire at us on sight. I decided we should fight our way through to the highway, where the SS were involved in a defensive struggle. My MG 42 rattled constantly into the hedges near the road and meadow, and this gave us a breathing space. The radio operator protected our backs with his MG. To the right opposite I spotted a sunken road I had not noticed before and called to the driver, 'Quick, go down there!' Probably we would not have been able to make the highway, and this sunken road with its hedges either side joined overhead in an arch was our salvation. We now came under friendly fire from the SS who thought we were Americans attacking them from the rear in armoured vehicles, but the sunken road was so overgrown that shooting had no effect and in the end they gave up. We drove the length of the sunken road and then headed for the highway and the SS, who by now had successfully fought off the attack. The Americans had withdrawn through the meadow back into the woods. Now we waited for Lieutenant Vogs to reappear.

Leaving the radio panzer under cover I walked towards where I had last seen the lieutenant's vehicle. At the edge of the bocage by the meadow a merry mood reigned in the SS trenches after their success, and now they were standing and talking in the open. A group of about ten of them were discussing their victory in loud voices on the highway. I made off into the wood about twenty metres from them and at once spotted a lurking, camouflaged American Sherman tank. I shouted a warning to the SS, but instead of going to ground first they surveyed the tank through binoculars. A split second later a shell exploded in front of them on the upward slope of the highway. They scattered but some received splinter wounds. They were lucky, the gunner fired short, otherwise the effect would have been far worse.

After my fruitless search for Lieutenant Vogs and his two crew I reported back to Battalion with the radio panzer. The lieutenant's gun wagon had been hit by enemy fire but the driver and gunner made their way back to Company a few days afterwards. Much later I discovered that Lieutenant Vogs had received a stomach wound and had been in the SS dressing station from where he became a prisoner of the Americans.

He did have a positive side. He kept a diary in which he logged every mission in which he had been involved and so, on 15 August 1944, the men of his reconnaissance patrol received the 25 Class to the Panzer Badge in Bronze signifying twenty-five days' hectic action at the front.

Chapter Three

Mid-July 1944:
A New Patrol Commander

Warrant Officer Otto Keichel was appointed the replacement for Lieutenant Vogs. Returning from an earlier reconnaissance mission, Keichel had run foul of an enemy tank column and his three reconnaissance vehicles had been destroyed. Keichel and some of the crew had made their way back to Company. My friend Werner Schröder from Criwitz in Mecklenburg lost his life when the radio panzer overturned. He was thrown out, but was then crushed to death by the panzer tracks.

Keichel was a WOII from Zossen south of Berlin and had served in North Africa with AA3. I knew him from Stahnsdorf where he had been a feared trainer of recruits. Of small stature, he had a large nose. At the beginning of 1944 we had met again at the Hohenlohe barracks, Nedlitz. Until then I had always avoided him and was therefore not delighted to have him as my new patrol leader. Now we were forced to depend on each other and as time went on our relationship improved. I was probably one of the few people who got on well with him. The missions under Keichel were not so unorthodox and dramatic as those with Lieutenant Vogs, but critical situations would crop up often enough.

The first operations were to establish contact with neighbouring divisions in order to report back on the situation in their sectors. Late on the evening of 20 July 1944 we returned to Company from a reconnaissance mission late and soaked to the skin by heavy rains. Colleagues told us of the attempt on the life of the Führer. At 22.00 hrs we listened to the German news broadcast in our radio panzer. An attempt had been made to kill the Führer and Supreme Commander of the German Wehrmacht. The Führer was almost unharmed and had suffered only bruises and light burns. We found it incomprehensible that Army officers had been behind this

51

attempted coup while here at the front we were risking our necks. I must confess I had a restless night.

When the military salute, placing the fingers of the right hand to one's cap, was universally replaced in the Wehrmacht a few days later by the Hitler salute with immediate effect, I was really annoyed at having been converted into a political soldier. We understood that it was the idea of Fat Hermann [Göring], whose troops were never seen in these parts. At Company we made our silent protest and stopped all saluting. Whoever forces a break with tradition should not be surprised at the consequences. If we young soldiers rejected it, how did the long-service veterans feel? Nobody in my company in the Afrika Korps ever gave the Hitler salute. Everybody wore his cap now and pleaded tennis elbow in the right arm.

At the beginning of July the Panzer Lehr Division had been transferred from Villers Bocage to the area west of St Lô, where it became involved in heavy fighting with the Americans. We were the liaison reconnaissance platoon to our neighbouring divisions and could thus monitor from a safe distance the murderous artillery fire and continuous fighter-bomber attacks. A cold drizzle had set in a few days previously, and this, together with the hedgerows, had slowed the American advance and been the cause of heavy casualties for them. One evening we saw them crossing the ruins of St Lô, which was defended by the paratroopers of the 3rd Parachute Division.

On the mapped front lines at that time I saw that the Allies had won control of a large part of the coast of Calvados. We had lost Caen and Cherbourg. If Allied armour now penetrated our front, we could lose all France, and who could stop them then? We had not been able to prevent their landings. There was no time to brood over this in the evenings for sleep was more important.

On 24 July our patrol set out for Périers to link up with SS units. At midday we watched a large bomber formation drop its bombs on St Lô, and it reminded me of the bombardment of our supply lines at Caen when my radio panzer was half buried. At Battalion that evening some grenadiers told us that the Americans had abandoned their position and they had wanted to take it over but permission had been refused.

Tuesday 25 July found us on the road again towards Périers. Because of enemy fighter-bomber activity Keichel decided to get off the St Lô–Périers main highway and go through the small villages south of it. Scarcely had we started than we were forced to take cover when many fighter-bombers came looking for us. It was simply impossible to make any progress. The devil and his angels were everywhere today, the sky was full of them! Next, heavy bombers droned in our direction and the earth trembled at the impact when the bombs hit. Dear Hermann, where are you? I had never in my life seen so many aircraft in the sky at one time. We were all shocked and bewildered, then heard that the target was somewhere west of St Lô. Keichel brought out his map and said, 'The target must be La Chapelle, which is our divisional HQ!' In dismay we watched as wave after wave of bombers arrived and unloaded their cargoes over the target, probably transforming it into a crater landscape and churning what had been below to the top. And what of the French civilians and German soldiers?

Since the bombing began we had not been able to contact HQ by radio and for that reason Keichel decided to suspend the mission and return to Battalion. There we found total chaos reigning. Many of the bombers had unloaded in the hinterland and our positions were now under constant artillery fire. The air raid had devastating consequences for our proud, powerful division. Our commander, Lieutenant General Bayerlein, had lost half of it. All our panzers in forward positions had been destroyed and the forward positions were an impassable moonscape. A catastrophe. In the evening the enemy radio station Calais reported that over 2,500 medium and heavy bombers had attacked ground targets and broken up the German front. They called it Operation 'Cobra' and its main targets had been our Panzer Lehr Division and a parachute regiment.

American tanks and infantry streamed through the destruction into open country and plunged us into wide-ranging mobile warfare. With our front demolished, German military commanders were totally blind as to the situation, and now began a period of great responsibility for the panzer reconnaissance patrols, whose task was to not lose sight of the fast advancing enemy. Our small armoured half-tracks proved themselves here, for the need arose occasionally to slink away cross-country if we found ourselves in a threatened position with regard to enemy spearheads. These missions would last two to four days during which time I would completely lose my feeling for time and space and I still cannot recall a single out-standing incident.

Seventh Army could not withstand the enemy pressure and was forced south away from the coast. Coutances was captured by an American armoured division. We no longer had a uniform defensive line and thus began for us the epoch of retreat. Western France lay open to the Allies. Our patrol went at once via Villebaudon-Villedieu as far as Avranches to reconnoitre the direction of the US armoured thrust.

Warrant Officer Keichel was a cautious commander who looked ahead to avoid casualties. Our radio operator Günter Fleischer had his morse key permanently in his hand sending encoded situation reports to Battalion and Division. Keichel had been ordered to scout towards Rennes but we got no farther than Fougeres. Our two vehicles waited in the small town while Keichel took his gun wagon to an area commandant's office to obtain information for his report. Suddenly a girl of twelve or thirteen years of age began dancing around our radio panzer, a merry song on her lips which I can still hear today:

Apres la guer fini
Soldat allemand parti
Hab mir am Alex die Pfeife verbrannt
Alles fürs Vaterland

('After the war ends, German soldier goes: On the Alex I burned out my pipe, All for the Fatherland'. By 'Alex' is presumably meant the Alexander Platz, a notorious locality for the sex trade in wartime Berlin. Tr.) While singing this she looked at us with such joy in her eyes that we looked down at her with great amusement. Probably some German wag had taught her the refrain, as to the meaning of which she remained innocent. We laughed a lot about this song but it gave us food for thought. Now that the American divisions had broken through, our days in France were numbered.

A radio message recalled us to Mortain to rejoin the remainder of our division. Together with 2nd SS Panzer Division we were to interrupt the Allied advance at Avranches. Our patrol would act as liaison to keep headquarters informed by radio of our successes. It began on the night of 7 August 1944. A ten-kilometre deep wedge was opened through the Allied line and our attack also recaptured additional ground. The following morning we had quite a new shock from the air. In our immediate vicinity we watched low-level fighter-bombers release fiery missiles at ground targets. In consternation we sought out the victims and saw wrecked panzers. The survivors told us that they had been under rocket fire. A couple missed, enabling us to confirm the fact for ourselves.

The Allied pilots seemed to have had some problems with the new rocket system. That evening the British radio station 'Calais' reported their RAF Hawker Typhoon aircraft as having been involved in the fighting at Mortain. These fighter-bombers equipped with eight rockets under the wings became the deadly enemy of the German panzers. It appeared that our powerful panzer formation had been destroyed solely by rockets. We were richer by one experience and now had to keep our eyes peeled for Typhoons. In the face of enemy air supremacy our thrust collapsed and we were forced back to where we started with heavy losses. Our forces were no longer adequate to prevent the enemy advancing.

Our patrol now accompanied elements of our division from Carrouges via Fromental to Falaise. The roads were blocked with German troops pulling back. From the north, British troops, Canadians and even a Polish armoured division, all with strong support from the US bomber squadrons, were bringing pressure on Falaise, while American forces pressed north via Argentan. The overall aim to create a pocket at Falaise was now obvious. We still had a corridor to the east but this was being closed down by the Allies and by daybreak it was almost impossible for a German vehicle to pass through it unseen. The encirclement was not complete but the situation grew worse for us daily. The town of Falaise itself had been so badly damaged by enemy bombing that it was impassable for vehicles. Luckily the surrounding region was very hilly with woods and bocage which at least gave our two patrol vehicles good cover against aircraft.

One evening Keichel informed us that our forces were trapped except for a five-kilometre wide corridor to the east which was receiving heavy artillery fire. At first light he would attempt to bring us out. This passed off more successfully than we thought it would:

daybreak was blessed with fog and under heavy covering fire we drove out without damage. We found parts of our division beyond the Falaise Pocket – these had either got out earlier or had never been inside it.

In the utter chaos of the withdrawal we had many adventures of which some have stuck in my memory. I would like to relate some of them, but such was the confusion of the retreat that I may be mistaken as to their location. The great catastrophe began to unfold before our eyes. The German support services to the rear lost their nerve and the Allied bombing caused panic. Reserve units, bakers and veterinary companies, supply and provisions battalions fled their quarters and bases, forming into columns of great length on the roads to the east and south-east. In many saloon cars of these retreating German columns I saw officers with French women. The town commandants, administration stallions and so forth who had had a bed of roses in France now set off with their mistresses, mostly in darkness just before dawn, some even heading for the Reich itself. The great danger now was that the front line troops would be infected by this chaos and defeatism and be swept along by it.

The success of the Anglo-American forces had encouraged the French Resistance organisation FFI to become more active, and they set out to ambush German supply columns and the army of military refugees. Convoys of lorries and cars would be found at a standstill in some locality, the drivers not daring to enter woodland for fear of coming under fire. Very often it was our job to go ahead with our armoured vehicles and force a way clear. When the partisans heard the rattle of our panzer tracks they would melt away, and the convoys could then proceed. The partisans never fired at us.

The Allies had found a reliable ally in the FFI ('Fifi'). These men and women, by day upright and harmless citizens, artisans, farmers and employees from cities and villages, had formed into a powerful militia led by former active officers of the French Army. They were constantly incited by British radio stations to engage in resistance to the Germans, and they took this to mean 'armed resistance'. They also proved very useful to the Allies by passing information on German movements and intentions. Soon they were a dangerous force not to be taken lightly, particularly with regard to supply columns. They also mistreated German prisoners they took.

When our patrol was on the road day or night it was the custom not to use the car-to-car voice radio because of the vehicle noise. Instead I would fire one or two rounds from my pistol into the air to attract Keichel's attention to the fact that I had something to communicate. At that he would stop and consult me.

It happened frequently that German infantry units which had been overwhelmed by the enemy armoured spearheads would make desperate efforts to rejoin our forces. Keichel received the order to meet up with a body of German troops and lead them along a safe path to our own lines. We made the rendezvous in a large French village. Keichel went to the command post while I took the vehicles into a meadow where fruit trees offered cover against enemy fighter-bombers. Apart from a couple of sentries I saw no infantry, probably all asleep in the village barns and houses. When Keichel arrived later, he told me that the infantry unit was made up of mixed contingents which had got here by night on foot. From the orchard I went to the main road to have a look at the situation in the village. I noticed many flowers in the windows of the houses which were presumably on hand ready for the triumphal reception of the Allied liberators, but instead an exhausted German unit had arrived.

Somebody shouted a warning that enemy tanks were approaching the village, and I ran back to our vehicles, for Keichel was still at the command post. I loaded the cannon with AP shells intending to sell our lives as dearly as possible. Two American M8 scout cars came down the village road unnoticed by the German infantry in their hideaways. One rifle shot rang out and I glimpsed both scout cars only briefly through a gap between two houses.

Late that afternoon Keichel came back. He informed me that the commander of the motley unit, a colonel, did not want to go north with us by a safe roundabout route but preferred to fight his way through to the German lines if necessary. In the evening I was astonished to see how many of them there were: it was a mystery how they had all managed to find somewhere to sleep all day.

The new, enlarged column had bicycles and cars in the van-guard thirty minutes ahead, then came two self-propelled assault guns, our two armoured reconnaissance vehicles, then troops on foot, more bicycles, horse-drawn wagons, handcarts and so on. We had to cross an Allied supply route. This was done under the protection of the two SP-guns which then resumed at the head of the column.

Jogging along in first gear we reached the houses of a village. In the darkness I saw how the road went uphill and then bore left over a bridge. On this road the outriders received fire, leaving two automobiles burning and the road lit by flames. The colonel decided that the two SP guns, our two reconnaissance vehicles and some engineer troops could secure the bridge in a surprise attack. Both SP guns went ahead to the bend in the road. Keichel's gun wagon was behind the second burning automobile and my radio panzer in front of it. Some dead German infantry were scattered across the road. Everything was eerily quiet, nobody was shooting and we assumed that the bridge sentries had decamped.

The first SP gun fired a single round towards the bridge. With this shot all hell broke loose and those who knew the Americans also knew that they would immediately make a great show of strength. Their infantry fire was so strong that we dared not raise our heads, let alone reply. Looking up I saw the tracer race by overhead. It rather reminded me of being in a Reichsbahn steam train and seeing the sparks from the locomotive flash past the windows in the night. Fire peppered the armour flanks of our radio panzer and I thought our last hour had come. During a minor lull in the shooting I heard Keichel shout, 'Henning, drive back, you are right in the glare from the fire!' In all the excitement I had not realised that. Kurtz my driver reversed the vehicle a few metres and the shooting at us abated. Then the two SP-guns came back like greased lightning and I thought we should be crushed, the first coming to a stop with a jerk just short of Keichel's gun wagon. I had my radio panzer trundle back to the protection of the houses from where I heard the colonel give Keichel a dressing down for not having fired.

The colonel now had a little think and lo and behold! Now he wanted to take the northern route suggested by Keichel at the outset. Keichel therefore took over at the head of the convoy. Passing the endless number of infantry I was astonished at how many of the various Wehrmacht branches made up the contingent. At walking pace, so that the column behind us could keep up, we followed the northern route to our lines unmolested. Whether the colonel ever acknowledged Keichel's successful leadership I never discovered.

Just short of a village while on reconnaissance one day a saloon car came racing towards us along the main highway, its passenger doors open. In the back seat and leg space in front of it were two wounded, boots protruding through the open door, a third wounded man hunched up in the passenger seat. The driver shouted: 'There are partisans in the next village and some of your people are already there!'

Keichel set off at once and outside the village we met Lieutenant Ziemke and his patrol. The commander of his radio panzer lay dead on the bonnet, a bullet through the head. Behind Lieutenant Ziemke's vehicle were twelve to fifteen paratroopers who had been marching through the village in file and had suddenly received fire from the houses. Apparently the partisans opened fire from the ventilation slots in the cowsheds and were not spotted. A rifle bullet hit the vision slit of my panzer and we had to put on our steel helmets.

The paratroopers wanted to mount an attack on the village using us for cover to get to their own vehicles and recover their dead and wounded. It was a large village with a ruler-straight road leading straight up to a tall church. Our three reconnaissance vehicles entered the village and the paratroopers forced entry into the first houses only to find them unoccupied. We drove forward a little but two paratroopers were not enough to search a house thoroughly as was evident when suddenly we came under fire from the rear of those houses which had already been searched. The exercise was clearly pointless and Lieutenant Ziemke called the whole thing off. We returned to our assembly point outside the village: we would need a full company to cleanse the village of partisans. Now and again a rifle round would come our way from the houses, then came one which hit my panzer from the left-hand side. This drew my attention to a large haystack in the field. I opened fire on it with tracer ammunition and a short while later it caught fire. Using the smoke for cover we saw the occupants of the haystack running for the village.

Hans Pischke, a friend of mine from Company, was gunner in Lieutenant Ziemke's gun wagon and covering the street with his weapons. Suddenly he fired the cannon. Near the church some cattle had wandered out of a side street and he fired on them in error. His nickname at Company was Pipel Pischke but from now on he was known as Pipel Cow-Killer. With our limited force there was nothing much we could do in this big village. The paratroopers divided up amongst our vehicles and we departed. As we drove away I saw men and women who must have been lying in the grass for an unknown purpose while all the shooting was going on.

The paratroopers directed us to a German supply depot located in a large underground gallery. The French were already there with their single-axle horse-drawn carts, stacked with delicacies which German troops rarely got to see. The paratroopers, still furious about the cowardly attack on them by the French in the village, began taking the wares for themselves, mainly tinned food. The French protested violently but the Germans had the guns. The locals were forced to assemble their carts for inspection. The gallery, large and long, had been almost cleared out by the French. It was very gloomy inside, and we feared to venture too far down the interior into the maze of side-tunnels even with flashlights, for one never knew what horrors might be lurking down there.

The German staff appeared to have abandoned the depot very suddenly. As always at such times, nothing had been parcelled out for passing hungry infantry except possibly at the last moment to induce a lift with the last of the fighting units, and they would actually rather leave it for the enemy to have. I had seen this kind of thing before in North Africa, both with the Tommies and our own administrative bureaucrats, whose ledgers had to balance even when it no longer mattered. Driving away I saw a stallion pestering a mare, forcing her ever closer to a precipice, and the single-axle cart rolled over taking both horses with it. It saddened me to see their love affair end in tragedy.

Time and again the American armoured spearheads thrusting forward caused us serious difficulties as we attempted to keep up and maintain contact. Often we had to slip away lightning fast into the hinterland. Sometimes we got behind the enemy lines and watched the French populace greeting Allied troops. The road through the village would be strewn with flowers and the French tricolor hung in all their windows. Sometimes the French would celebrate our arrival in their village by mistake. Our reconnaissance vehicles were carefully camouflaged with branches so as not to be immediately recognisable, but even so we had to be sure there were no enemy in the village. This was always a tense venture. Keichel was very careful about having a line of retreat if rumbled. He had lost a crew for this reason once before. Furthermore, the very last thing we wanted was to fall into the hands of the French Resistance, whose members committed atrocities against their German prisoners.

On one of these excursions behind enemy lines, when we mostly used country lanes and by-ways, two young cyclists approached us in high spirits, believing us to be their liberators. Carried away by their exuberance, they told Keichel at once where the hated Germans were, then recognised their mistake and their faces fell. Keichel signalled to me to bring the radio panzer closer to ask these French boys some questions. At that they hurled their bicycles aside and with three or four long leaps disappeared into the woods. We had neither pistols nor machine-pistols to hand and could not fire after them. Presumably they were Resistance fighters on a mission. The only thing left to do was pile up the two bicycles and run the panzers over them.

Very often radio contact to Battalion would be lost. We would have to find high ground to enable us to regain contact and for Battalion to tell us their new location, and then we would have to pore over the map for the small French village they had chosen this time. We operated from Battalion, refuelling and reprovisioning there. Sometimes we might be several days late in reporting in to Company and they would sometimes write us off. When we then appeared unexpectedly we would always receive an uproarious welcome back. Colleagues would supply us with food and drink unbidden and we would feel safe and secure in familiar company.

As panzer reconnaissance men we were trained to notice details about the terrain and look ahead to spot the enemy or possible dangers. Battle experience was of inestimable value, and in the war years we had it to excess. 'See much, be seen little' was hammered into us from recruit training onwards.

Our patrol was driving along a country road in France which followed a river lined by trees and bushes on the left hand side. Keichel was driving very cautiously and watchfully in the leading gun wagon, for we could not bear off the road and if danger threatened we would have to turn back immediately. Keichel stopped his vehicle, looked back to me, pointed ahead and moved his arm horizontally. I saw at once between the trees the barrel of a tank gun covering the road. From the shape of the muzzle it was a German Mark IV. Keichel got out and advanced gingerly, for we could not know if the panzer crew would react nervously. Our two vehicles followed him. A panzer battalion was in the village covering all roads leading into it. A river flowed through the village, and all bridges had been prepared with explosives. While Keichel went to the command post I led both our vehicles to cover along an avenue of birch trees, after which we threw ourselves into a convenient haystack to enjoy the warm August sun. About midday Keichel came back and we drove to the highway through the avenue of birches, our purpose now being to reconnoitre the whereabouts of the American armoured spearhead to the south.

Just short of the highway I noticed to my right, near the first house of the village, a Mark IV, and another to the left of the birch trees in open country near a large grove of bushes. On the highway a haze shimmered above the asphalt due to the heat and I doubted if we would able to see danger approaching – it reminded me of similar effects in North Africa and I ran to Keichel to persuade him to wait until it was cooler and the shimmer lessened. As an old Afrikaner himself he recognised the danger from experience and allowed himself to be convinced. We went back to our haystack, had something to eat and then all stretched out in the soft straw. Because of the panzer battalion nearby we felt totally secure against future surprises.

In the afternoon, when the temperature dropped, the crew was rudely awakened by Keichel and reminded of the job in hand. At the highway junction we saw the Mark IV which had been near the bushes trundling slowly back towards the village with its gun pointing astern. Next I saw tanks approaching about two kilometres distant and drew Keichel's attention to them. Through binoculars he recognised them at once as the American armoured spearhead and called up the crew of the Mark IV. They did not seem to realise the danger, and Keichel left his own vehicle to run and warn them. On they clanked, showing their lightly armoured rear towards the enemy. We had no idea how long the Americans had been watching the panzers, sizing up the most favourable position for the attack. When Keichel came back he said to me, 'I am going to watch this panzer duel from close range' and crossed the highway to a ditch. The patrol was now my responsibility and I brought our two vehicles so far back along the avenue of birches that I lost sight of the enemy tanks. Suddenly a hail of steel fell around us. We were taken completely by surprise and shocked at the amount of tanks and artillery the Americans had brought up. A brutal force began to lay the trees flat on either side of our avenue as if these tall birches formed some kind of protective wall. Leaves, branches and steel splinters rained down. We reversed farther back down the avenue. The firing was constant, the road surface before us festooned green with branches and upturned trees. I found a blind spot from the shelling but from there I was unable to see the highway and did not know how the Germans' panzers had fared. I was also concerned for Keichel.

The barrage ceased and abruptly silence fell. No bird song could be heard, they had all fled before this American rumpus. What of Keichel? I had to get up and find him, I climbed over branches and fallen trees on the road and just short of the highway he came running up, completely filthy. 'Man, oh man, what do you look like?' I greeted him. He cursed: 'The Americans laid it down so thick that never once did I raise my head. I had to crawl away through a drainage pipe to get across the road.' This gave me some pleasure. Keichel always had to see the enemy situation for himself. If a battalion or company command post informed him where the front lines were, he always had to go there first to check before he sent his signal. If they told him there were two or three enemy tanks in the field he would go there and see for himself. This often brought us into dangerous situations, causing us to rage inwardly and wish he was somewhere else. I must also acknowledge that he was extremely conscientious and undertook every operation with caution and careful consideration unlike his predecessor Lieutenant Vogs, who rushed from one disaster to another and came to a tragic end.

Keichel said he had derived something from his solo mission and so we drove into the village, which lay protected in a river valley. The Americans fired at it only sporadically but once there we took cover, placing both vehicles behind a house while Keichel went to the panzer command post. Suddenly a shell crashed into the roof of a neighbouring house and the entire roof disappeared. Even today I cannot understand how a single shell could have done that. I have seen several times how not a rafter remained in place, but generally the chimney would survive.

A Mark IV drove past us and I looked at the tank commander in disbelief. He had only one arm. My God, had the German Wehrmacht come this far that a one-armed panzer commander was fit for the front? We had a lively discussion afterwards about whether that was what 'total war' meant.

Keichel returned from the command post, sent off his signals and then we headed over one of the river bridges for the high ground to the north, immediately sighting the enemy tank column again. Presumably they were replenishing for their next sortie and so left us unmolested.

After a while we drove up a country lane to a ridge and saw below us on the highway, about a kilometre away, a horse-drawn artillery battery. It was a fascinating sight for a panzer soldier. In all my military career it was the first time I had seen such a unit. In North Africa and even in Normandy our fighting units had always been motorised. Watching this unique theatre I saw the plodding battery suddenly become animated, speeding up as though crazed. The horses were released into a field and the guns unlimbered and turned to face us. Keichel lined up our two vehicles towards the battery. Surveying the region we saw neither friend nor foe and realised we were the target. We waved. Standing on the panzer bonnet I flourished our panzer flag. By their reaction we noticed that they had identified us and we drove downhill to meet them.

Keichel had some harsh words for the battery commander, and since he did not dismount from his vehicle, the battery commander did not know with whom he had the pleasure. Some of the gunners came up to my radio panzer and said, 'You were lucky, we were about to turn you into mincemeat!'

'If you go down there for about 15 kilometres the Americans will make mincemeat of you, and all I shall pity is your fine horses. Have you enough shells or do they bring them to you in a horse and cart?' In this loutish manner we responded to their insinuations of their great strength. My God, what would become of them up against a

The four inseparables, in comradely solidarity, from the left G. Rusch, E. Sigle, the author, and H. Brünje.

Recruit training at Stahnsdorf on the eight-wheeled Sd.Kfz 233 with the short 7.5cm gun.

On the way to live-fire training with AP and HE shells.

The author, left, with a live round.

On Christmas leave in 1943 after successful completion of training. Note the Afrika cuff-title.

The author on sentry duty guarding vehicles at Bruck an der Leitha.

Our panzer reconnaissance troop, from left, Fleskes, Suse, Vogs, Kurz, the author, unidentified man, Mahnkopf and Fleischer.

The author by the radio panzer in snow and slush at Bruck an der Leitha, early March 1944.

The first rays of the sun fall on the haystack at Nagytarcsa. In the background the radio panzer.

The radio panzer crew at Raab. The author wearing the greatcoat, driver Kurz, and radio operator Fleischer.

Hungarians civilians admiring German vehicles, April 1944.

Lieutenant General Fritz Bayerlein, commander of the Panzer Lehr Division, and Captain von Fallois in Hungary, April 1944.

The author's reconnaissance troop leader Lieutenant Vogs in France, June 1944.

The author as a corporal in the Normandy bocage, sporting a daring Rommel-type scarf.

US-Operationen
zwischen Omaha, Cherbourg und Avranches

Landungsköpfe der Alliierten am Abend des 6.Juni 1944
Frontverlauf am 12.Juni 1944
Frontverlauf am 20.Juni 1944
Frontverlauf zwischen dem 18.und 24.Juli 1944
Frontverlauf am 31.Juli 1944

Sketch of the invasion coast with the various front lines until the end of July 1944.

Field Marshal Rommel inspecting a wrecked US Horsa glider inland from the invasion coast.

Sketch map of the failed counter-offensive by the seriously depleted Panzer Lehr Division.

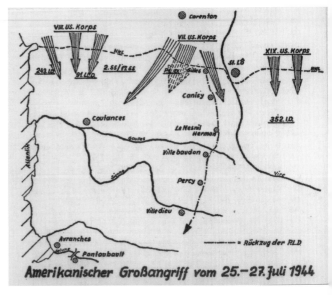

Amerikanischer Großangriff vom 25.–27. Juli 1944

Wrecked British tanks, a Sherman Firefly (right) and a Cromwell, after the victorious armoured skirmish at Villers-Bocage.

A fairly battered armoured scout car of No 3 Company

Cleaning the barrel of the 5cm L/24 gun of a Puma (Sd.Kfz 234/2), HQ Company.

Belated certificate dated 15 August 1944 awarding the author in France the Panzer Combat Badge in Bronze.

Certificate awarding the Panzer Combat Badge 25 Class in Bronze (twenty-five days in action at the front).

BESITZZEUGNIS

DEM Unteroffizier
(DIENSTGRAD)

Otto Henning
(VOR- UND FAMILIENNAME)

2./ Panzer – Aufkl. Lehr – Abt. 130
(TRUPPENTEIL)

VERLEIHE ICH FÜR TAPFERE TEILNAHME

AN 25 EINSATZTAGEN

DIE II . STUFE ZUM
PANZERKAMPFABZEICHEN
IN BRONZE

Abt. Gef.Stand, den 15. August 1944
(ORT UND DATUM)

(UNTERSCHRIFT)

Major u. Abt. – Kommandeur
(DIENSTGRAD UND DIENSTSTELLUNG)

Family photo taken during author's last leave at Grevesmühlen, Mecklenburg, October 1944.

German Panther tank ready to move out.

German grenadiers
fight on past
wrecked US Army
half-tracks during
the Ardennes
offensive.

A German motorcyclist
attempting to start his
machine, by vehicles
and guns from a US
convoy.

Not so often this way round! American soldiers taken prisoner by the Germans.

German wounded passing a US convoy.

The author's reconnaissance-troop leader Warrant Officer Keichel, awarded the Knight's Cross 18 January 1945, fell 14 April 1945.

A German Jagdtiger abandoned in a village at the end of the war.

US troops passing ruined buildings on the way into the Reich.

The end of the war. German PoWs head towards an uncertain future

The author wearing the civilian suit he escaped from the French in.

fully motorised Allied tank column and Allied air supremacy?

After a couple of days at Company refuelling, reprovisioning and sleeping our fill on straw in a barn we were back in action. Our job was to keep reporting the changing locations of the enemy armoured spearheads. We spent one whole day retreating before one such American unit. Mostly they would rest in a village in late afternoon, get settled in for the night and set off again next morning. Occasionally they would duel when their path was blocked by German panzers or anti-tank guns, finally pulling out along some side road to get round the problem. Thus our little patrol had to be always very alert for enemy armour and our own defences.

Mostly we stalked the enemy armour along roads and country lanes, since they customarily used the main highways for their advance. Late one afternoon we drove through a village. Many of the French inhabitants were standing in their porches in joyful expectation of the arrival of their liberators. This would probably not occur until the following morning. Keichel kept a respectful distance back from the next village, which was hidden behind a bushy plantation and in enemy hands. We also knew that behind us German panzers were hidden in woodland from where they controlled the highway and would engage the enemy armour when it showed up.

We spent the night in the country with alternating watches and through the morning mist saw vague shapes approaching. We saw them, and then they vanished. The purest phantoms in the morning fog. We aimed our weapons at them, assuming this was an enemy foot patrol. It had not been our experience previously that the Americans sent out foot patrols ahead of their armour to scout. The mist had made fools of us. There were a few small trees and bushes occasionally just visible through the swathes of mist and then disappearing. It was one of those things that set one's nerves on edge day after day.

At daybreak we heard the first enemy tanks switch on their engines and gradually the noise got ever louder. In about an hour the entire armada set off again eastwards, and our radio operator transmitted his first encoded messages as to time, location and direction of advance of the enemy armoured column.

Our own motors were not running and we listened to the noise and clanking of their tracks. Their advance began and we withdrew a little further at speed along hidden paths. In the woods we halted on a track to one side of our security line and although we could see nothing we heard the enemy armour rolling up. Next our panzers fired as the leading tank crossed their field of fire. There was a short engagement after which a strange silence fell in the wood with no firing or tank movement to be heard. Our radio operator reported the engagement in code to Division.

We received a new assignment by radio. The Americans were now regrouping their spearhead and were intent upon pushing east along parallel roads. On the way to the new operational area we observed panic break out amongst some German vehicles approaching us. Infantrymen came running up shouting, arms flailing while others set their vehicles on fire. The sight of burning lorries made an appalling sight on the long, tree-lined highway. The first Sherman tanks fired at the column as they passed on their way towards us. We drove at once into the vegetation. Ever more infantry came running up pleading to be taken with us. In the radio panzer we could hardly move. Men were crouching on the armoured bonnet forward, blocking vision through the driver's viewing slit while others balanced on the trailer coupling of either vehicle. We found a woodland path to evade the enemy column, crossed their line of advance to reach the German lines and discharged our human freight. In these cross-country detours our small half-track reconnaissance wagons proved their worth outstandingly. With wheeled vehicles we would have been hopelessly bogged down.

Our operational missions brought us ever nearer to Paris. I saw road signs advertising Versailles and soon we were rolling past the magnificent palace of Louis XIV. I drew my pistol and fired once into the air. Keichel heard it, turned and I signalled him to stop. Keichel stopped at once and I requested making a brief detour through the grounds of the palace. Unfortunately he was unsympathetic for his orders said he should report to a village in woods north of Paris. My plea that here was a unique opportunity, which might never recur in our lifetimes, failed to change his decision. How I should have liked to walk those famous gardens and the grand edifice in which in 1919 the fateful peace treaty was negotiated against Germany.

At Maisons-Laffitte we reached a ferry across the Seine, but had to wait for the following morning. It was a small ferry and could only take a few vehicles at a time. When we were finally halfway across, some enemy fighter-bombers arrived at low level. Shocked and defenceless I was in two minds. Should I jump into the water or into the radio panzer? As a land rat it was a totally new situation for me, and with no cover in sight for miles. My fears were groundless for the nine aircraft continued in the direction of Paris having a more important mission than the sinking of a small ferry.

Our two vehicles arrived in the village north of Paris as ordered to find none of the Company there. Keichel compared the signal with his map to make sure we were in the right place. We parked on the village square opposite a bar which was quickly investigated by the crew. Some Frenchmen sitting inside it looked up at them with obvious displeasure. Two German sailors asked at the radio panzer what we were doing here. 'Our company is being given quarters in this village. We are the advance party but that is all I can say!' I replied.

'Then come to our château, a convalescent home for U-boat men, and plenty of room for all!'

This was naturally an alluring offer and I informed Keichel at once. The two sailors got into my vehicle and showed us the way. The château was set in glorious parkland with a large open-air swimming pool at the edge of a wood. We accepted the offer with thanks and gradually all the reconnaissance troops of Nos 1 and 2 Companies were accommodated in single or double rooms. An older Lieutenant Commander was in charge of the home, assisted by his sailors and the French domestic staff, mainly women, who did the cooking and cleaning.

The naval men were very pleased to have us at the château and leave our vehicles parked at the main entrance to the building on account of the partisans of the Free French organisations in the woods. We were told horrific stories of partisan atrocities against German personnel, and it was best to go to any lengths to avoid falling into their hands. Next day the naval commander showed me a case containing French egg-type hand grenades and asked if I knew how they worked and could I arm them with a fuze. I preferred not to interfere with these weapons and declined to experiment.

We enjoyed a few wonderfully quiet days at the home, with outstanding food and service in the dining room, music room and reading rooms, and slept in great comfort in excellent beds. After a sumptuous breakfast we could swim in the pool under the August sun. We lived like gods in France and would dearly have stayed there until the war's end. The Allies were advancing on Paris, however, and after three days our naval hosts headed back to Germany leaving us as lords of the château with all its glories. Against my will, and only by reason of my slight knowledge of French, the company commander and Spiess appointed me administrator. This required me to liaise with the French staff. In this period of political change they no longer wanted to do the jobs for which they were employed, but spent much of their time hunting for anything edible in and around the château. One had to watch them like a hawk or they would have had the bed linen as well.

Next day I was told to organise an NCOs' evening. The cellars were still well stocked with fine wines, champagne, Calvados, aperitifs and bottled beer, and as we preferred this not to fall into the hands of the wives of Frenchmen and the Americans, the need arose for an arranged 'comradeship evening'. After a short opening address by the company commander and the subsequent banquet there was a general relaxation. Once the mass of them started up with the old chant 'Comrades, eat and drink up, the peace will be awful', the whole event began to get out of control and degenerated into a booze-up. People formed into individual groups to discuss war and peace, life and death, happiness and sorrow and again and again, Raise your glasses!

Being unable to hold my drink I was carried by two men to my room. This was situated on the first floor in the centre section of the château at the back with a view across parkland. That night I was awoken by a dreadful din, shouts and cries for medics, all of which I found incomprehensible in my befuddled state. I thought that partisans must be attacking the château because people kept shouting for medics. I was unable to rise to my feet and investigate the cause for myself and not until next day did I discover what the problem had been.

At the rear of the château and below my window was a large outside staircase with a heavy stone balustrade. Some corporals and sergeants were discussing God and The World with a lieutenant who had just been transferred to the Company. They were sitting on the balustrade and others were leaning against it when suddenly it gave way, causing some of the group to fall to the paving below. The lieutenant broke his neck and died instantly. His body was then buried beneath a great tree in the park.

The company and its commander now had a major problem. The lieutenant had not been in action with us and his father was a senior officer who would certainly instigate enquiries into his son's sudden death in order to be in possession of those facts enabling him to claim that his son had died for Führer, Folk and Fatherland. One could hardly report to the parents that their officer son had died by tragic accident at an NCOs' booze-up, for this would have repercussions on the Company. Exactly how the commander got round it was never revealed.

Next day our Spiess, Senior Warrant Officer Petschner, told me to photograph the grave. I took two photos. Unfortunately the headstone and cross were located under thick leafy branches against a raised bank and came out very dark. The stairway with the collapsed balustrade on the other hand came out excellently in the clear sunshine.

A number of panzer reconnaissance crews had arrived at the château with their vehicles but no orders. On the way some of the crews had been involved in shooting incidents with the Maquis in the environs of Paris. This surplus of vehicles meant that we could form a three-car patrol and I was given command of a gun wagon, a half-track with 5cm gun. After five or six days at our wonderfully peaceful retreat we were obliged to leave. The reality of war had us in its jaws again. We took with us additional provisions both liquid and solid from the richly stocked food stores: as house superintendent my time had not been spent unprofitably. Two days later on a mission we happened to be passing the château and I asked Keichel for a half hour stop there but he was not interested. His order said he had to reconnoitre north of Paris and east of the bends in the Seine and thus we were back in the thick of it.

On one of these bends we saw for the first time a large formation of Me 109 fighter-bombers diving to attack enemy positions on the western bank. They were met by wild anti-aircraft fire and we saw one Me 109 make a wheels-up landing after being hit. We drove by the casualty and the pilot, uninjured, climbed into the radio panzer. He described having bombed a gigantic camp of tents and was happy that his belly landing had gone off so well.

An American corps had broken through between Rheims and Paris and we were sent there at once. We arrived at a village where an SS unit was in position. We left our half-tracks concealed from aviation in the yard of a small factory while Keichel went to the SS command post. The factory owner, a very friendly elderly gentleman, showed me over his business which produced baby food from bananas, oranges and so on, sold in glass containers. For the moment the business could not obtain fruit from the south of France.

The crews got bored just sitting on the vehicles and they suggested we enjoy a French liqueur. We had left the château with all we could gather from the stock in the cellar and now each man had a case of Curacao, Chartreuse, a French herb-flavoured liqueur, and some bottles with a high alcohol percentage plus food, delicacies and a wagon-wheel of Swiss cheese, all kept in the radio panzer. Many of the men had also helped themselves to small mementoes of the U-boat convalescent home. Our radio operator, Günter Fleischer, acquired an accordion, of which he was a masterly player though I limited myself to a beautiful white blanket and two recorders. My two daughters were still playing these long after the war. When Keichel was absent I had command and now agreed to one bottle doing the rounds. It was soon empty and since this had now given us the taste for it ('It is very late in the afternoon and we shall not be making a reconnaissance sortie today, so let's have another bottle of cognac'), against my better judgement I again approved the suggestion. The mood became ever more joyful, jokes were told, most heard often before because we had long been a group in the Company. Then Hans Suse brought out the batch of love letters with all their sexual innuendoes which a young French girl had written to her German panzer corporal, and the mood grew ever merrier. The war with all its cruelties and misery was forgotten and we looked forward to a quiet night under the protection of the SS battalion.

Suddenly the small door in the big yard gate was thrown open and Keichel stood there with a grave expression. The bottles disappeared lightning-fast and we looked at our commander with happy faces. He gave us each a glare. 'I am so glad to find you all in fine humour, just in the right mood for a patrol!' We looked at each other in dismay. Mamma mia, we were not fit to go forth in this state. I knew only too well that alcohol and a patrol did not mix, one got light-headed very easily and the result could be fatal. I knew all that and yet had let myself be persuaded to open a few bottles.

Keichel described our mission briefly: 'We have lost contact with the enemy while retreating and have to re-establish it. We shall accompany an SS platoon on an aggressive reconnaissance until we find the enemy. The operation is not without its dangers, keep your eyes and ears open and watch out for fighter-bombers, we shall be travelling on the main highway to the west!' and with that he ordered 'Courtyard gate open – mount up – march!' His vehicle led the way. My driver, an old senior private who had been in the early Polish and French campaigns and was then wounded in Russia, grazed the courtyard gate while turning into the street. This was a good start. I saw Keichel shake his head at our driving. Outside the village we met up with the SS. Keichel and the SS Lieutenant discussed briefly how they would proceed. Our patrol would lead and the SS would follow in three lorries. They would stop short of each village, the SS would get out and comb through the village along the main road while we waited to give covering fire if required. On the highway Keichel's gun wagon drove on one side of the road while I took the other at an angle well behind him so as to always have a free field of fire. The radio panzer was third and then the SS lorries at a distance.

This procedure was followed through several villages and at the end of the sweep of each village our radio operator would signal our location to Battalion. Always, as we drove past the SS men forming up at the end of a village, we would look down smugly upon them from where we perched in our turrets. After driving through the last village we stood sentry waiting for the lorries on the highway, which rose along the side of a hill and bore left behind it. Keichel's vehicle was about eighty metres ahead of mine, and on the bend I could look back down into the village and far out over the countryside. Suddenly I saw a column of vehicles approaching on the road which led into the village below us. In our fuzzy condition, my gunner and I could not make out whether these were friend or foe. Not until shortly before they entered the village did we recognise them as enemy by their aircraft recognition banners. They were two American scout cars and three jeeps with mounted MGs.

The SS were still boarding their lorries and had no knowledge that an American reconnaissance unit had arrived. We could not see the enemy patrol in the village but guessed that the French would warn them there were SS present. Because of the trees on the highway we had to manoeuvre the two rear vehicles to find a good shooting position. We checked our weapons and I put a mixture of AP and HE shells in the magazine for the gun. Now the Americans came racing back the way they had come, but at my order 'Fire at will!' the gunner realised with horror that he could not depress the barrel of the gun sufficiently and so the enemy vehicles passed below our gun and MG 42 unmolested. Seeing our hectic reactions in the turret, Keichel saw at once that something was wrong, drove back and now glimpsed the fleeing enemy reconnaissance patrol. He started a mighty palaver with me at once and now, his face florid with anger, realised that his whole troop was drunk. His own driver could hardly walk, although he was still able to drive. Keichel had just started to really take me to task when the first SS lorry came round the bend and he had to moderate his tone. What would the SS think of a joint operation with the Wehrmacht in which the men in the latter were the worse for drink? In an undertone he threatened me with repercussions later. In fact nothing ever came of it and the incident was soon forgotten. I took the lesson to heart and never drank again on duty or allowed myself to be beguiled into allowing schnapps to be delivered to crewmen before a reconnaissance operation.

Keichel informed the SS commander that an enemy reconnaissance unit had just left the village in great haste, from which it was to be inferred that the enemy held the next village on. At that the SS dug in on the hill and our three vehicles scouted ahead alone. About five kilometres forward Keichel saw through binoculars the enemy armoured spearhead standing outside the next village. Because of the trees on the highway and the back slope our patrol was difficult to see. In the joyous celebration of their liberation the civilians and particularly the women were on the enemy tanks and no doubt this distracted the enemy crews. We established that the enemy armour was settling down for the night in the village, and we reported accordingly. Late that evening we were recalled by radio to the SS base.

As the result of losses to vehicles, the company was being restructured behind Rheims. I had to give my gun wagon to another patrol and became instead commander of Lieutenant Ziemke's radio panzer. He had been a reconnaissance patrol leader with AA3 in the Afrika Korps and wore the German Cross in Gold. His gunner Hans Pischke from Cottbus was my friend in the Company and now we were together in the same patrol.

Chapter Four

Late August 1944: Lieutenant Ziemke becomes my Patrol Leader

A new period of my military service began under Lieutenant Ziemke. I gained new insight into patrol procedures and signals formulations. On the very first mission I got to know his qualities of leadership in which he made the safety of the men in his patrol the first priority and demanded quality reporting by signal to HQ on the results of his reconnaissance. 'See much and be seen little' was a motto of panzer reconnaissance in recruit training and at NCO school. This meant not engaging the enemy, but detecting enemy armour spearheads and the direction of their advance. This information was of decisive importance for German military commanders in the face of the fluid changes of position in France.

I was impressed by Lieutenant Ziemke's circumspection in protecting his patrol against air attack and artillery bombardments, and also the receipt and transmission of radio signals which I studied very closely. I learnt much from this for my own later activities as patrol leader. Despite the dangers to which we were always prey in advance of our own front line, on patrol with Lieutenant Ziemke I felt safer than with my two predecessors, Lieutenant Vogs and Warrant Officer Keichel, with whom we always had lucky escapes from disaster at the last moment.

During one of our constant changes of base, our patrol was stationed one day at a crossroads in the hope that the enemy armour, whose position we did not know for sure, would show up there. There were no German troops anywhere to be seen. Three automobiles came driving up from our rear and for safety's sake we manned our weapons. There were German officers in these cars and Lieutenant Ziemke halted them. He gave the regular military salute with a hand to the cap at which the senior ranking officer asked him, 'Can't you get used to the new salute?' meaning the

Hitler salute imposed universally in the Wehrmacht after the 20 July plot.

Lieutenant Ziemke advised the officers that they could not proceed beyond this point for there were no German troops ahead and after driving a short distance they would meet the enemy. The officers asked to be shown the situation on a map and enquired if the enemy ahead was British, American or French. After being told that we had before us a US armoured unit, the senior officer (unfortunately I do not remember his rank) said that he wanted to gain an impression of the enemy situation personally and would therefore drive towards the enemy. Thunderstruck we watched the cars drive on and a vigorous discussion developed about 'even officers defecting now'. Lieutenant Ziemke intervened and forbade anything further being said for nothing could be proved. All the same, they never returned and we heard no shooting, and so all we were left with was suspicion.

Our company had now pulled back in the direction of Verdun, the battlefield of our fathers in 1916. As contact keepers we were aware that an enemy armoured push was heading directly for Verdun to capture the bridge there intact. At the beginning of September 1944 our patrol reached the city and saw at the railway station a transport train loaded with panzers. Lieutenant Ziemke ran to the transport commander and informed him of the enemy armour approaching the city. They began unloading the panzers at once. Scarcely were the first panzers off the low-loaders than they were fighting the enemy armour and thus stopped their advance at the last moment. In my immediate vicinity, a panzer opened fire while still coming off the loading ramp. My radio operator was so surprised that he dropped his Morse key.

I ran at once to Lieutenant Ziemke, asking him to cross the bridge over the Meuse quickly before it was blown up. Since our mission here was more or less ended and we could not fight tanks, we crossed the Meuse. On the bridge I saw that the engineers had made the necessary preparations to destroy it. There were funny-looking 'milk churns' everywhere. My God, I thought, if a shell lands here, we will all go up with the whole shit.

Arriving on the east bank of the Meuse after leaving Verdun, Lieutenant Ziemke deployed us to cover between the highway and the river so as to view the other side of the water. Suddenly there was an explosion and the bridge over the Meuse collapsed. Shortly afterwards on the other side we saw American tanks coming cross-country to face us. Lieutenant Ziemke then went to the command post outside the city for some time and temporarily left me in command of the patrol.

Soon groups of infantry ten to fifteen strong, some armed, some not, began to arrive along the highway from Verdun. Their idea was to keep going along the undefended road, which ran beside the Meuse for about three miles, to woods with high ground to the right. We could see the grassy craters on the height left by the artillery shelling of 1916. I stopped the first group and ordered them emphatically not to proceed because American tanks had drawn up on the other side of the river. They could see our highway and fire on it.

These were young soldiers, naval infantry not yet out of basic training and sent to the front line at Verdun to defend it. These survivors of the unequal battle were now arming, depressed and totally disorganised, and intent upon leaving the city. More and more were coming up, determined to get through. With machine-pistol at my chest I convinced the first of them to run 10 metres apart, but after a while they bunched up again. Amongst them were some training staff whom I tried to enlist to my aid and so prevent these boys dying on the highway. They ignored my pleas and pushed past, probably in the arrogant assumption that a panzer corporal could not order a naval infantryman what to do. Whatever the reason, they failed to recognise the terrible danger into which they were now running at full tilt.

The highway was filling with increasingly large groups of young soldiers lacking battle experience. We heard the bark of tank cannon and then HE shells ripped into a cluster of boys who, instead of going to ground or finding cover, tried to go up the unprotected slope. Since they attempted this in groups it provided the tank machine-gunners with a fresh target, and we looked on helplessly as they were picked off. Veterans of the front and training instructors drilled in infantry techniques would have been spared this senseless bloodshed. The real culprit with blood on his hands was their commanding officer for sending recruits from mid-training direct to the front line.

After a while Lieutenant Ziemke returned from his situation conference. He proposed driving down this highway for the three kilometres to the woods. I informed him at once about the disaster involving the naval infantry and showed him the Sherman tanks facing us on the other bank of the Meuse. He replied that he had an important assignment and no time to detour. He had orders to proceed at top speed and we were not to stop for any reason whatever. Swiftly we camouflaged our vehicles with fresh branches, more importantly on the side towards the enemy, and in the end we must have looked like a large bush.

Ziemke led, tracks clanking and rattling at 60 kms/hr and I followed half a kilometre behind. We passed the horrific scene of the massacred naval infantry. My radio operator and I settled down low in our seats and I watched the road through the lateral viewing slit near the driver. I saw some shells land near Ziemke's vehicle: whether the American tanks were also firing at us I could not determine because the tracks were making so much noise. About halfway there I saw a column of lorries come out of the wood. My God, we were still well short and had to stop them. Fortunately for them they noticed our difficulty at once, their passengers leapt out and went to cover. The lorries then made an about-turn smartly and returned to the woods and safety. One by one the infantry disappeared into the roadside ditches. By their steel helmets and packs we recognised them as paratroopers. They would have battle experience and would know how to move about the country. Lieutenant Ziemke discussed the Verdun situation with their commander.

Over the next few days we crabbed to the west around Verdun and ferreted out the enemy armoured spearheads which had broken through. On the German side there was chaos and Lieutenant Ziemke had to be very careful not to come across this armour unexpectedly. We sweated blood whenever we were near them. Our gun wagon with its 20mm cannon and light armour plate was hopelessly inferior to a tank. In these circumstances it required battle experience and alertness to save our skins again and again, and permanent good luck!

On this excursion we ran across scattered naval infantry roaming the countryside. From a large expanse of woodland I took two of them aboard my radio panzer. They were boys still in recruit training tossed into the fighting prematurely. I remembered how I had been at that age – I had my first battle experience in North Africa when I was eighteen – but by then I had completed recruit training and was given a lot of luck to help overcome my inexperience.

One of the two boys looked very pale and said he had been shot through the stomach. I thought this was unlikely. 'You mean you've got a graze on your tummy,' I tried to convince him. 'No,' his colleague said, 'he really has been shot in the stomach, and it came out of his back!' I found this incredible, for from experience I knew that an exit wound would be large. He did look very cheesy and exhausted I had to admit, but I was convinced he must be imagining it. At the next stop he showed us his wounds. We could scarcely believe our eyes, there were the entry and exit wounds and almost healed. He had not even covered them with a first aid dressing. I called Lieutenant Ziemke over and we all stood staring at the wounds in disbelief. The lieutenant decided to get him to the nearest dressing station for the doctors to take a look, and give him an emergency dressing to keep the wounds clean. The ambulance people were very annoyed to be called out for such nonsense but after a look at him placed him on a stretcher and we left his colleague with him. What became of him subsequently I do not know but at Company we often spoke of that miracle.

We got quarters in a French village and put our vehicles in a barn. Our company at that time had two patrols active using four vehicles in all. We took on provisions, refuelled and collected our mail. After finishing the necessities we relaxed on our vehicles which were lined up in the barn one behind the other. We had a bottle of schnapps but kept it out of sight to avoid problems with Ziemke. We always had children playing near us who would quickly get up to mischief. The bottle of schnapps was on the front mudguard, where a young teenage boy kept taking little sips from it. Hans Pischke said, 'Keep your eye on that urchin, he'll empty the bottle!' I took possession of it and sent the boy home. While crossing the road to his parents' house he began to stagger. My colleagues and the other kids found this very funny and did a burlesque, but it worried me; perhaps he had alcohol poisoning and could die from it?

'Ziemke's coming!' Everybody scurried back to the rear of the barn with their bad consciences and I was forced to remain seated on the armoured car while the French children watched uncomprehendingly.

'What's going on here and where are the men?'

'Nothing to report, Herr Leutnant! The men are doing something behind the barn.'

'What was that business with the boy reeling in the street?'

'I saw no such boy, Herr Leutnant.'

'Did you give him anything alcoholic to drink?'

'Herr Leutnant, everybody here is straight as a die!'

That was an end to it and Ziemke told me we were leaving on patrol very early next morning and I had to report to him when men and vehicles were at readiness for the mission. The following evening when we returned to our quarters in the barn the boy was absent. Presumably his parents had told him not to come near us again.

In the course of the retreat we crossed into Luxembourg. The people were very friendly to us but had nothing good to say about the 'Golden Pheasants' (Nazi Party functionaries who wore mustard-coloured uniforms). Only once did we experience a problem. We wanted to park our vehicles on a farm. The old lady refused us entry to her land with outspread arms, shouting and crying blue murder. We could have ignored her and just rolled in but Lieutenant Ziemke preferred not to use force and we drove our half-tracks to the neighbouring barn instead.

Of our entire company, Lieutenant Ziemke's patrol with one gun wagon and a radio panzer was the only one actually operational. For that reason we were on the road constantly. A little beyond Mersch while covering the roads for the infantry we saw three American jeeps approaching slowly. Ziemke obtained the agreement of the infantry commander not to shoot because he wanted to bag the jeeps. Unfortunately some of the infantry got nervous and opened fire without orders. The Americans jumped out of their vehicles and found cover. Annoyed at the premature firing Ziemke went forward and took nine Americans prisoner. Two lightly wounded were patched up by their colleagues and then handed over to our infantry. Unfortunately two of the jeeps with the mounted MGs were now useless but the radio jeep was still a runner and I had to drive it back.

As I drove up I saw a heated argument in progress between Lieutenant Ziemke and the infantry commander. Basically, if the infantry idiots had not fired early they could have had two jeeps, but now they had to cobble together a serviceable jeep from the two damaged ones. The radio was still working on my jeep and I attempted to contact the Americans to let them know that their specialists were safely in German hands but for some reason I could not get through. In a meadow I examined my jeep with its all-wheel drive. We knew jeeps from North Africa, but this was the first one I had driven myself. After a while Lieutenant Ziemke came up with the two half-tracks and took the jeep as his personal possession. When we left for patrol he used to entrust it to our vehicle maintenance staff.

Lieutenant Ziemke's jeep and our two reconnaissance vehicles crossed the border to Oer and then to Irrel, where we found quarters with friendly people. Together with the maintenance crew of three or four men this was the only operational patrol of No. 2 Company. I crossed the German border with mixed feelings expecting scorn and ridicule for returning as part of a beaten army, but the contrary was the case for we were received with open arms wherever we went.

At Irrel I got to know a girl whose parents owned a joinery. They often invited me to lunch. They wanted to know what to do when the front line came nearer – flee or stay? Which of us could advise on that? If the front hardened into trench warfare it was better to leave. If there were no peace negotiations and the war rolled past the district and civilians were not interfered with, as mostly happened in France, it was better to stay and guard against looting. For the first time I saw refugees with horse and carts piled high with their belongings on the high road between Echternach and Irrel. What we could not understand was why they were leaving Luxembourg.

All night long I tormented myself with the question whether German artillery would fire on an enemy-occupied village if there were German women and children present. Could a German battery commander square it with his conscience to fire on German towns and villages? I could not imagine it. I had volunteered for the Wehrmacht to help defend my country and not to destroy it. This was a completely new situation for me and kept me awake at night.

After a week's rest and recovery at Irrel Lieutenant Ziemke instructed me to take the patrol to Battalion HQ near Trier. He would drive the jeep there himself. At the same time he told me that the whole Division was to be taken over by the Waffen-SS; if that happened I was to bring the patrol back to Irrel immediately. He wanted to prevent the Panzer Lehr Division being incorporated into the SS at all costs, and we ourselves were not enthusiastic about becoming SS. At a crossroads near our Battalion HQ I asked a sentry of our Company about the SS rumour. Because he could not give me a satisfactory answer I took a chance and approached the place cautiously. At HQ they told me the Battalion was to be re-formed at the Neckar river.

The Battalion moved in stages via Baumholder, Kaiserslautern and Heidelberg to the Heilbronn area and No. 2 Company found quarters in Bachenau, near Gundelsheim on the Neckar. I was billeted with the Holder family at Bachenau, and they treated me as their own son. (I still correspond today with their daughter Martha.) After the great strain of the invasion and the retreat across France it was a wonderful drive in September weather. Lieutenant Ziemke led with the jeep, which still had the white star on the bonnet. As he told me after the war, he had a few difficult situations because Wehrmacht bases wanted to confiscate the vehicle. I commanded the two half-tracks through western Germany. The people were extremely friendly and if we stayed any length of time at a location we would be given food and drink. If we stopped in a village in the late afternoon soon we would be offered lodgings for the night. Unfortunately next day we would have to be up and off to meet the next stage on the timetable.

The rear-echelon services at Bachenau were organised only slowly and there seemed to be no rush. At the fire-brigade station some infantry were serving short prison sentences. On three consecutive days I was sent out with two men in the hunt for RAF officers who had escaped from a German PoW camp. We searched the woods near Tiefenbach with our machine-pistols and sunned ourselves. At midday a farmer's daughter would cycle out from Tiefenbach with lunch. It was the season for apple-and-plum tarts and over the wine of Baden many troths were plighted with the local girls. After the war quite a number of No. 2 Company men returned to Bachenau and married there.

After about three weeks the wonderful time in Bachenau with fruit tarts and wine came to an end and with heavy heart we took our leave of the fine land of Swabia. We loaded aboard a train at Bad Friedrichshall and headed for Westphalia, unloading at Paderborn and driving from there to Bad Driburg.

I was given quarters with a colleague on a large farm. Two Russian PoWs tended the horses there. They both spoke very good German and so we had interesting conversations with them. They laid special emphasis on being Ukrainian and not Russians. At the time I could not see the difference, for me every Soviet soldier was a Russian, but that probably resulted from my ignorance of the situation in the USSR and my great fortune in never having to fight there.

Chapter Five

October 1944:
My Last Home Leave of the War

To my surprise at the beginning of October 1944 together with other comrades I received fourteen days' home leave. The leave pass was endorsed 'Leave by Order of the Führer' which legend was intended to protect us against the bloodhounds of the heroic field gendarmerie. Shortly before midnight I took a train at Höxter and went to Lübeck via Hannover and Hamburg, arriving next morning. At Lübeck I had a wait and left the station building where I ran into the arms of three field-gendarmes who had been watching it.

'Where are you going then on a Sunday morning?'

'Me? I want to stretch my legs here.'

'Stretch your legs?' the senior sergeant snapped venomously, 'Man, you must have lost your senses. You will tell me where you are coming from and going to.'

'I am coming from the front and going home, I am on leave.'

'Leeeeave?' he hissed. 'In this fifth year of the war you're on leave? Where did you get permission?'

'I happen to have leave by order of the Führer.'

'Well, that's a new one! Show me your Führer order!'

I produced my leave pass from my tunic pocket. A second sergeant wanted to see my paybook and finally all three of them were sorting through my documents.

Standing before them guileless, my God how fearsome they looked, the horror of the infantry. With steel helmet and harsh service poker face, the embossed inverted half-moon lead plate on the breast hanging from chains around the neck, sharp creases in grey trousers, field boots: it was best not to provoke them in any way. They could always find something to take objection to in the uniform, an incorrect manner of reporting oneself, or not appearing to be subservient enough to them. (In a packed Berlin tavern one of these field-gendarmes told me I should stand to attention while he was checking my leave pass.)

'All correct, enjoy your leave!' With that they returned my papers and without a further word I was dismissed.

A short while later I heard martial music and saw flags waving above the heads of a crowd lining the street. A military band led followed by a company with shouldered arms. Behind them marched civilians, some wearing a steel helmet or cap and carrying long rifles of a type unknown to me. Others had a Panzerfaust on their shoulder, a jacket with or without a belt, the leaders attempting to keep in step with the music, but those at the rear were all at sixes and sevens. These were middle-aged men with stony faces who appeared to me in my youthfulness to be old men.

I watched the march-past at a suitable distance to avoid having to salute the flag (we soldiers were forced to give the Hitler-salute and would always attempt to avoid this). I asked a woman standing near me what the march-past was for. 'That is the Volkssturm,' she replied. Volkssturm – what was that? I mulled it over but could never remember hearing of such an organisation.

That Sunday afternoon I turned up at home unexpectedly. They were naturally all overjoyed. For now we had total war and there was only ever bad news regarding our circle of friends and acquaintances – fallen, missing, wounded. I asked my father about the Volkssturm. 'The Volkssturm are the last reserves in the defence of the Homeland,' he explained. Even he had been recruited to the second line. I looked at him in incredulity. 'But you've only got one leg.' (He had lost a leg in the First World War and wore an artificial limb.)

'We, the cripples of the second line of defence will be those who hold our ground in the final battles because we are unable to run away. That is now, I suspect, the reasoning in the Party leadership!' Dear Fatherland, have you come to this?

In my home town there was nothing for a 20-year-old war veteran to do. Everything was grey in total war. In a sawmill near my training shop for apprentices they were building fuselages for fighter aircraft. Production had been transferred here because of the air raids in the province. Our town also had air raid warnings on many days, when whole convoys of fire engines with exhausted firemen would drive through the town, either going to or returning from Stettin or Hamburg, or any place which the terror-bombers laid waste in the last months of the war.

One afternoon with Lieutenant Rosenow, a school friend, we visited the mother of our school friend Otto Göwe, who had fallen in North Africa. Frau Göwe had had twins and believed now that her son must have received news of their birth before he was killed at Fuqa. It is hard to visit the parents of fallen school friends. One mother was so bitter over the loss of her son that she would never receive any of his old friends.

An acquaintance I often met had lost both legs below the knee in Russia. During a Russian air raid he jumped out of a barracks window and noticed that his feet were missing when he tried to run off. Some of my female school friends were already war widows, and the newspapers were full of obituaries, 'Fallen for Führer, Volk and Fatherland'. My sister's fiancée had also fallen before I had the chance to meet him.

Even though the Homeland was now so bleak and cheerless, it was still nice to sleep in my own bed and know my parents once more. But was that enough for a young man, thirsting for action, who wanted to dance, have experiences and be happy? I found it scarcely comprehensible but I was nostalgic for the comrades of my company, where I would be amongst those who thought like me and suffered the same problems. Above all at Company I had close friends with whom I spent every moment which offered itself. One soon forgot the worst days at the front, and the good times in the circle of one's friends impressed themselves deeply.

Accordingly, my departure from home – boarding the train to rejoin my unit – was not so difficult to endure. My mother had baked some biscuits which now filled my map-case. At Lübeck a naval auxiliary got into my compartment, a feast for the eyes in her naval uniform, and she made my heart beat faster at once. Soon we were engrossed in conversation while nibbling my mother's biscuits. At Hamburg our paths divided, for I had to go on to Hannover. With a handshake, a deep look into her eyes and a last wave goodbye she disappeared from my view on the platform. It was enough to make one weep. I had twelve days' leave behind me, found nothing to enjoy and right here in the train Cupid fired an arrow into my heart. This girl could have made my leave very sweet, and also my departure from Mecklenburg much harder to bear.

In reflective mood while waiting for the train to make its move for Hannover I heard on the platform such shouting and bawling – my God, whatever can be up? From the window I saw some U-boat men taking their leave of others of their crew, all probably just back from a patrol. The racket could be heard all over the station, and their language, probably customary on their U-boat, would certainly have caused some female blushes at the main rail terminus. It was dark, however, and the station only dimly lit.

At Hannover I took the local train for Paderborn. The compartment had facing bench seats and a door at either side. There was no lighting or heating. Only at a station could one see by its dull lighting if there was a place free. A girl sat opposite me, as I saw when entering and by her conversation, but the other occupants were all middle-aged women. Because of a preliminary air raid warning the train left Hannover early and moved sluggishly between each village halt. It was very cold in the compartment and sitting hunched forward for warmth I happened to touch the girl. She did not shrink back and cautiously I began to play with her hands. Only when a station came up with its poor lighting did we separate. We played this game in the darkness and soon our cheeks were touching. I had a warm feeling in the heart and grew less aware of the cold. The girl's hands got warm and the touch of our cheeks was sweet. I do not know if she was sitting with her mother, for the conversation flagged and words were only exchanged at the stations. Otherwise it was quiet in the compartment but we could feel our pulses through the contact of our cheeks. Then another station came as we saw by the lighting and we fell back. The women and the girl alighted. Without a word of farewell, without having exchanged a word, the contact was broken. In the cold compartment my hands and cheeks cooled slowly.

I arrived at Paderborn in the middle of the night and received directions to a barracks. The duty NCO put me into a recruits' room where I climbed into an empty top bunk. At reveille I did not get up because I was still on leave. After a while the duty NCO came back and ripped away my blanket. In a reflex action I kicked him in the face with my bare feet and the affair escalated. He said he would report the matter to the duty officer and asked the recruits present if anybody had witnessed the incident, but apparently nobody had. From this altercation the recruits saw that a quite different tone existed between front soldiers than in the barracks. I breakfasted with the recruits and the duty NCO stayed away. I took the bus to Bad Driburg and reported back to my company.

Chapter Six

Keichel Picks Me Again

Whilst I was on leave the company received new vehicles and the crews were redistributed. During this latter operation every patrol leader did what he could to grab people from the former permanent cadre. One's relationship to the Spiess naturally played a major role in all this and accordingly Warrant Officer Keichel clawed me back. Since all the paperwork had already been filed I could no longer appeal in the hope of remaining with Lieutenant Ziemke.

The company had been fully re-equipped with new vehicles and each reconnaissance patrol had two Sd.Kfz 250/9 gun wagons and a Sd.Kfz 250/3 radio panzer. I was now commander of the No. 2 gun wagon and deputy patrol commander. My driver was a veteran senior private who had been on the Russian Front and my gunner one of the new NCO trainees with us to gain experience at the front.

We familiarised ourselves with the new vehicles and went through various exercises with the new crews. In between we helped our host harvest sugar beet. At the beginning we kept up with the farm labourers but, not being used to the work, soon we could hardly stand. At the beginning of November 1944 we drove to Höxter and loaded our vehicles on railway trucks. The gun wagons with their 2cm cannon were distributed along the individual trains as flak. In the Hunsrück we unloaded them and went to quarters on the Hunsrück-Höhenstrasse. The reactivated 130 Panzer Lehr Reconnaissance Battalion was now re-formed as follows:

Headquarters Company (sixteen Puma eight-wheel armoured reconnaissance vehicles).
No. 1 Armoured Reconnaissance Company (twenty-five half-track armoured reconnaissance vehicles).
Nos. 2 and 3 Light Armoured Reconnaissance Companies (light

and medium armoured infantry half-tracks).

No 4 Heavy Company (artillery, mortar, anti-tank and engineer platoons).

Support and Supply Company.

The north wind blew fiercely over the uplands. At Company we discussed where our next deployment would be. One cloudless day we saw three parachutes drifting far inland from a great height. We guessed they would be crew from a shot-down bomber.

My friend Hans Pischke had been billeted with a middle-aged woman whose husband was in Russia. The easy life we had behind the lines and the relaxed duty schedule prevailing in our company irritated her and she would often lecture us: 'My dear Lord, if I knew that my husband was being ordered about by young boys like you I should go mad!'

'Yes, madam,' we would reply, 'But service is service and schnapps is schnapps! When we go out on patrol all the fun stops, each trip is a suicide mission and we can never be sure that we will be returning home safely. So behind the lines we make the best of it!'

Around 20 November 1944 the battalion was ordered to join the flank of the Panzer Lehr Division against American forces which had broken through at Strasbourg. We transferred to the Nieder-bronn area in haste and from there we sortied almost daily south of the Moder and near Haguenau. There was no clear front line. The Americans would liberate a village and then leave it to us, and we had to be extremely careful not to be ambushed. Every road leading to a village had its anti-tank obstacles but remained open.

The people of Alsace were well disposed towards us having been Germans themselves in the past and I detected no enmity. (When Alsace was re-annexed in 1940, the inhabitants either had to accept German nationality or abandon the province to live in France.) When we spoke with them in the houses where we were billeted they were very forthcoming and praised the earlier successes of the Wehrmacht. There were many men from Alsace in the Wehrmacht, even some in our battalion. They had no good word to say about the 'Golden Pheasants'. Even here an old lady barred our way into her farmyard with much ado. She was concerned that having our reconnaissance vehicles parked there would attract enemy fighter-bombers, and so we had to settle for the farm next door. During all my service I never once saw civilians forced to let us in; our patrol commanders always tried to settle things peaceably.

While on patrol between two villages we came across a married couple pulling a small cart. The man wore a Reichsbahn uniform. Keichel stopped him and asked if there were German soldiers in the next village. We were wearing camouflage combinations and the man did not recognise us as German. He embarked upon an accurate description of the places still held by the Germans, their strengths and which bases their reconnaissance vehicles operated from. I had driven up quite close and could hear every word. The wife now got involved in the conversation and said excitedly how happy they were that the Americans had come at last and were hunting the damned Germans to the devil. Keichel was initially speechless, then grabbed the man's collar and called him a traitor, a man wearing German railway uniform with the eagle and swastika on the cap. Did he know what we did with traitors today? Both suddenly recognised the danger they had talked themselves into and went to pieces. The woman whimpered and the railway trousers trembled at the knees. In disgust Keichel told them, 'Go to the devil' and then gave his driver the order 'March!'.

Even now I still do not know what to make of it. Are the bilingual people of Alsace more in favour of being part of France or Germany? In my Afrika Korps company we had armoured infantry carriers bearing the legend 'Elsäss und Lothringen' – Alsace and Lorraine. In my present company I had often talked to Alsatian people and never heard them speak deprecatingly of the worsening political situation. In the radio panzer we listened regularly to the forbidden enemy broadcasts. Probably it is always the case in border provinces that when one side gets the upper hand in war, the inner conviction tends to wander into the victor's camp. (When our battalion retreated from Alsace, our Alsatian colleagues all suddenly disappeared.)

Our patrol approached the next large village with caution. I moved up to second place in the column with my gun wagon behind Keichel's so that we both had a clear field of fire. The radio panzer brought up the rear. At the entrance to the village we drove through the anti-tank obstacle, not yet firmly installed. The place looked deserted. From behind their curtains the local population had seen the Americans come and go, and now they had German armoured vehicles again. The village street forked. One road went ahead, the other curved to the right. Keichel took the latter and suddenly his MG was firing. I drove up tight in support and opened up on an American scouting party with four jeeps. At this distance it was not so important to hit but to be the first to fire, and the 2cm cannon and MG 42 made a wonderful racket between the houses.

The Americans were so surprised that they never returned fire but leapt out of their jeeps at once and fled into the houses. Keichel's gunner Lambert Fleskes, who had been in my company in Africa, had reacted correctly and opened fire without pausing to aim, at which the Americans had taken flight. We destroyed their jeeps afterwards. In our reconnaissance company our motto was: 'Whoever shoots first lives longer'. We returned the way we had come and I secured the road near the tank obstacle with my half-track.

Keichel came over and said he was going on foot patrol along a by-way with the commander of the radio panzer. I told my young gunner, until now without experience of the front, to point the weapon ready to fire at the bend in the road. To quieten his nerves I explained that anything coming up from ahead would be enemy but he should fire only on my command. Keep calm, don't panic, I kept telling him.

Suddenly a single jeep came along and I said at once, 'Don't shoot, don't shoot, let him get closer then we'll have him.' Then we saw them waving and I recognised Keichel and the commander of the radio panzer. They had gone down the by-way to the jeeps, found three of them unserviceable but this one, a bit farther back, still idling in neutral. Things could naturally turn very nasty when an enemy vehicle arrived unexpectedly with a German crew and nerves were on edge. We brought the jeep back to Company as spoils of war.

On another patrol our vehicles were unprotected and about 100 metres from a railway embankment. Keichel was at the radio panzer dictating a signal for the radio operator to transmit to Battalion. Suddenly two enemy fighter-bombers roared over us at low level, banked high and we saw at once that they had seen us. We sprinted to our vehicles and headed at full pelt for the railway bridge. The two aircraft had turned and made for our starting position but could not find us since we were now under cover. They did not give up so easily and came round the other side of the embankment to attack. Still unable to see us under the bridge they opened fire anyway. We anticipated this move and had pulled back sufficiently to watch their MG rounds kicking up clouds of dust in front of us. They tried the same thing from the other side again but we merely shifted our position under the bridge and frustrated them anew. Luckily for us they had no bombs. I certainly would not have wanted to have been at the mercy of these two bloodthirsty leeches in open country, for then we should never have got away with it.

After some initial successes, the Panzer Lehr Division clashed with the US Third Army and was forced on the defensive. This was the army of General Patton, our adversary from Tunisia in 1943. Our patrol now drove to call on various security positions. On a ridge we saw Luftwaffe ground forces for the first time, a field unit digging slit trenches. To the south a country lane lined with bushes, hedges and sporadic trees ran down into a valley. Keichel put both gun wagons under cover along this lane for safety and then went to the Luftwaffe command post. We also knew that in the valley, panzer-grenadiers from our battalion were guarding access along the approach road.

Being trained reconnaissance men we always kept our surroundings under close observation and at once through binoculars I saw a few American tanks and a howitzer battery moving into position on a distant ridge. On our own ridge some NCOs were walking about as though on some airfield at a Luftwaffe base. I drew the attention of a warrant officer to the danger they were courting if they continued to wander around in the open. He was not really interested and so they carried on as before with the Luftwaffe soldiers going from trench to trench and standing around in groups smoking.

When a Luftwaffe corporal came to our vehicle I pointed out the danger but again I met nonchalant indifference and he replied, 'Don't shit your pants in your tin can.' His attitude took my breath away and I retorted, 'Take care, the Americans will soon winkle you out of your trenches.' With a glance at the enemy howitzer battery on the peak opposite I saw that it would not be long before they put an end to the peaceful comings and goings on this side of the uplands, and I warned my crews, 'Nobody leave his vehicle!'

After a while we saw flashes from the American guns. We kept our heads down and soon the 15.5cm shells arrived and exploded all along our ridge. They sent over only three salvoes before all fell quiet, except for the shouting for medics. Keichel came running up to find out what had happened, but we were in the sunken road out of harm's way while the Luftwaffe warriors were pouring out of their trenches looking shocked and bewildered.

Keichel returned to the command post while we guarded the sunken road towards the south. Shooting with infantry weapons in the valley became louder. After a while some grenadiers came panting up, firing back at where they had come from, and went to ground nearby. I checked our field of fire and the line of retreat. Finally some Americans in their typical rounded steel helmets came in sight and we opened fire with both 2cm cannon and the MG 42s, supported by the panzer-grenadiers near and behind us. This forced the Americans to pull back, pursued by the grenadiers firing at them at the gallop. Keichel reappeared, but by now the danger had passed. Radio signals were sent, and after a pause our new orders were morsed over.

Returning from a patrol we were given quarters in private houses in Haguenau, where we thought we might spend a few hours of peace and quiet. During the hours of darkness, however, the town came under continuous enemy artillery fire forcing us to shelter all night in the cellars with the occupants. The Americans had probably taken bearings on our battalion's radio stations and called out their night shift. Our cellar had extra support from planking but we thought a direct hit would probably come right through. As front veterans we did not like to cower defenceless and unprotected in the cellars of civilian houses, but how much worse was it for the women and children, crying and screaming, clinging to us desperately when near-misses blew out the candles. Next day we surveyed the damage. A column of cyclists had chained all their machines together against the wall of a house, a shell had hit and now the machines lay in a tangle of metal tubing. Colleagues from my company described how a shell had penetrated the cellar roof and come to rest hanging down between the bracing struts of the cellar supports. In shock everybody had scampered out into the street. They were very lucky. Again and again one heard the most incredible things which happen in wartime.

Chapter Seven

The Ardennes Offensive

At the beginning of December 1944 the battalion, now deployed along the Moder river near Pfaffenhofen, was relieved by an infantry division and transferred by train to Traben-Trarbach and Bernkastel-Kues on the river Moselle. Our Sd.Kfz 250/9 gun wagons were placed as flak protection in the middle of the trains. While we were loading them aboard, two enemy reconnaissance aircraft spent a long time circling the station and I feared the worst for our transporters. We arrived safely to Traben-Trarbach without incident, however.

Part of the journey took us along the Rhine. My driver, a senior private from the Rhineland, disappeared suddenly and could not be found anywhere on the train. I was at a loss as to whether I should inform the patrol commander and Company. If he had deserted and was not back by the time we unloaded I would have a major problem for failing to report his absence. If he turned up at unloading and I had already reported his absence, it would be he who had the big problem. Knowing my company commander Lieutenant Gavenat, my driver would be arrested for absence without leave. Thus during the entire journey I had this damned unpleasant knot in my stomach. At unloading he reappeared. He had alighted near his home town, visited his parents who owned a hotel, and then caught us up using local trains.

Our No. 1 Company was given quarters at Bad Wilstein and Kautenbach. The street snaked through mountainous country with a stream alongside. From my window the mountains blocked the sky. I often went walking in Traben-Trarbach with my friend Hans Pischke. We crossed the bridge over the Moselle and spat into its waters. There was absolutely nothing to do in the village. One Saturday evening we asked a local man on convalescent leave where there was any night life. 'You must go to "The Wild Man", but they won't let you in unless you knock three times.' He took us there, knocked three times, and we were admitted. In the public bar the innkeeper called out 'Flak men, arm yourselves, the panzers are coming!' These were flak infantry, who guarded the Moselle bridges, with their wives and girlfriends and were probably regular customers.

The innkeeper noticed from our 'Afrika' cuff-titles that Pischke and I had both served in North Africa. Immediately a close bond was established between us all, for during the First World War he had served in the German South-West African colonies [modern Namibia]. Thus we were old Africa comrades and the whole evening he served us young Moselle wine without charge. With the flak men and their female consorts we had a very merry time and sang many old songs – *Wir lagen vor Madegascar und hatten die Pest an Bord* ('We lay off Madagascar and had the plague on board') and also the old hunting song from colonial times *Haie Safari!* which the Afrika Korps adopted with new lyrics.

When we took our leave and Pischke and I went out into the fresh air, the young wine hit us. Now we had to walk five kilometres along the serpentine road, alongside the babbling brook, to our quarters. That walk is a total blank for me. Finally when we peered around the corner of the house at daybreak, the Company had paraded and the Spiess stood before them. We could not allow ourselves to be seen in such a state and slunk off to our quarters to freshen up and make ourselves presentable. The landlady covered her face with her hands when she saw me.

Some time later, after the Company had been dismissed, we reported to Senior Warrant Officer Petschner, the Spiess. He took a light view of the affair. 'Lucky you did not come on parade in that state or I would have had to report you to the Company commander. For missing morning parade you will each do three days' Duty NCO', and at that he grinned, having spared himself six days as Duty NCO. Petschner had been in North Afrika as AA3 commander, wore the Iron Cross 1st Class and the German Cross in Gold and now had an understanding with his young NCOs. The punishment hit Pischke and me hard for we were always together and now we had to loaf for three days alone.

The men had quarters in a school, corporals, sergeants and officers in private homes. Whoever wanted to go out had to sign the Guard Book: the men had to report back by 22.00 hrs, corporals by midnight and sergeants by 01.00 hrs. The Guard Book was controlled by the Duty NCO to ensure that these curfew hours were observed, and a report had to be made next morning to the Spiess. Whoever failed to note his departure in the Guard Book had to be mighty careful not to be spotted. The company commander had seen two infantrymen who had neglected to sign out in Traben-Trarbach and these received jail time. Thus everybody was forewarned.

At midnight when I checked the Guard Book five corporals had not signed back in. Shortly before 0130 hrs the Duty Private, whose turn ran from midnight to reveille, woke me and said I should come to the Duty NCO's room. The five corporals wanted their arrival to be entered as midnight. Falsification of the Guard Book was a serious military offence. I had to find some way round it. I sent the Duty Private off on a round of the sleeping quarters and to check on the sentries. I said to the corporals, 'Here is the Guard Book, five corporals are missing but if the entries are there in the early morning, perhaps I dreamt it!' Next morning I reported to the Spiess, 'On watch nothing to report!'

Unfortunately some sergeants seated in a tavern at midnight had seen the corporals pass by singing. They checked the Watch Book next day and found that everybody had been entered as returning at the correct hour. At about ten the hypocrite Keichel asked me if there had been any events of note on the last watch. I knew at once what this was about and told him that at midnight a number of corporals had not returned but that next morning, without any complicity on my part of course, they were all entered correctly. 'Well Henning, you have a millstone around your neck, for that is a guard offence.' At that he told me that some sergeants had seen the corporals after midnight and had informed the Spiess of an alleged falsification of the Watch Book.

After afternoon roll call I had to appear before the Spiess so that he could make his report to the company commander about the guard offence after interviewing me first. In the meantime I had consulted the corporals and drawn up a plan of defence. I would say that, as I understood it, the corporals had not been in the locality of the tavern until after 01.00 hrs, and no sergeant had signed the

Guard Book after 01.00 hrs. This meant that the several sergeants making the complaint must have been absent without leave themselves in order to see the corporals singing in the street, and had themselves falsified the Guard Book. Petschner saw at once that it would cause havoc if he took action against all the corporals and sergeants involved. He grinned and said, 'OK Henning, I shall talk to the sergeants and then decide if the company commander needs to be told.' I made a smart about-turn knowing at once that that was an end to it, for most of the sergeants, including Keichel, had been with Petschner in AA3 in North Africa and, as is well known, crows do not peck each other's eyes out.

Starting on 13 December 1944, and over a two-day period, we went by road to Krautscheid via Wittlich, Kyllburg and Waxweiler. We moved only by night and camouflaged the vehicles carefully by day, generally finding a barn to park them in. Everything was a big secret, although an attack was rumoured. In Krautscheid our recon-naissance company was the only combat unit we saw, and in the neighbouring village they had set up a veterinary hospital, but otherwise there were no other troops anywhere. Our battalion and also our company was up to strength in vehicles and personnel and had been given full provisions, ammunition and fuel.

On the afternoon of Friday 15 December 1944 the company was put on high-alert readiness. From now on nobody could leave the unit. When dark fell Keichel came back from a conference and told us: 'At 05.30 hrs on 16 December 1944 we shall attack the enemy after an artillery bombardment over the river Our. The recon-naissance company will be reinforced by one panzer company, one anti-tank company and a light howitzer company, and these will form the spearhead battalion of the Panzer Lehr Division. A Volksgrenadier Division will build bridgeheads over the Our and Clerf, and the Panzer Lehr will push ahead as quickly as possible via Bastogne to the Meuse at Dinant. So much for Battalion and Division! And now the most important thing for ourselves. Two patrols have been earmarked for "nuisance duty". After breaking through the enemy lines they will be free to create panic in the enemy rear. Those patrols are of Lieutenant X and ourselves!' Shock and horror all round! A suicide mission in the fifth year of the war was no morale-booster. The old hands amongst us knew what it meant and we exchanged anxious glances.

'But that will hardly be possible with the kind of highway and territory we will have in Luxembourg,' I pointed out. 'Recently with Lieutenant Ziemke we came back through Luxembourg, and therefore I know what I am talking about. It is just not possible for us to hide in the bushes in those hills when tanks turn up!'

'We have a mission and we shall carry it out,' Keichel snapped, 'End of discussion, we leave for the departure area at 23.30 hrs and you, Henning, will report the operational readiness of the patrol to me!'. At that he swept off to his next conference and left us with our gloomy thoughts. We did not know whether only our division was to attack or if the whole army in the West would be involved. We had seen no attack troops. Not until later did we realise how perfectly the preparations had been organised so that even ourselves as participants knew nothing of the attack troops moving forward.

The radio operator obtained his signals and codebooks from the battalion signals officer. Absolute radio silence was in force. Swiftly I got hold of a couple of General Staff maps on the 1:100,000 scale for the assumed areas of advance in Luxembourg and Belgium. It was always a good thing to know exactly where we were in a crisis situation. In France I often used to purloin maps from my patrol commanders because they could get replacements at any time from the map office. Therefore I always knew where we were geographically.

The time passed slowly until 23.30 hrs when both patrols set off into the cold, dark winter's night. It was a very difficult drive over those smooth, hilly roads and the commanders often had to walk ahead of the vehicles to mark the centre of the road to prevent them slipping off into the abyss. As we discovered later, the lieutenant's patrol had an accident on a snowbound highway and was forced to abandon the mission. Throughout the drive we met no other traffic except for two lorries near Preischeid whose drivers had probably parked for some sleep. We got to the prescribed crossroads but all was quiet, no panzers, no vehicles and also no signposts. We looked at each other aghast. Keichel said: 'Perhaps the whole attack has been aborted and they forgot to tell us.' It was eerily quiet all round, even the nearby front line was peaceful.

Keichel turned us back and we drove along the stretch which ran at an angle to the front. Suddenly he stopped and summoned me. 'Henning, have a look at the map. What is your opinion of where we are?' In the light of my pocket lamp I showed him right away, I had been following our route secretly.

'I am of the same opinion, but there are no troops here at all. At 05.30 hrs all our artillery is supposed to fire, pioneers and panzers will destroy the enemy positions so that we can be pushed through into the enemy rear!'

'Why don't we go back to those two lorries and ask if they have heard any troop movements during the night?' I suggested. He thought this was a good idea and we awoke the lorry drivers. They said they had heard us but nobody else. They were loath to get down from their cabs, being probably well wrapped up in blankets against the beastly cold.

We returned to the rendezvous point and suddenly all hell broke loose. The crossroads and the village were full of panzers and combat vehicles. Keichel got a rocket from the commanders because he had not been at the position ordered. Because of him the whole plan was in chaos and could not proceed as directed. Keichel, who always talked big himself, now had to do the listening and he was threatened with consequences! We were told to insert our three half-tracks into the column, but progress was halting. Dawn found us still on the German side of the Our. Can't the pioneers put a damn bridge up?

Early on this 16 December 1944 there was a frost with low cloud so that enemy air activity was restricted. The fighter-bombers would have been overjoyed to find us all laid out here like a string of pearls. At midday we had got as far as Untereisenbach with a tall, precipitous cliff to our left and the basin of the Our to our right. Now the fighter-bombers appeared. Because of the cliff it was difficult for them to attack the convoy. Directly to the rear of my gun wagon was a quadruple 2cm flak firing almost vertically upwards. In the turret we wore our steel helmets just in case a shell exploded in a barrel or during its flight, something I had experienced during panzer training. An enemy machine came for straight for us at low level from three o'clock. My gunner was bemused by the shooting of the flak quadruple and slow to grasp the situation. I gave him a few blows on the steel helmet with the reserve barrel of the MG to get him to react faster, take aim and finally open fire. The pilot of the aircraft fired a burst into the cliffs and flew off without damage.

On 17 December 1944 we finally reached the main highway in Luxembourg. The situation remained totally confused, our advance having been considerably delayed by the unexpected resistance of the Americans and the almost insuperable difficulties presented by the terrain. This rendered our 'nuisance' patrol in the hinterland behind the enemy lines simply impossible. Our battalion was forced to intervene at Hosingen and Wahlhausen in support of the Volksgrenadiers. We patrolled towards Hosingen and Drauffelt in order to cross the Clervè which we did at 18.12 hrs. Once there, our patrol was recalled by radio and redirected via Kautenbach towards Wiltz where we spent a quiet night. Next morning my gun wagon was stationary on the outskirts of a village on guard when ten to twelve Americans emerged from a wood across the snow-covered fields towards us, hands on their steel helmets in the gesture of surrender. The gunner manned the MG while I went to meet them. I indicated they should lower their hands and sent them into the village. It was obvious that they had been lost in the woods for some time and were at the end of their strength. In North Africa it was our custom to have a relaxed attitude towards PoWs. The Afrika Korps held strictly to the rules and were a model for our younger soldiers now. We never frisked or abused prisoners, knowing that in a flash the tables could be turned and we would be in the same situation. We hoped for humane treatment for ourselves accordingly. Perhaps at collection points the treatment was different, but that is only a guess since I never saw a German PoW camp at any time during my military service. In the radio panzer we were always tuned in to the enemy German-language broadcasts. After a few days we heard accusations that German SS soldiers had shot US prisoners at Malmèdy. We simply refused to believe this and considered it enemy atrocity propaganda.

We accompanied the panzer spearhead towards Bastogne. We continually came across intact groups of small American units in pockets of resistance whose purpose was to disrupt our lines of supply. In the woods American engineers had blown up tree after great tree to block the roads along which we were advancing, and had also laid mines. These all had to be cleared by our engineers first of all, and this cost us time. After three days we were south east of Bastogne at Wardin and Marvie, involved in bitter fighting with heavy losses to both sides. Keichel remained convinced that with a concentrated effort Bastogne could have been taken. He told me that according to the orders it should have fallen to us by 16.00 hrs on the first day, but that was the planning of staff officers who still had the successes of May 1940 in their heads. The reality against US forces in 1944 was quite different.

The advance continued after we were reinforced by a panzer engineer battalion. We passed Bastogne to the south and after a short fight captured a long transport convoy on the US corps main supply route between Tillet and Moircy. At Piranpré our patrol captured material, including Christmas mail. We transferred the Christmas parcels into our half-tracks and so full did they become that we could hardly train the turrets. Most of the packets were tossed into the radio panzer and then Keichel urged us forward.

Next we halted for lack of fuel. I was told to go back with my gun wagon and bring up the supply column which had got stuck somewhere. It was a long haul back. I found the lorries, all held up by dispersed groups of enemy troops. I reported to the transport officer, who was in conference with other officers in a house, and urged him to get through quickly. They could not go by way of the track along which I had arrived; the heavy lorries needed an asphalt highway and the snow did not make it any easier. My gun wagon was appointed leader for the journey. Everything started well, though too slowly for my liking. Shortly before dark fell I was halted by infantry at the entrance to a village. The Americans had blocked the road ahead. The transport commander had all the lorry crews form a circular defence in the village while my vehicle was ordered forward on sentry duty off the road. Some infantry dug in ahead of us near the road. During the night it began to snow heavily and soon we were snowed in.

Firing was heard from up ahead, at which the lorry crews moved up behind my gun wagon. We removed the canvas covers which protected our weapons from the elements and released the safety catches. Two infantrymen came to report that figures in snow suits had been seen advancing along the road towards them. We could see no such figures but fired off a magazine with explosive rounds in the general direction indicated. The fire was not returned.

At daybreak I had to reconnoitre the road to ensure it was free of the enemy. There was no sign of them and so the convoy continued its journey to Battalion, where we were received with joy. Keichel was very happy to have me back and the patrol at full strength again. After refuelling we headed for St Hubert. In a field we discovered a whole battery of enemy artillery, all the guns arrayed as if for a parade. Keichel notified Battalion by radio, and after a while some panzers turned up. The Americans had their gun barrels horizontal, probably in expectation of the German attack. Self-propelled guns and some Panzer Mk IVs came up from a depression and in a brief exchange of fire the American guns were over-whelmed. The survivors abandoned the artillery and ran up the snow-covered slope into the houses. After the skirmish we saw trails of blood in the snow and German medics went into the houses to tend the American wounded.

Late on the morning of 23 December, St Hubert fell to our battalion and now our armour assembled there in order to attack beyond Rochefort on the Meuse. At midday the weather cleared somewhat, but the temperature remained at -10°C. A host of low-flying two-engined aircraft came droning over St Hubert. I went hot and cold. If they turned back and bombed these roads crammed with vehicles our whole battalion was mincemeat. I directed my driver at once alongside the wall of a house for better protection in the event of a bomber attack. With relief we watched them fly off. About half an hour later they were back over St Hubert. By the open hatches and doors it was obvious that they had dropped supplies to American troops bottled up at Bastogne. In the afternoon we got to the area east of Rochefort, but our attempt to capture it came to nothing.

A close friendship had developed between our patrol and one of the lorry crews following our capture of American material. When we arrived at Battalion both men had arranged quarters for us and for this service we invited them to share in our captured provisions. They cooked, buttered bread and made a cold buffet for us. They always kept fuel and spare parts in reserve for us on their lorry. The driver was from Pomerania and had been valet and cook to a general in Russia. The driver's mate was a Berliner of full figure, a hairdresser by trade who had styled the hair of the female world in Ahlbeck and Heringsdorf before the war and now amused us with the stories of his courtships of the lonely ladies at a spa. We nicknamed him 'Graf Alfi'. Our excellent collaboration came to a terrible end. Returning from patrol one day we were told that their lorry had received a direct hit from artillery while distributing petrol. One of them was dead, the other seriously wounded. We were all greatly saddened and missed very much our two friends, so different from us in their way of life.

On the morning of 24 December 1944 the Belgian town of Rochefort finally fell to our battalion in conjunction with an engineer battalion which had been rushed up. Our patrol followed two Panzer Mk V Panthers along an approach road where our gun wagons gave covering fire in house-to-house fighting. Engineer groups pressed forward beside us and to our rear. Just behind a sharp right-hand bend two American anti-tank guns held the road bridge over the Lomme. As the first Panther appeared at the bend it received two hits, but the shells bounced off and struck the upper storey of a nearby house. The Panther withdrew at once behind the corner of the house.

It was difficult to decide how to root out the anti-tank guns. After a conference of panzer commanders they thought that at this short range the shells would not develop their full hitting power. The lieutenant remounted his panzer and with mixed feelings we watched how it would go. With motor screeching the panzer came round the corner of the house. Both anti-tank guns fired at once, again the shells bounced off the armour and hit the upper storey of the building and then the Panther replied. We followed behind it. Both anti-tank guns were taken out together with a pretty café with a green ceramic facade which had been near them. (M. Florent Lambert told me in the year 2000 that this café was owned by M. Désiré Fievet.) As soon as the leading Panther arrived at the bridge over the Lomme, American engineers blew it up. This put an end to our progress. In the fighting for Rochefort our battalion commander, Major von Born-Fallois, was wounded. Our engineers cleared the houses of American troops in hiding but still the occasional shot rang out. An engineer was wounded in the leg near my vehicle. Later that afternoon some engineers told us that they found an

American sniper in a house they had suspected. He was hiding amongst potato crates.

The destruction of the bridge now offered us a chance to rest, and with three men I took quarters in a house nearby. The Belgian occupants were obviously not delighted at our sudden arrival, but by mutual agreement we settled in the kitchen. We had agreed amongst ourselves that each crew would have a parcel of their choice from the captured American Christmas post for Christmas Eve, and these parcels could not be opened beforehand. That afternoon our driver arrived with a tree which he erected in the kitchen. The occupants, particularly the children, helped us decorate it with candles, balls and cotton wool.

Keichel had been at Battalion since midday and as his deputy I was responsible for refuelling, replenishing and also for our small Christmas celebration. After our work was finished we had thoughts only for the festivities, peace and quiet, and sleep. I had stretched out on the sofa in the kitchen and my thoughts wandered to home and elsewhere, but I was restless after the tensions of the last few days.

I can understand why the Belgians would have been prickly towards us, but in this house we did not feel it. The family was reserved but not unfriendly. When my hand fell from the sofa as I slept, the lady of the house replaced it on my chest. We Germans were in their country for the fourth time since the reign of Napoleon and each time the damage and devastation from ever more modern weapons was greater. We, like Napoleon, had had half of Europe under our jackboots and now half the world was driving us back to the point from where we set out. My God, how I feared to peer into the future and imagine what would become of us if we lost. What awaited us in the Homeland after the Allied carpet-bombing of our cities? And now here, was our entire advance at an end because of this fallen bridge? If I survived this war then the peace would be awful and we would all have to atone for what we had done in the name of the Greater German Reich.

I was twenty and this was my fourth Christmas of the war. From experience I knew that in the Army one should not plan ahead, for generally things turned out differently to what one expected. For Christmas 1942 in the Afrika Korps we had planned a quiet

Christmas Eve for our reconnaissance company after the long retreat from El Alamein. Then at 22.00 hrs came the alarm and we spent the whole night and Christmas Day on the road in the eight-wheeler. The British were to the south with a huge armada of vehicles aiming to bottle us up in the north.

Thinking of Christmas Eve I was overtaken by sleep. Suddenly the door was thrown open and Keichel, map under his arm, awoke us rudely from our anticipated Christmas reveries. 'Up, up, you lazy shower, we're leaving on reconnaissance immediately!' We reacted sluggishly and I thought, My God, what must they have said at Battalion to ginger up this poison dwarf (Keichel) for the next operation? Perhaps my sleepy face seemed defiant to him, for he snapped, 'Get your arse off your mattress Henning, in ten minutes we have an officers' reconnaissance patrol!' A what? I rose slowly from my sofa while Keichel drummed up the rest of the men from the other houses. At our vehicles he explained the orders. 'Because the bridge is down we have lost contact with the enemy, and our patrol has the task of establishing where the enemy front line runs and the interception points they have set up. The operation is so important that we shall be accompanied by two jeeps with officers.'

This being Christmas Eve the orders brought forth no shouts of enthusiasm and everybody looked to me to express an opinion to Keichel. 'This is a pure suicide mission again and how do we cross the water? And will the officers lead or follow us?' Keichel replied in poisonous tones: 'From you all I want to know is if the vehicles are fuelled up, replenished and the patrol is ready. In five minutes we go!' Shit, our Christmas was down the drain. I returned quickly to the Belgian family to bid our hosts farewell, we all shook hands and the old granny said in passable German that she wished me luck to come safely through the war.

The two captured jeeps, each crewed by one officer, a driver and two panzer grenadiers with machine-pistols drove up and we left at once. I had been on reconnaissance often enough in North Africa and France, but this particular Christmas Eve of 1944 I had the most damned unhealthy feeling and felt sure it was not going to go well. It was bitterly cold as the patrol headed downstream from the wrecked bridge on the Lomme. The river flowed very quickly here, smooth and wide. Only along the river banks was there a layer of ice. Keichel was thinking about trying to ford the river with the half-tracks because he knew the river bed was stony. I called out to him, 'If you get stuck in the middle I'm not getting out into the water!' This gave him pause for thought and then he joined all the tow ropes together and secured them to his vehicle so that if necessary we could haul him back. He made it across however. We dragged the elongated rope back, attached one jeep each to the two remaining half-tracks and so we all got through the cold water. It was now fully dark before moonrise and we drove up to the bridgehead crew on the enemy side to report. Some engineers approached and asked where we were going so late in the evening.

'On patrol, so that you people can have a quiet Christmas!'

'We'd rather not be in your shoes!'

We could only shrug our shoulders about this mission. The patrol closed up, for with every kilometre west we drove it got more dangerous. Keichel led in the first gun wagon, then came the radio panzer and I secured the rear with the second gun wagon. The two jeeps followed behind. Every thirty minutes we had to transmit a coded message to Battalion giving our position. This would be monitored by Division. Thus Keichel was being hard pressed by both headquarters for results.

The first kilometres were quickly behind us and then we introduced a routine in which we stopped every kilometre, each driver would switch off his engine and we would listen for sounds in the night. In the patrol this was carried out in exemplary fashion for we were all experienced men selected by Keichel and of proven mettle. Only the two jeeps failed to get the point and their engines thundered in neutral in the silent winter night. I got out twice to tell the jeep drivers what they were supposed to do, but it was beyond them. The officers' jeeps were already proving a liability.

The greatest danger for us came from the west, behind the clouds, for the full moon had risen. In bright moonlight we should be easily visible to the enemy. Furthermore this would provide good flying weather for enemy fighter-bombers following the recent overcast days during our advance. We drove on through the moonlit night, our legs, arms and above all our knees frozen stiff and painful. I would not have trusted myself to leap out of the half-track in that condition. We wore camouflage combinations over our black panzer uniforms. We could not wear a greatcoat on patrol because it would impede out immediate escape should our narrow armoured box be hit. There was no issue of purpose-made winter clothing.

Some houses came into sight and we slowed. They were not occupied by the enemy and we drove on. Stopped on a slope a large puddle appeared below my vehicle. I reported to Keichel that I was losing fuel. He came back with me, put a finger in the puddle, smelled and licked it and concluded: 'That is water. Today you and I must drink our fill from the cup of bitter sorrow.' The word he used, 'Kelch', is an ecclesiastical term. Whether it was an augury for what he sense would happen ahead that Christmas morning only he could tell. On the slope, the water collected from the river crossing had flowed out from the undercarriage of my half-track.

In the moonlight the distance between the patrol and the jeeps kept increasing. After a few kilometres the first jeep fell back after consulting Keichel, and a short while later the second jeep also decided not to continue with us. Apparently they did not like the way we did things. I was pleased to be rid of them, always tailing along behind, for they neither could nor wanted to go along with the tactics of a reconnaissance patrol.

The patrol proceeded alone. Outside Ciergnon I had to go on foot patrol with Keichel as so often before, one of us either side of the road with machine-pistol at the ready, the two gun wagons following at the limit of visual range to give covering fire. We approached the houses cautiously, but they were not occupied by the enemy. In one of them we found a couple of men with a sergeant from 2nd Panzer Division. They told us that the division must be somewhere ahead of us to the north although they could not supply better details. Keichel sent a signal regarding Ciergnon and now we headed north- west. The aim was to approach the Meuse and Dinant on by-roads north of the Lesse, practically by the back door. Keichel halted on a right-hand bend and from this elevated position we had a grand panorama over the snowy landscape, lit by the moon. After the first foot patrol I joined Keichel at a longish halt to discuss our next move. We could hear dogs barking in the villages ahead of us which might have indicated unrest there because of enemy strangers. We decided therefore to call a halt until daybreak.

Studying the map, Keichel identified a bridge over a stream about two kilometres ahead and decided to investigate if the bridge had enemy sentries on it or was mined. If not we would secure the bridge in the night for the advance of the Division. We set out on foot patrol again with the vehicles following at the limit of vision. After a left-hand bend we saw the bridge railings gleaming in the moonlight. We held off the vehicles and crept forward to the bridge using all available cover. (From experience we knew that when we came across American sentries, there was always a fireworks display with their explosive shells. Then we would have to stay in cover, keep quiet and not try to advance. Only when they had expended enough ammunition to convince themselves we must be done for would they reduce their fire allowing us to sneak through.) We confirmed that the bridge was neither mined nor guarded, and Keichel positioned his gun wagon to protect it, the radio panzer in the centre, where a country lane crossed, and my vehicle protecting the road behind. Here we were in No-Man's Land and danger could threaten from anywhere. Battalion was informed of our intentions by radio.

Now we had a little time to ourselves and we could begin our Christmas festivities. Each crewman unwrapped his Christmas parcel which had been sent by American families to their brave soldiers. We had to do this inside our vehicles because we were not allowed to dismount. The parcels contained mainly Christmas edibles, candles, cakes, pastries and chocolate. The cake was very dry after the long journey and the crumbs stuck in the throat because we had nothing to drink. We liked the kisses impressed on paper best. In the beastly cold we thought wistfully of our planned Christmas in Rochefort with the Belgian family. Most of all we missed the warm kitchen and soft sofa.

I spent some time in Keichel's vehicle and we talked about Christmases we had had in Germany and in the Wehrmacht, also about our service in North Africa with its tropical heat, so different to this lousy cold here. Kaichel and his driver Hans Suse had been with AA3 in the Afrika Korps, his gunner Lambert Fleskes and I in a panzer reconnaissance company of AA580. Five members of this patrol were former Afrikaners.

Listening in the night, suddenly we heard footsteps on the road coming towards us. They stopped frequently. We suspected at once an enemy patrol intending to blow up or mine the bridge. I wanted to creep back to my own vehicle quickly but Keichel held me back. For safety's sake I climbed on the bonnet to one side of the driver's viewing slit while Keichel and Fleskes peered above the turret coaming into the darkness. The footsteps came ever nearer, occasionally stopping. The first of them had now reached the bridge where they halted. We estimated at least a platoon. I thought, if we open fire on them with our 2cm HE shells and the MG 42 we shall have a nice Christmas bloodbath. Moreover, every reconnaissance man is mindful of the motto, 'Whoever fires first lives longer!' Keichel hesitated with the order to fire until they were all on the bridge about thirty paces away and nicely grouped up.

'Open fire!' Keichel ordered. I ducked my head in expectation of return fire but Fleskes had failed to comply with the order. Had his gun jammed or was it a religious thing about not firing first on Christmas Day? He came from Kleve, a strongly Catholic region. Even later we never got a proper explanation about why he disobeyed the order.

'Don't shoot, don't shoot, German soldiers here!' came the shout from the bridge. Keichel told me, 'Henning, go and see what they are.' Aha, this was why he had held me back as a witness for his pyrotechnics! I slid off the engine plating with my machine-pistol and called out to Fleskes, 'Don't drill me in the back, Lambert!' and, keeping to the edge of the road, made my way cautiously to the platoon which had stopped and not moved again. I called one of them forward to me for questioning, for precautions in war are doubly advisable. I was greatly relieved to find that they actually were German infantry, all not-so-young comrades from 2nd Panzer Division, who had been only a short time in uniform and were probably the last reserves for Final Victory. Some of them were so exhausted that they hit the ground trembling and I couldn't talk to them. The group was fifteen or sixteen strong and had gone astray cross-country before finding this bridge. They thought it would have enemy sentries and expected to be captured. They were unable to provide us with any information of where they had come from and where they were going. Once they had collected themselves a little we gave them precise instructions how to get to Rochefort, and advised Battalion by radio to expect them, since they might be in danger from the German sentries guarding the Rochefort bridgehead.

We of the patrol were none of us beginners in this war, but this order 'Open fire!' at our own comrades gave us a sickening feeling. Every one of us closed our eyes and reflected on how he would have come to terms with shooting dead our own comrades on Christmas morning. Keichel never brought the matter up later and we never spoke of it. Therefore I cannot say why Fleskes chose to ignore the order. For myself in any case I always recall that patrol on Christmas morning 1944 with the order to fire on our own comrades and what Keichel had said earlier about drinking our fill of the cup of bitter sorrow.

At daybreak we headed for the Meuse on back roads and secret paths for a while before receiving the recall by radio to the Battalion position on the Rochefort-Boissonville highway. On the way back we happened to be in terrain off the road when we saw a long gun barrel and a German Panther appear slowly around a street corner. Now we had to be very careful for we did not know if the panzer crew had knowledge of our reconnaissance patrol. Our vehicles were camouflaged with fir branches and we observed the panzer very watchfully without moving. After thirty minutes it rolled back and disappeared. We followed slowly and rejoined the highway to Rochefort.

At midnight on Christmas Eve, troops of the Panzer Lehr Division had assembled around Rochefort in order to help the hard-pressed 2nd Panzer Division near Dinant, and ran into strong resistance at Boissonville. Our patrol knew nothing of the division's change of direction to the north. As we approached Rochefort we heard a terrible artillery barrage hitting north of the town. On the outskirts of Rochefort we saw many mushroom-like columns of smoke rising up in the woods to the left of the road. An aircraft, which we assumed was the artillery spotter, was circling over the wood. Many residents were out of doors and watching with horror, no doubt full of concern that this murderous bombardment could spread to the town. Keichel brought the patrol close to leafy cover and watched helplessly as the American heavy howitzer batteries fired ceaselessly into the woods. It was so bad that Keichel did not want to risk the drive to Battalion: that was how bad it was. He often told me when he returned from operational conferences that enemy armour could be withdrawn from Aachen to penetrate our spearhead, and now they had done so.

The Panzer Lehr Division made two further attempts to get 2nd Panzer Division out of the encirclement, but both were thwarted by RAF Typhoons. Their reconnaissance and artillery observers identified our panzer positions and attacked our Mk IVs and Panthers with rockets. Then came American fighter-bombers and we dared not leave cover, let alone change position.

Enemy resistance over the two days of Christmas increased because the weather conditions had improved to such an extent that by the evening of Boxing Day 1944 we knew that the Ardennes Offensive must fail. When it got dark we retired west of St Hubert to join elements of the sadly reduced forward battalion of 2nd Panzer Division coming out from Celles near Dinant. The Panzer ALA proceeded as ordered to a position from where in deep snow and bitter cold we had to defend the sector against British forces.

Our patrol was now well forward in what has become known as the Bulge, and received quarters in a village with the remnants of the armoured reconnaissance company. My crew and I lodged in a two-storey farmhouse. The farmer's wife gave us a room at the rear of this house which was unfortunately situated near a crossroads and often received enemy nuisance fire day and night. When it started up at night the old lady, her daughter and two children would come and sleep with us in the same room on the side of the house farthest from the shelling. The two husbands were away. The two women were not delighted to have us as guests but there were no problems or rancour. The daughter told us that one of the village girls had had a baby by a German soldier.

From positions in the surrounding woods the grenadiers of the Panzer ALA were defending the forward spearhead against British troops from positions. Twice daily we drove both gun wagons to the panzer grenadier trenches. Later, when fuel began to run short, we used only one. Keichel went in the morning, myself shortly before dark to give the panzer grenadiers moral support. In their trenches in deep snow and bitter cold their situation was unenviable. We on the other hand had the warm guest room which Keichel had arranged for us.

112

Because of the bestial weather in a cold metal box on wheels I had pain in the joints of both knees which caused me difficulty in standing. In the wardrobe of our room I found a pair of ladies' knitted socks of thick wool and great length. I requisitioned them and wore them over my long underpants, and I hope that both ladies forgave me the theft. I do know that in their house throughout the war to the moment of our departure they suffered no damage and I think that if they got through the Second World War minus only a pair of knitted socks they did not fare so badly.

Whilst our position at the head of the German spearhead was relatively quiet, and we only left it to visit the panzer grenadiers, from 30 December 1944 the Americans began a great pincer movement to trap us in the Bulge by heading towards Bastogne to the north while the British [actually US VII Corps under Montgomery's command. Ed] went south from Houffalize on 3 January. Keichel often spoke of the heavy fighting at Bastogne when he returned from conferences at Battalion. He related how General Bayerlein had said that he had fired more ammunition at Bastogne than throughout the entire war up to that point. Because of this murderous German artillery fire, General Patton's VIII Corps had been forced to abandon its intentions. In the evenings in the radio panzer we would always tune in to the Allied radio station 'Calais' to obtain a very accurate picture of the situation at the front. At Houffalize the Allies were slowly squeezing the Bulge and sitting here at the front of it we began to see a future for ourselves as prisoners of war.

On 10 January 1945 orders came to withdraw that night. There was only one road passable to escape the encirclement, and this was exposed to heavy artillery fire. Individual timetables had been precisely worked out to avoid bottlenecks and congestion. It was bitterly cold with sub-zero temperatures and the roads were made difficult to manoeuvre on by snow and icy surfaces. Whoever slipped off the highway or broke down would be pushed aside ruthlessly to leave the path clear for the next convoy.

Our patrol was to pull out at 23.30 hrs and we gathered in a room at the restaurant where Keichel was billeted, the three half-tracks outside. We were nice and cosy and the room was heated to get us all warmed up for departure. Suddenly panzer grenadiers began firing furiously and we ran out to get our vehicles into cover off the road. The grenadiers came up in their armoured carriers, stopped, shouted that the Tommies were attacking and then retired. It was almost 22.00 hrs and the night was silent, no sounds of street barricades being moved, and nobody was shooting. We were flabbergasted at how quiet it was. The grenadiers were not supposed to abandon their trenches, and without attracting attention that they were doing so, until after we had left. Finally we concluded that an MG burst had been released unintentionally and they had pulled out believing incorrectly that not to do so would cost them their chance to get out of the Bulge.

Keichel ordered me to guard the road with my gun wagon. We had become the most westerly border point in Belgium. I sat with my crew in the cold, my knees hurting so much that I could neither sit nor stand, nor get out of my panzer. At 22.30 hrs on the dot Keichel led us out. It went better than expected, for the retreat had been organised in exemplary fashion. We were probably amongst the last to leave the Bulge and had a fairly free drive. There was some enemy artillery fire to deter us but we emerged unscathed. We suspected that the Bulge was next to empty now anyway and the enemy would be very upset at his failure to close the bag earlier.

The Panzer ALA was on the move once more after the trench war around St Hubert and we performed some reconnaissance missions. On one of these we scouted the battle area around Houffalize, where bloody fighting was continuing in the face of the enemy advance. It was a difficult struggle in winter temperatures in the gorges and woods with much commitment in material by both sides.

Our engineers were in their element laying mines, as I remember their having done during our retreat in North Africa. One evening as we were driving through a village they stopped us: 'For God's sake go no further, we have mined everything, streets and houses. Don't enter any house, if you touch the latch the front door will blow up in your face and the chimney will fall around your ears.' 'Pure novelties', as they described them, had been fixed in all kinds of places and I had the feeling that they had gone too far, and nobody really knew who had put what where. Keichel went to their command post and we alighted. I heard a piano playing in a house, felt my way across the dark floor with the toe of my boot, stubbed

114

against something soft and yielding and got to the living room door. The engineers had lit some Hindenburg candles, by the light of which one of them was seated at the piano singing as he played: 'Everything will pass, All this will pass away, For after this war ends, Comes another May!' The choir, clad in their white battledress, had all been drinking and sang along lustily. There was plenty of gallows humour being so close to the enemy. Whoever lives in danger every day becomes blunted emotionally after a time but they still managed to win a few happy moments. Their lieutenant entered and ended the singing. As I was leaving my boots came in contact with the soft object on the dark floor of the house, and somebody called out, 'Don't forget to take Karl with you on your vehicle!' Then I saw two engineers lay their dead comrade, wrapped in a blanket, on the bonnet of their armoured carrier. Karl was the object which I had encountered with the toecap of my boots.

Next day we were scouting in the vicinity of Houffalize again and arrived in the dark by a back road on the outskirts of a small town. Nobody was shooting, absolute quiet reigned. Keichel stopped short of the highway to look for the command post. I heard the un-mistakeable noise which jolting spades and gas masks make when infantry run. These men were coming up one behind the other in single file along the house walls. I could tell at once that they were experienced soldiers and thus we needed to be doubly cautious. At once I gave the order, 'Nobody leave the vehicles!'

About ten minutes later a shell was fired from the neighbouring heights into the town, which lay in a valley below them. There was no delay between the enemy 15.5cm howitzer battery firing and the shells exploding. We put on our steel helmets immediately and drove our vehicles close to the house walls for some protection. The enemy gunners must have finished their coffee break or unloading a fresh supply of ammunition, for now they all started up together.

Where the hell was Keichel, I fumed, why must he stick his arse into every shithole? He had to come back soon or I would have to go and look for him in this hail of shells and flying splinters. Probably he had found himself a cellar to shelter in and was waiting for the opportune moment to return. Time went on and I had no idea what I should do – drive out of the immediate zone of danger or stay put and hope we didn't get hit? Suddenly he came dashing between two salvoes, filthy but in one piece, and jumped into his vehicle. Instead of leaving the village he now decided to drive through it, and we had to follow. The main road was blocked with vehicles of all kinds and the infantry were crouching in the cellars of the houses. We rolled slowly along the house fronts on the right hand side, over front gardens and pavements in the shadow of the firing, ruthlessly forcing aside any vehicle in our path and all the while I was thinking that at any moment our vehicles are going to be flattened by one of these shells roaring over.

Almost at the end of the village there was a by-road to the right which rose up a slope. Keichel chose this way to escape the enemy artillery. He had not gone far before he stopped; the road ahead was receiving fire from a light howitzer battery. The shells were exploding damned close together on the road between the houses, which were detached and in their own grounds. As I had noticed repeatedly, the spread of salvoes from German guns was much less tight. We moved forward and now, of course, the shells were exploding around us. Keichel was peering over the edge of turret into the darkness. Suddenly he withdrew his head lightning fast but left his arms clinging to the turret. His vehicle stopped and he shouted: 'Damn, I'm wounded, Henning, come here!' Another salvo landed close by and I called to his gunner Lambert Fleskes, 'Drive forward a bit out of the firing!' We advanced another 200 metres and now I could bandage Keichel's forearm and fit a sling. He was in shock and out of it completely. I radioed our position and reported: 'Patrol commander wounded – I am returning.'

Keichel did not want to go back through the village with all the artillery fire, but there was no other way open. He was ranting and raving about this and I was forced to take the initiative. I led the patrol a little farther up the sloping road to get free of the shelling and this calmed him somewhat. Driving ahead I saw that the lane fell away, and I put my turret to six o'clock to enable us to make a speedier getaway should an enemy tank appear. I put Keichel into the radio panzer to give him more space. From the crest of the road we spotted the two enemy batteries by their muzzle flashes on hilly terrain not too far off. The report of the guns firing was louder than the shells exploding. Over to one side behind us a single German gun was firing in slow motion. From my experience in North Africa

I recognised it as an 8.8cm by its hard, dry sound. It was the battle of a dwarf against Goliath, as we had known in this war so often. The German gunners probably carried their ammunition with them in a rucksack. We heard a vehicle approaching slowly along the lane. I remounted my gun wagon and released the safety catches on the weapons. When it was close to us I called out: 'Halt, who's there?'

'Don't shoot, German radio platoon!' They were a telephone crew taking up the landline. 'You can't go any further,' they said, 'The Americans are at the crossroads below. We had to leave everything there and get round the bend fast!'

I radioed their report to Battalion. I had to return there to obtain medical treatment for Keichel. We placed the radio panzer between the two gun wagons and went back the way we had come through the village in the valley. As the rear wagon passed a house a shell hit the roof and loose rafters and tiles landed on the machine. The panzer was covered in dirt but emerged undamaged. I brought Keichel to our staff surgeon and reported the patrol back to Lieutenant Werren, who was commanding Panzer ALA since Major von Born-Fallois had been wounded.

We knew that Warrant Officer Keichel had been recommended for the Knight's Cross because his patrol had made the farthest reconnaissance westwards ahead of the division. We heard it later in the Wehrmacht Bulletin that he received the award in the military hospital. The rest of the patrol got nothing. In the citations for 'Knight's Cross Holders of the Army' it states: 'Warrant Officer Otto Keichel, attached to 130 Panzer Lehr Reconnaissance Battalion of the Panzer Lehr Division, distinguished himself during the Ardennes Offensive in December 1944. The Division sustained heavy losses in bitter fighting after the Allied landings in Normandy. Fully rested in late autumn 1944 around Paderborn, it took part in the last major German offensive in the West in the winter of 1944/1945. By his personal bravery and skill Keichel proved himself as a Warrant Officer Class II and reconnaissance patrol leader. His soldierly achievements found their recognition on 18 January 1945 with the award of the Knight's Cross.'

On 29 January 1945, Major Gerd von Born-Fallois, late commander of Panzer ALA 130, also received the Knight's Cross.

Chapter Eight

I Become Patrol Leader

Next day Lieutenant Gavenat, my company commander, told me that I had been appointed to lead Keichel's patrol and I had to report to Battalion early next morning for a mission. It was the last thing I had expected, to command a reconnaissance patrol as a corporal aged twenty.

As commander of a patrol vehicle I had brought my crew through all dangers without injury. I had learned how to move through enemy-occupied territory without being seen, knew how to read a map and prepare radio messages. Now, however, I had to work on my own initiative and make decisions, call in at company, battalion and regimental command posts to obtain important information about friendly and enemy forces and to report my findings by encoded radio signal. I had not been trained for this by my previous patrol commander and therein I saw my major problems. As a Mecklenburger I did not have the kind of ready tongue needed to involve myself in every discussion of this and that. That night we billeted in a Belgian school. I could not sleep.

Next morning at Battalion I received my orders from Lieutenant Werren: 'Reconnoitre the front X to Y, establish the positions of German and enemy forces, and the enemy's intentions. For your first patrol I wish you much soldier's luck!' With that I was dismissed, my head full of problems.

The drive to the operational area in snow, sub-zero temperatures and icy roads went ahead without mishap and I sent my first operational signal. Then the trouble started. Near the main front line I came to a crossroads with my three vehicles and saw some Panzer Mk IVs in a small wood. I wanted to speak to the unit commander and noticed that all the crews were inside the panzers with nobody nearby or sitting on the hull. This was not a good sign. I banged on the armour with a stick to attract attention and an officer of captain's rank put his head out of the commander's round hatch. The panzers were on guard duty here but under cover against fighter-bombers. Suddenly the enemy began to shell the little wood: trees snapped and metal splinters whirred. I took cover near the panzer tracks and when the shelling ceased jumped up and ran back to my own vehicle. I had just made it when the next salvoes hit the woods. The Americans must have had their stock of ammunition replenished. I would have had a few more questions for the panzer captain, but did not dare go back into the wood.

Suddenly my radio panzer set off down a lane without orders, obviously intent upon getting clear of the shelling. Unfortunately this lane was under enemy observation and so we tried to recall it by waving. (In action we rarely had our car-to-car radio switched on.) Both gun wagons stopped and the radio panzer came rolling back. Immediately afterwards a salvo landed in the lane. I told the driver to get out and made it crystal-clear to him that in action no vehicle leaves the patrol without my order. On reconnaissance patrols everybody must be able to rely unconditionally on the next man. From experience I knew that at the beginning of a new mission one had to establish firm control or discipline would collapse when danger threatened. For that reason, operations and relaxing behind the lines had to be clearly distinguished. By radio I notified Pz ALA of my position, five Panzer Mk IVs at readiness and artillery firing on my location.

At a grenadier battalion command post a major informed me that he had only 150 men, was in desperate need of reinforcements and panzer support or else he could not hold his position. By radio came new orders. When I arrived at the spot indicated enemy tanks were attacking and gaining ground. I radioed at once that the enemy armoured spearhead was heading for Battalion. After a while, radio contact was disrupted and my radio operator could no longer raise Pz ALA. (Later the Battalion radio operators told my own operator that enemy tanks had suddenly begun firing on the village and Battalion had had to evacuate with all haste.)

To avoid being cut off without radio contact in the operational area, I attempted to regain our lines. The Ardennes consist of heavily wooded low mountains and valleys of such a nature that progress by armoured vehicles is only possible using roads and lanes, and not cross-country. Suddenly we were fired upon by tanks advancing from our side. We sought cover at once and barely escaped. My radio operator still had no contact with Battalion and from the map it looked as though we were trapped. There was no road or lane out of it. We could destroy our vehicles and head for our lines on foot through the woods, but what soldier abandons his vehicle except in the most hopeless situation?

On the map I sought the shortest route to our lines. It had a path sketched in on a patch of woodland which fell steeply into a glade but went no further. I took the drivers with me in search of this path to see if it would be driveable. It went down a wooded slope and had probably been created for a single-axle ox cart. Suddenly an infantryman came running up to report tanks approaching our position. Thus the Americans put an end to all discussion of the pros and cons: we were forced to try it.

All three vehicle commanders had to walk ahead of their vehicles to follow the path and so prevent the vehicle careering off into the abyss. My gun wagon led and I drew the driver's attention to the need to keep the right wheel and track always close to the right side of the path and in the snowdrifts. There was a crash and the right wheel hit a rock projecting up out of the ground but hidden under the snow. When the vehicle rolled back the wheel came off and the axle lay on the ground. The drivers knew how to solve this. The axle was winched up, a tree felled and secured with ropes as a kind of skid. We could only go forwards and we had to steer using the brakes on the caterpillar tracks. At the bottom we found a large meadow through which flowed a small but deep brook. There was a bridge across it but it was too weak to bear the weight of our vehicles. We looked for somewhere to ford it. The meadow was frozen over. We felled some trees and threw them into the brook enabling all three vehicles to cross successfully. All the time we could see two enemy reconnaissance aircraft constantly circling above us.

Now the vehicles faced a climb up the wooded slope on the other side and I went ahead to find the most favourable route through the trees. The operation went better than expected, the tracks gripping the snow-covered leafy ground beautifully. We did have a few awkward moments but the tracks proved adequate to the task. Finally we came to a wide highway running through woodland.

Infantry there shook their heads as these crazy panzer people suddenly came up through the trees. Once on the asphalted road we were safe and proceeded slowly with our half skid-half-track panzer to Company. The repair squad got to work on it straight away and next day my gun wagon was operational again.

On my first assignment as patrol commander I had forgotten one very important thing, namely always to have an escape route in mind to protect the patrol against danger of annihilation. Because of the disruption to radio traffic, we had been unable to warn Battalion of the imminent danger of encirclement by the enemy.

We had one day to rest and a mission the following day. Our operational area was Vielsalm–Wemperhardt–St Vith. Under constant pressure from massed artillery, tanks and fighter-bombers, our infantry units and pioneers pulled back with heavy losses. The supply situation of the fighting troops grew worse daily. I went with the patrol to command posts only to confirm they were still there and to determine the position of the main enemy forces and my information was then transmitted to Battalion and Division.

At these command posts I gained an insight into the constantly increasing heavy losses of our fighting units. I also studied the different characters of the officers in these outposts. When I reported myself in the correct manner, with rank and as a reconnaissance commander from the Panzer Lehr Division, I received correct but wounding responses. 'Send us reinforcements, ammunition or panzers rather than come snooping round here!' was one example. A gnarled Army jackass ignored me completely, I assume on the basis that 'I am not going to discuss the military situation in my battalion's sector with a corporal!'

I always got precise answers in the foremost command posts and was briefed correctly for my signals to Battalion. I must also add that without exception all Waffen-SS command posts gave correct answers. My map board was much appreciated in the Staffs. On the reverse I had glued coloured photos of scantily-clad ladies of the American silk-stocking industry with immaculate, endlessly long legs and the most forward Company command posts always pored over them with juicy remarks.

On 20 January 1945 the Panzer Lehr Division was withdrawn from the battle zone and we moved with Pz ALA into the snowy Eiffel.

The patrols made their way back individually to the Reich border through congested roads under cover of darkness. At a snail's pace we crossed the makeshift bridge over the Our, but where the road began its ascent everything was at a standstill. About thirty metres away was a Panzer Mk IV in a meadow, and all traffic had to ford the steam instead of using the bridge. I noticed a small flame inside the panzer but did not realise the significance. Perhaps they were spot-welding something – we all carried a soldering torch in our vehicles. The patrol waited and waited. Then a panzer crewman came along, asking every driver in the convoy if they had a fire extinguisher. This was a stupid question, and of course nobody had one. What he should have said was 'Quick, quick, for God's sake your fire extinguisher, we have a fire in the panzer carburettor and it will explode!' This might have awakened somebody's interest in the convoy to assist on this freezing-cold night. Even my patrol might have helped. But nothing happened and the infantry dozed. Suddenly the Panzer Mk IV blew up with a fearful explosion. More explosions followed – probably the ammunition – and terrified people from the cars and lorries in the convoy came running to find protection behind our armour from metal splinters and flying wreckage. I did not know the cause, but a fire in the carburettor or engine was the most likely. Finally, after hours of waiting, we began our ascent over the first mountain. Vehicles which gave up the ghost were pushed out of the way and over the hillside without regard to the circumstances, as we often saw.

In a village of the snowy Eiffel the company arranged quarters for the next morning and we had to spend the first night freezing in a barn with our vehicles. By day our crews went into the family's big kitchen and thus friction with the farmer's wife was already simmering. We patrol commanders spent most of our time with the company commander, for the Panzer Lehr Division was to be transferred to the Eastern Front and there were preparations to be taken in hand for the train journey. A change of fighting front, up against the Soviets, was not a captivating idea. 'Well see here, Henning, against the Soviets you will have to change your operational tactics. They are quite a different kettle of fish to the British and Americans.' Such was the lofty advice I received from other commanders who had already had their experience in Russia.

One happy day we were told to stand down, we would be staying on the Western Front, since Sixth SS Panzer Army was going to counter the major Soviet offensive that had begun on 12 January 1945. Our staying on was a factor which escalated the struggle between my crews and the farmer's wife in the kitchen and I had to intervene as mediator. One had to have sympathy for her, always having to put up with soldiers warming themselves in her kitchen and even at midday when she was cooking the soup.

Upstairs two men from a supply company had been occupying a room for some time, and on the same floor as a family, with two daughters aged thirteen and fifteen, who had been bombed out. The farmer's wife complained to me that one of these soldiers used to wander about stark naked to draw water from the tap and was ignoring her pleas to desist. I spoke to the man and told him that if I received another complaint that he had been seen naked by the wife and daughters I would see to it he was drafted to the infantry and then to a place where his hot passions would be suitably cooled. These two supply soldiers relieved their frustration by stepping on the toes of my crews at every suitable opportunity.

During the day all road traffic was suspended by enemy fighter-bomber activity. They were always present and sometimes flew low over our village. We could see them through the open chimney above the big kitchen range, and it did not escape notice that the chimney was used as a chamber to smoke meat.

The altercations with our hosts grew more violent until one day the old farmer threatened one of my men with a big frying pan. This was the first time in my war service at home or abroad that I had experienced problems with billet hosts. A satisfactory compromise was not possible and so I sought a new billet for the patrol. I found a house at the end of the village and the nine of us slept in a small unheated room on the first floor. This took up all the floor space and to move about one had to feel one's way with one's feet.

Because of daily missions to the front and the cold, hygiene had suffered and the numbers of lice found in our clothing, particularly as a result of our sleeping conditions, had increased dramatically. We had a major delousing session morning and evening. We heated the room with a powerful stream of fire from two blow lamps, undressed and then searched for the critters.

Early one morning our Spiess, Petschner, and the village commandant, a lieutenant relieved of patrol duties because of his huge casualty rate in men and vehicles, stood in our doorway. We were all laid out on the floor like sardines, covered in blankets and overcoats.

'Henning,' the Spiess said, 'have your people swiped a pig in the village?' As usual he had an impish grin on his face.

'What? Someone stole a whole pig? But surely somebody would have heard that.'

'When we find these people who steal so brazenly from their German racial colleagues engaged in total war, they will receive the most severe punishment,' the lieutenant chipped in. At that he had a look in the corners of the room and also the stairway leading upstairs to see if he could find anything.

'We do have lice, Herr Leutnant, but that is all you will discover here,' I called after him as he went downstairs. The pair of them searched our vehicles and then headed back to Company. My driver Hans Suse and the driver of the second gun wagon, a senior private, were tugging nervously at some blankets in the effort to cover over something. I became suspicious, pulled the blanket off and saw two bulging sacks.

'What are these?' I enquired.

'That is the pig they were looking for,' Suse replied.

'Are you out of your mind? Where did you take it from and how long has it been here?'

'Since this evening. We took it from the smoke chamber!'

'You get it out of here – now! In five minutes I want it gone!'

I could not shout at him for fear of being heard by the other occupants of the house below us. They placed the smoked hams in the legs of their combinations and hid them in the high snowdrift behind the house, where they would be out of sight but preserved. When we left they collected them. An hour later there was a big raid on our room and vehicles. The village commandant and another officer not known to us came looking for the pig. They now knew its origins but finding nothing withdrew to search elsewhere shaking their heads.

Meanwhile I had found out the *modus operandi*. Both drivers had had sentry duty that night and had borrowed a sledge from our house to visit the farmhouse and remove the pork, bacon and sides of ham from the smoke chamber. This theft was committed without the knowledge of other members of the patrol and was justified as revenge for the ill-treatment we had received.

On reflection what steps should I have taken? I prefer to adhere to the old adage 'Speech is silver but silence is golden'. Moreover, Army rations were no longer what they should have been and so as we entered the sixth year of the war at least we had a little supplement, for who knew what was still to come?

Only limited reinforcements came to the hamlets in the High Eiffel. There were not so many reserves in the reserve units any longer. Fuel was so scarce that we stood practically immobile. Thus dawned the epoch of self-supply, such as we always experienced when retreating, and it heralded the defeat.

It was a good time now to have people with organisational talent in one's patrol, and the man who fitted the bill was my driver Hans Suse from Berlin. If there was nothing to be had anywhere, he would always find something. (We met again after the war.) One day my people arrived with some parcels which they had 'organised' from lorries in an SS supply convoy. (The word 'thieved' or 'stole' was avoided in the military and 'organised' meant the same thing.) These were so-called 'Adolf Hitler parcels' which their recipients would not now be receiving as 2 February gifts (a special day in the National Socialist and SS neo-pagan calendar). The parcels were much more valuable than the American ones, and the various new owners of them transferred the alcoholic contents to water canisters to be on the safe side.

At the beginning of February 1945 I was twenty-one years of age and had consolidated my position as patrol commander with the battalion. I was known in the company as a good map reader, and when we were transferred anywhere I would generally be the first to arrive with my patrol. Whenever the Company commander was explaining how to get to the new location the Spiess would always add, 'And the field-kitchen lorry will follow Henning.'

The field-kitchen was probably the most important item of equipment in any unit, but ours had gone astray once or twice. Our Sergeant Furier, a baker by trade, who otherwise did a good job for the company, found it all too easy to get lost in transit. With the field-kitchen in tow our patrol went through Schleiden and Zülpich in the Cologne area. The company arrived at Ahrem, where I was given quarters with a nice family. On the first Sunday the company was deloused at Lechenich. All our clothing was put into a steam oven and we showered thoroughly. My billet hosts used to love talking about the Cologne carnival and I was all ears. The Rhinelanders were lively and merry and their radio station broadcast dance music and even told jokes. I felt really content in the Rhineland. Compared to these people, those in the Eiffel were taciturn and difficult to approach. They listened only to the news and then turned their radios off. They shook their heads in disapproval at the music playing in our radio panzer.

The autobahn ran east of Ahlem. Fighter-bombers attacked supply columns on it every day and bomb splinters would often hit our houses. One day I was walking across the enclosed yard without giving a thought to fighter-bombers. A large bomb splinter came flying through the big gate and tore my black panzer trousers and hit my right shin but without injuring the bone and ended up in the dung heap. All I needed was a light dressing. The farmer picked the splinter out of the manure and kept it as a souvenir.

Just as we were beginning to get nicely settled in we had to transfer to Fellerhöfe near Willich. In the afternoon we got quarters on a big farm and put the vehicles in a barn. I got to know a pretty young girl by the name of Resi. We chatted over supper and then had a long and interesting conversation strolling the village street. Suddenly a soldier came running up and took me to the company commander, where I received immediate orders for transfer to Kamp-Lintfort. I had just time enough to exchange addresses with Resi before waving goodbye and going. We spent probably no more than an hour together and, mutually attracted, had a wonderful talk. That was the fate of the panzer reconnaissance man, however, for we were a fast, mobile unit used as a 'fire brigade' and sent to any trouble spot or to plug a gap in the front line. For the making of a relationship there was simply no time.

It was now mid-February 1945 and the Panzer Lehr Division was to counter-attack to stop the British in the Lower Rhineland. Scarcely had we occupied quarters in the village of Issum than I had to set out on patrol. Despite my protests to the company commander I had to give up my second gun wagon because of a shortage of vehicles, and so I set out with one gun wagon and the radio panzer. My orders were to reconnoitre via Xanten and Calcar to Kleve and Reichswald.

It is always difficult for a patrol leader to obtain an idea of friendly and enemy activity in terms of artillery, tanks and aircraft from a quick overview of a sector to which he is new. On the second day he will begin to have a picture of the dangers at ground level and from the air. Besides these problems however, on this patrol the whole battle zone lay under a carpet of snow through which we had to drive without cover, victims waiting for fighter-bombers. At Xanten I drove to the command post of a panzer engineer battalion which had just arrived and whose commander asked if he could be linked in to our radio net. This meant that the radio operators had to exchange code books. Beyond Calcar came to the main front line and called on several company command posts.

The British were attacking from the Reichswald with a Polish brigade and had strong artillery and armoured support. Gocher Heide was open country and I had to be constantly alert for enemy fighter-bombers skilled in picking off vehicles whose drivers put themselves in harm's way through inattention or inexperience. The German front line consisted mainly of a series of outposts and so I felt my way from one to another, advising Battalion and Division of my observations about enemy dispositions and our own forces. The officers complained bitterly at their losses in the companies and having to hold out in their provisional footholds in sub-zero temperatures without adequate food.

My gun wagon had gearbox damage and the driver found it difficult changing gear. I radioed: 'Gun wagon out of service – gearbox damage – patrol not operational – am returning.' The answer came back immediately: 'Radio wagon remains operational'. Now I had to transfer to the radio wagon. In all my reconnaissance service I had never operated in action with only one vehicle. There had to be a serious situation at Battalion if they could not conjure up a replacement.

During the night the front had to be pulled back and we drove along a path through a field while under artillery fire. Suddenly there was a rattling sound from the tracks. With a flashlight I saw that we had run over a cart and two dead horses which had received a direct hit just before. There was absolutely no point in pressing forward. I found a good spot to spend the night and imposed radio silence until 06.00 hrs.

On 22 February 1945 the Panzer Lehr Division, reinforced by a panzer engineer battalion, attacked in the effort to win back the positions they had lost. After initial success the enemy replied with masses of artillery and defended so resolutely with their armour that our attack faltered. My radio panzer was under continual infantry fire from individual farms which the enemy had overrun. The attack relieved the pressure on 15th Panzer Grenadier Division south west of Udem, which held its positions with the help of a Volks artillery division.

We were now in our third day at the front with only the radio panzer. Around midday we came to a spot where two paths crossed. Here the vehicle sank through the surface earth into a morass up to the belly. We were unable to get unstuck by use of the tracks. We were in open country and around us we saw the dark impressions of shell hits in the snow. I radioed: 'Stuck in a morass'. The radio operator switched off the equipment and the three of us attempted to get the vehicle back up. We winched it up and put stones under the tracks. This was an awful job, our boots and combinations half full of frozen mud. How we cursed Battalion for ordering us to continue our reconnaissance with only one panzer. Finally we got it up. Exhausted, weak and weary I now radioed: 'Vehicle driveable – am returning'.

My team had arranged quarters for us at Company so that we could go straight to bed. The billet hostess washed my combinations and underwear while I slept. As so happens when soldiers are in a village there is always sport with the local lovelies. Next day the girls hid my boots before morning parade and I had to fall in wearing house slippers. I inveigled myself into the rear rank and the Spiess did not notice, otherwise I should have had some awkward questions to answer and given the infantry something to laugh about. We had scarcely got warmed up in the village than the threat of an enemy breakthrough at Mönchen Gladbach developed and the Battalion had to relocate there at once. My gun wagon was short of parts which meant I would be delayed leaving since I would have to wait for the crew to fit them. The company commander told me the rough new location behind the front line and if they moved out I was to ask the burgomaster [mayor] for directions. We spoke to the latter a few hours later but he had nothing for us. It was already afternoon and I suggested to my crew that we return to our former quarters at Fellerhöfe, for the farmer there had given us a good supper and might do so again. At the same time I hoped to see Resi. It was already dark when we arrived at Fellerhöfe and we were given a friendly reception by the farmer's wife, who guaranteed us supper. We drove the panzer into the barn. I told the driver to remove one of the track bolts and drive forward a little so that the track fell off. It was a precaution in case the field gendarmes or over-zealous 'Golden Pheasants' should ask difficult questions about our battalion or company, as to whose whereabouts at that moment we unfortunately knew nothing. So we had a 'damaged track' which was a ten-minute repair job, although it could be spun out for an hour. When the Army was in trouble there were always these 'field courts' dispensing summary justice and one had to guard against it. Field gendarmes and other highwaymen were always scouring the rear areas for the last reserves to press into service and woe to him who had no plausible explanation for being where they found him. I spoke to Resi only briefly during the evening and quickly took my leave at her window next morning.

My panzer drove towards Mönchen-Gladbach via Willich and before we got to the town I diverted to Korschebroich in search of Battalion. Halfway down the road was a three-man heroic field-gendarme posse who signalled us to stop, a captain and two warrant officers with half-moon breast-shield, steel helmet and each carrying a machine-pistol.

'Where have you come from – where are you going – what is your unit?'

'I am driving to my unit – Panzer Lehr Division!' I replied from the turret.

'Listen! The enemy has broken through at Korschenbroich-Büttgen and must be stopped. You go ahead and hold the road against any future attacks!'

'I have just come from the workshop and first have to fill up and replenish with ammunition.' At that the captain went to the rear and lifted our petrol cans. 'These are full!' he shouted. I ducked below and shouted to the driver, 'Get going!' He reacted at once and we careered off down the empty road. The gunner and I kept our heads down for safety's sake just in case the gendarmes decided to open fire on us but probably they chose discretion because our gun was bigger than theirs.

Scarcely had we got past the first houses than I spotted the enemy armoured spearhead advancing at Kaarts with damned fighter-bombers circling overhead. I drove at once to cover alongside a house. There was no sign anywhere of my battalion or company. The Thunderbolts fired at anything that moved and any pockets of resistance. Their presence threatened my vehicle and I remained in cover. We knew from France that once they nailed us down it would take time before we could slip away. Now we had to keep our nerve; any movement could have fatal consequences. A group of grenadiers came running by, some soaked after wading across a tributary of the Niers, and in this cold! 'Pull out!' they shouted before disappearing behind the houses. They had gone and we still cowered under cover, fearing to move because of the fighter-bombers. Luckily the main thrust of the enemy attack was targeted on Kaarts to our flank and with so many tanks and armoured vehicles that we gave up counting. Hans Suse and Lambert Fleskes were calmness personified and we kept our nerve. Both had been in North Africa, Fleskes in the same panzer reconnaissance company as I.

The enemy armour spearhead had passed us by and the Thunderbolts were now circling farther on. The time was ripe for us to retire and so we trundled back down the empty road towards Mönchen-Gladbach. The heroic field-gendarmes were at the same spot in the centre of the road signalling us to stop. 'Step on the gas and keep going!' A conversation with them could have fatal consequences for us and both my crewmen knew it. We had all heard rumours of Field Marshal Model's 'field hunters' and the fear which officers and men adrift had of them. At high speed, with the tracks rattling and clanking, we bore down on them, obviously never going to stop, and at the last moment they dived off the road for safety. What vengeful thoughts crossed their minds? On the outskirts of Mönchen-Gladbach I saw our battalion shield on a signpost which I had missed the first time. I located our company in the south-west of the city and parked my gun wagon near my radio panzer and

130

other reconnaissance vehicles in a schoolyard, then reported to my company commander.

'Man, Henning, where have you come from?'

'I was pinned down by fighter-bombers at Korschenbroich. Couldn't move forward or back.'

'Then you have come out of the frying pan into the fire, for we are sitting here with Battalion and elements of Division in a trap!'

'Early this morning I came here from Willich with no problem.'

Suddenly there was an explosion very close by; we ducked together – a salvo of artillery shells detonated in the schoolyard. I feared the worst and, concerned for my men, sprinted outside, unnecessarily as it happened, as nobody had a scratch. No doubt the enemy had triangulated our location from our heavy radio traffic and therefore our street had attracted a lot of attention from their artillery. We sought the hindmost shadow of the houses for protection against the shellfire. Many infantry were sheltering in cellars with the house occupants. The 'organisational' talents in the Company 'organised' food and preserved fruit from cellars left unattended and this provoked complaints to the company commander. He issued an order strongly forbidding the unauthorised taking of food from the population.

As patrol commander, I had to visit the battalion command post set up in a large building and I passed the time in a relatively safe cellar. Artillery could not touch us there, but the houses in the street were badly damaged by the endless shelling.

On the afternoon of 1 March 1945 I left Mönchen-Gladbach with my patrol, almost the last Army vehicles to go. Many women and old men waved us off from the entrance to the city's big air-raid shelter. Some of the women were weeping. I was not sure whether they were sad because familiar faces were leaving the city and they felt uncertain at the prospect of enemy soldiers arriving, or they were happy because the artillery bombardments by the enemy would now cease. I asked myself often whether German artillery would fire at the enemy occupying German towns where their own women and children were living. Unfortunately I bore witness that no difference was drawn between Homeland and 'Enemyland'. At that time the Homeland meant very, very much to us and we soldiers made great sacrifices and suffered deprivation for it.

During the night in the divisional command post I received instructions to ascertain if the Rhine bridge facing Düsseldorf at Neuss was still intact. If it was, it would enable the division to escape the encirclement by crossing the river. The mission had to be carried out without delay and was of the greatest importance. On the outskirts of Schiefbahn I was stopped by panzer covering troops and told I could not proceed on the road because American armour was waiting around the next bend. I sent my first radio message about these German and American positions.

So far as I could make out in the darkness, the village had come in for heavy shelling and most roofs were badly damaged. With the agreement of the officer responsible for the Panzer Mk IV covering force I decided to attempt to break through south of the road through fields to Meerbusch. This meant passing wrecked American tanks east of Schiefbahn. One of them was still burning fiercely with two dead Americans alongside. Both bodies were giving off white steam. This was not an encouraging omen for our operation.

With great caution and keeping the terrain under constant obser-vation we felt our way eastwards. Through my binoculars half right I saw a German armoured infantry carrier head into a farmyard. There was a brief exchange of fire and then all fell quiet. This indicated that the enemy occupied the farmyard. We kept on over countless tank tracks heading north and I guessed that the enemy was north of us around Willich-Osterath. Suddenly we came under wild infantry bazooka fire from our left. 'Keep going, full speed!' I shouted to my driver and with motor screaming, the radio panzer close behind us, we evaded this murderous fire in a shallow valley, where I halted the vehicles, got out and went forward on foot, the two vehicles following a good distance behind. After a while I had them pull over near the cover of a hedgerow and continued reconnoitring the path and countryside ahead. It was eerily quiet, no shooting, and therefore I had no idea of the enemy's location.

After a while I recognised before me the road between Kaarts and Osterath and heard engine noises, whether German or enemy was impossible to tell. Creeping closer to listen intently for the direction of their movement, and noting the tank impressions which led here, I had to conclude that they must be enemy. Then came the distinct sound of tanks which confirmed it. There was no way through for us and so I returned to the vehicles and radioed Division: 'My coordinates – infantry fire from north – many tank tracks to Willich-Osterath – enemy tanks at Meerbusch – returning.'

I discussed our withdrawal with my other vehicle commander. With motors well throttled back we rolled back down into the shallow valley for a situation conference. It was quiet there, although we guessed that the Americans would give us a hot reception, for they knew we had to come back their way. It was decided that I would lead at full speed, attracting their fire to my vehicle and once we were more or less through it the radio panzer would follow flat out. We reckoned the enemy would then concentrate on the radio panzer and squander their opportunity to destroy my gun wagon. Right, mount up, steel helmets on and let's go. The radio panzer crew wished us 'Hals und Beinbruch' – 'Hope you break your neck and legs', the usual German military salutation for good luck in parting.

My driver took off at once and soon the first flares shot skywards. Dribs and drabs of infantry rounds bounced off our armour and mortar shells exploded around us. Fleskes and I kept very low, hanging on grimly as the gun wagon rattled and shook its way down the field path. The firing petered out and we were through it. In the glare of the Very lights I watched the radio panzer run the gauntlet, but the enemy fire was less venomous than for us. From experience we had judged the Americans right. They started off by firing wildly with everything they had, having as they did an inexhaustible supply of ammunition, but without much clear purpose. We Germans on the other hand were obliged to make each round count because of our chronic shortage of ammunition.

We reached the first houses of Mönchen-Gladbach-Neuwerk and I saw white flags in the street. I stopped, shocked. Were the Americans here already? Then in the darkness I made out the armoured infantry carriers of the panzer grenadiers pressed close to the house walls. The whole street was hanging out white flags. For me it was a grotesque sight. Until then in German streets I had only ever seen swastika flags waving on political occasions of all kinds. This demonstration had probably occurred without any uniform decision on the part of the occupants, but in the darkness against the dark walls of the houses the white flags stood out very noticeably. White flags to show they were giving in, German military vehicles below them and no German soldier took umbrage. In this sixth year of the war probably all soldiers had had enough of fighting and the Homeland being bombed to rubble, and now longed for peace.

I reported back to the divisional command post and was immediately ordered to scout Viersen-Tönisvorst, south of Krefeld, and towards Osterath. I got to Krefeld during the night without problem and now felt my way cautiously to the outskirts of Fischeln, where I met some Volkssturm men and a couple of self-propelled assault guns on piquet duty near the end of a housing block. I radioed my coordinates and reported the weak German defences to Division. The night was relatively bright, and from the edge of the village through binoculars I could make out the shadowy houses of Fellerhöfe where we had billeted the previous night. The intervening territory between the two villages was absolutely silent with no shooting. Aware of the impending attack by the Americans I was just about to order the patrol to head for our previous billet hosts and Resi's family when a Volkssturm man stopped me.

'Where are you heading?'

'To Fellerhöfe.'

'You can't, enemy tanks have been there since late afternoon.' What luck he stopped us. Running into the enemy armour in that terrain without cover would have been very nasty. To be on the safe side I drew back a little into Fischeln to get us some rest or sleep, and we parked near a small square. I knocked on a door and asked the owner if he could put us up. He invited us in at once and, as they say today, we crashed, dog-tired and just as we were, on couch, settee or carpet. The occupants then went down to the cellar.

It was still dark next morning when fierce shooting awoke us. Startled, we jumped up and ran to our vehicles. I approached the SP-guns for information. Just ahead one of them had been hit, probably by a bazooka, and was burning. My driver braked and reversed. The Volkssturm had probably dispersed during the night and now American assault forces were at the first houses. We drove slowly to the main highway to Krefeld and I hid the vehicles alongside a house on a bend so as to keep the road under observation before radioing the new situation to Battalion.

After a while, chains of American infantry made their shadowy advance on both sides of the road. This presented us with a good opportunity to give them something to think about for waking us up so early. We let them approach and then opened fire on them with the 2cm cannon and the MG 42. They spread out along the house walls for cover, returned a hesitant fire and retired. Unfortunately we were unable to operate effectively on our side of the road without the second gun wagon, with which we could have dominated the road on both sides. I took us farther back into the city for fear of being cut off if the enemy came down a back street behind us. From the map I selected the far side of a crossroads to observe the traffic. It was relatively quiet in the city with little shooting, and even then impossible to determine which side was firing. Our alertness gradually began to falter and our eyes closed 'just to rest them'. Suddenly my gunner nudged me and whispered: 'There are two American scout cars alongside.' I chilled. German voices addressed us and the mystery was solved. They were two American vehicles captured by the Waffen-SS who now proposed doing something heroic with them. They had come up on us quietly from behind and unseen while the drivers of my patrol were looking towards our direction of flight.

The SS patrol leader asked me for our observations. I told him that the enemy was attacking with infantry, and on the road ahead we had exchanged fire with an assault platoon. The US armour spearhead was outside Krefeld and would probably attack at daybreak. Then he wanted to know exactly where we had had the fight with the assault platoon and informed me, 'We shall have a look for ourselves!'.

'Take care, the Americans destroyed the SP-guns with bazookas,' I replied. With a couple of jerks like a billy goat the first SS vehicle set off at top speed traversing the crossroads and disappeared into the darkness. The second captured vehicle was nothing like so hasty and when the driver put it into gear, the commander almost strangled him from behind.

'That looks promising,' I told my gunner, Fleskes. Then came a muzzle flash ahead, an explosion and some infantry weapons began to chatter. The second SS vehicle braked, skidded on the crossroads and stopped facing to the left, mounted the pavement, slipped back on the road and disappeared. We were all spectators to the entire drama and the radio panzer commander said to us: 'That's what a hobo with two days' stubble gets you in a panzer, the Knight's Cross or death!'

'We sleepy heads ought to hold a funeral oration for them. We were all asleep together on reconnaissance and the SS woke us up,' I reminded him. I was still wild that nobody had seen them creep up on us.

Slowly it grew light, the new day began and fresh business awaited us. By radio I received orders to scout Lanklatum. We mounted up and headed for the new operational area via Gellepstratum.

From a farmyard near Lanklatum I saw clearly the enemy advance into Krefeld and informed Battalion and Division. The Americans seemed to meet no German resistance. Protected against being surprised by swampy ground and a stream we watched vehicle after vehicle pass along the Willich highway towards Krefeld without any German defensive fire. Unexpectedly, some German field gunners arrived nearby to set up an observation post to direct fire on the enemy columns. I had a friendly talk with the artillery sergeant and we put our two vehicles closer to them against a house wall for cover against the air. The battery was located on the other side of the Rhine, he told me. The readiness to fire was delayed and delayed. I crouched waiting for the order to fire to come from the observation post, and I was hoping to see the shooting skills of the artillery sowing disorder amongst the American columns. I had the equivalent of a front seat on the platform of honour at training depot, and would have something for my radio operator to transmit when we saw the results.

Finally they were ready. The sergeant said, 'Better come to cover with us.' This was a wall about four feet high.

'Is your shooting that bad?' I asked him.

'Precaution is better than hindsight,' he replied as I moved down from my seat in the grandstand. A roar came from behind, and we were sprayed with dirt from fifty metres away. The first shell exploded short of the highway, the rest in the meadow except the last, close to us.

I looked at the sergeant in dismay. 'What, that's it? But you haven't hit the highway yet!' The Americans did not appear concerned about the 10.5cm howitzer battery and their traffic kept rolling. The second salvo was better, but widely dispersed, like through a watering can.

'We are used to something different to this. When the Americans shell a street we are always left with a lot of matchwood,' I told the gunner.

'Yes, yes, I know,' the sergeant responded, 'it used to be like that with us, but what do you expect from our old, worn-out howitzers? There are no spare parts and so we shall have to see in Final Victory with these!'

I left them in disappointment. Meanwhile my radio operator had discovered that our battalion had relocated at Oberhausen on the other side of the Rhine. On the map I found the road near Krefeld which passed close to a big bend in the river to the west. Now I would have to be very cautious that we were not cut off near Uerdingen. My two crews, already veterans, urged me to go there to determine the enemy situation. On the way the radio panzer had gearbox trouble and was no longer fully operational. I went back to it and had the driver explain. I also knew that with this kind of pre-select gearbox the repair had to be done by a specialist. My drivers were nobody's fools and, with a glance at the map, they were really keen to reach the hinterland in the Rhine bend near Lanklatum. In view of the situation at the front I had to admit to myself that the breakdown of the radio panzer was not untimely and I wirelessed: 'Radio panzer damaged gearbox – returning.'

Unimpeded by the enemy infantry we crossed the Rhine bridge at Duisburg and obtained quarters in a private house at Oberhausen. The remnants of the Panzer Lehr Division had crossed the Rhine at Wesel after brushing aside delaying resistance. By the time I made my report to the company commander, quarters had already been arranged for us. My crew and I were lodged with very friendly people on the upper floor of a semi-detached house, where we slept three men to a room. The owners had three daughters of about fifteen to nineteen years of age who in their willingness to make our stay comfortable did everything conceivably possible. They brought us pillows embroidered 'Sweet Dreams' and 'The Lord protect you'. The girls cared for us devotedly but unfortunately their overflowing friendliness was overwhelming. After we had settled in, washed, shaved and cleaned our boots, we withdrew discreetly from the close attentions of the three young ladies.

Just back from a mission at the front and glad to have left the western bank of the Rhine, we decided to have a look at the local talent in Oberhausen. We got to know three Rhineland girls for a laugh and a joke. Because the March weather in Oberhausen is not so agreeable, it occurred to Hans Suse that we could continue our outing in our room. I thought this was stretching it but allowed myself to be persuaded on the condition that we all had to keep very quiet. We went upstairs unnoticed and spoke softly so that our billet hosts would not be aware what was going on. After a while we were called down to supper and treated kind-heartedly by the parents and daughters. Conversations developed in which we had to speak and answer questions, but my thoughts were one floor higher. I cursed at my having let my crew have their way since I could sense trouble ahead. We took leave of our hosts with probably too much haste, thanking them for supper. They thought we must be very weary after such a tiring day, to which we could only answer with a nod of the head. The girls upstairs had become restless at so long an absence and we found them reading our paybooks to see if we were married. We were very young, of course, and the war had left us with no time to make relationships of depth with girls eager to marry.

As time went on our conversation must have become audible below for there was suddenly a shout and I found the gentleman of the house at our door asking if we had girls in our room. I answered truthfully, that we would talk quietly and the girls were leaving in an hour. He seemed satisfied with this answer and left. It looked as though it had gone off well but I warned everybody to keep quiet. Shortly afterwards he called up: 'The girls must leave the house at once!'

'Yes, yes, they are going immediately,' I replied and to the circle: 'We'd better break it up or they will get really annoyed.'

Suddenly our host called up again: 'The women have to leave the house this very instant!' The terminology was clearly sharpening and we saw the lady of the house at his side, telling him what to say. She passed him some new threat and he relayed it forcefully as we came down the staircase: 'These hussies should be ashamed of themselves, going into a room with strange men. Go to the devil!'

At that the girl I had befriended considered this an insult to her honour and the indignation poured out of her mouth like a waterfall and rushed past my ears so fast that I can neither repeat nor write down anything she actually said. We had our work cut out to calm her down. As we left I apologised again to our hosts, to which the lady responded, foaming at the mouth: 'That is the thanks we get, taking you into our house and you bring women in!' and her husband added: 'Tomorrow I shall go to the company commander and complain of your conduct!'

'By all means do, the Company Office is one street away.' I doubted he would. We took the girls home, and I gave my female friend a piece of my mind for her aggression towards the house owners. One thing led to another and I took my leave of her abruptly in front of her parents' house. One shitty evening in Oberhausen with nothing but problems.

Next morning a messenger came with orders for me to report at once to the Company Office. The Spiess received me grinning. Whatever had we set in motion this time? A man had come wanting to speak to nobody but the company commander. Then in high dudgeon he had complained we had had women in the room which was not tolerated in their house. The Spiess had tried to calm the man: 'These boys have just come back from reconnaissance at the front and now need to relax. Behind the lines they can go a bit too far but one should not take it so seriously!'

The man was not satisfied with this answer, Petschner told me. He was resolved to speak to the company commander. I told the Spiess that the people had three daughters who had cared for us most devotedly but all three were and looked soppy and the parents were probably more upset because we had found three other girls. 'Well, Henning, you are in for it now. The commander just looks for such incidents in the Company!'

Shortly afterwards I reported to Lieutenant Gavenat in his private rooms. I knocked, went in and reported. At once he snapped: 'Wait outside until I call you in!' Thus I waited in the hall as ordered. The house owners were also there and looked at me with vexation. Now I simmered with anger myself. After half an hour I knocked again and entered. 'Do you have difficulty understanding? Kindly wait outside until I call you in!' I took him literally this time and waited outside the house because the stares of the house owners were getting on my nerves. This also gave me the opportunity to think about some counter arguments.

Around midday the commander emerged and let loose a tirade at finding me outside the house. 'I have obeyed your order correctly and waited outside, Herr Lieutenant,' I replied. Back inside, I had to stand to attention and listen to his sermon on morality.

'With your crew you have been guilty of a serious offence such that the billet hosts had to complain to me. You and your crew admitted to your room women of doubtful repute and offended against decency and morality to the most punishable levels!' he spluttered.

'I know no immoral, indecent German women, Herr Lieutenant. We ignored the crude attempts to associate with us made by their rather stupid daughters. Apart from that I know of no infractions of morality.'

'You therefore challenge the complaint, in my view justified, made by the billet hosts?'

'Indeed, we conversed quietly and in a disciplined manner with some German Hitler Youth girls, and there was no more to it than that!'

The German BDM girls took the wind out of the lieutenant's sails.

'Shut your trap! I shall discuss with Senior Warrant Officer Petschner the disciplinary action we shall take against you and your crew. Now go and apologise to the billet hosts, make things right and woe betide you if any more complaints reach my ears!' With that I was dismissed and now it was past midday.

When I got back, my crew had already moved into the neighbour's house, the other dwelling of the semi-detached house. Upon entering our room I saw driver Hans Suse's girlfriend sitting there. 'Are you out of your mind? I have just been hauled over the coals by the company commander and here you are doing the same thing all over again.'

'No problem, our new hosts know the girl and have no objection to her being here!' The girl was apprenticed to a nearby food business and therefore knew both women well. The over-reaction of the other landlady probably had more to do with our ignoring her own daughters than in having girls in our room without permission. Rudi Petschner, himself a former patrol leader, poured oil on troubled waters with the company commander. I got three days Duty NCO and the other two received three nights' extra guard duty.

Around the fourth day our stay in Oberhausen came to an end and we transferred to Kettwig. As we drove off it was dark and my driver, upset at the unjustified guard duty, tried to demolish the garden wall of our dear neighbour by reversing into it accidentally, but I was able to prevent this. Quite enough damage had already been caused in the Ruhr by the Allied bombing raids.

At Kettwig I was given quarters in the house of a master painter on the main road. One day we experienced an Allied air raid in which the earth shook. The neighbours were of the opinion that Essen had been bombed, but it was foggy and we could not see the aircraft. Our stay at Kettwig also ended after three days and we transferred to Hösel near Heiligenhaus, where I had quarters with a nice married couple on Bahnhof-Strasse. Since 10 March 1945, HQ Company, with its eight-wheeled armoured reconnaissance vehicles led by Lieutenant Gollwitzer, had been in the front line opposing the American bridgehead at Remagen, while we spent a few quiet days at Hösel. Some female Luftwaffe signals auxiliaries were stationed at Heiligenhaus. We spent some happy hours with them in the Hösel restaurant. My friend Hans Pischke and I got to know two girls well. One, a senior auxiliary from Düsseldorf, had been engaged to a U-boat man lost in action. They were stationed at Brest and then Cherbourg, and after the invasion of Normandy had been forced to return through France to Germany by thumbing lifts from lorries. Several German lorry drivers took advantage of their plight by offering the journey in exchange for sex. If they refused, they were set down by the wayside. At Heiligenhaus the girls were housed in barracks and when we met them there problems always surfaced with the Luftwaffe men who considered the girls their own property and would not allow panzer soldiers near them. Upon taking our leave of the girls we advised them to wear civilian clothes when the Americans came, because they made even uniformed women into prisoners of war.

At Hösel, Warrant Officer Keichel returned wearing his Knight's Cross and recovered from his wound. As expected, he demanded his old patrol back with the original crews since all of us were still there, having survived thus far. I was keen to rejoin his patrol as an armoured car commander since it was better to go on patrols with a Knight's Cross holder than be exposed forever to the pressure of Battalion for results. Things turned out quite differently, however.

I accompanied the company commander to the commanding officer, who informed me that I had been detached to the War Academy [for officer training] and I was to travel to Potsdam with a courier. I should have gone to War Academy earlier from Bachenau, but a move had prevented it. Perhaps the Americans would roll things up locally and I would get out of it unscathed; from experience I knew that young junior lieutenants at the front had a short life-expectancy. My prayers were answered when the Americans broke out of their bridgehead at Remagen on 25 March, pressed forward smartly, causing my drafting to be scrapped.

I remained a reconnaissance patrol commander despite my youth. I took charge of a new patrol with fresh men and prepared quickly for a new mission. My gunner and the commander of the radio panzer were from NCO school and had been trained for a military career from childhood. They were enthusiastic young men who obtained their front experience with us.

Elements of our division were in action at Remagen, but the enemy expanded the bridgehead at Bad Honnef and Königswinter with strong forces. I had the best information about the front line from an enemy radio station. It was strictly forbidden to listen in, but at Company nobody cared. On Sunday 25 March 1945 the Company was put on alert and I took my patrol via Wuppertal-Elberfeld to Gummersbach, where I received orders to establish in which direction the armour spearheads of the US First Army were advancing, to remain in touch with them and report their position by radio. I was informed briefly that the German defensive positions ran along the Sieg river from Siegburg to Siegen. I discovered that the enemy had thrust rapidly from south of the Sieg eastwards and his armour was already at Siegen-Haiger. Everything was now moving very rapidly and I had to take the greatest care not to be overtaken by it.

My biggest problem was not the enemy but obtaining petrol. We sniffed it out mostly from the civilian population, and thus I got fuel

from Party offices and fuel dumps, always emphasising the importance of our reconnaissance missions. We noticed how the chaotic
situation grew worse daily. Our numerically inferior troop numbers
could not hold the enemy advance. All resistance was broken within
a short time by superior artillery and the circling fighter-bombers,
and should our young infantry still show the will to resist, they were
crushed by the enemy armour. In the regiments a physical lack of
vigour set in and the infantry succumbed to this feeling of
exhaustion.

Enemy radio broadcasts reported that Tommy had crossed the
Rhine at Wesel and was heading east. With a glance at my maps it
was easy to anticipate his intention. The encirclement of the Ruhr
was still not complete, and so far I had come safely out of each bulge
and pocket with the Panzer Lehr Division, but I had to watch closely
to get my timing right.

We established that the American armour spearhead was turning
north around the Rothaar uplands. This certainly looked like a move
to create a pocket. My patrol was waiting near woodland at Brilon,
and I was undecided whether to go east or return to Battalion and
Company in the developing encirclement. The crew was divided –
those who lived westward of our position wanted to go back into
the pocket and the rest could not make up their minds. A radio
message decided for us: 'Return to Schmallenberg.' The remnants
of the Panzer Lehr Division and a panzer grenadier division had
been assembled to break out to the east around Winterberg and we
had to join them so as not to miss the thrust into open country to the
east.

The attack south-east of Winterberg began on Good Friday, 30
March 1945. We followed the armour spearhead via Küstelberg
towards Medebach, but on Easter Sunday in the State forest we
could go no farther forwards. The word was passed from vehicle to
vehicle in the convoys: 'The route east is free,' but it did not look
like it. By radio I was ordered to the Kahler Asten ridge in order to
observe the enemy movements in the valley along the highway near
Beiasten.

From the heights west of Kahler Asten I came across the
observation post for an 8.8cm flak battery on a wooded slope. This
outpost had been here for some days and I arranged with the

sergeant in charge to send my signals from there. On our forays along the slopes we came across some isolated houses and barracks in the woods served only by a beaten track. The houses were occupied mostly by women, children and old men, and from conversations with them we learned they were refugees or people bombed out from the Winterberg region. The sergeant observed: 'One could lodge here for the rest of the war and wait for it to end. The Americans would never find you on these wooded slopes!' The idea was appealing, but my thinking had not yet progressed that far. Two days later the sergeant advised me that his battery was being relocated.

While motoring through the Rothaar uplands there arose problems with the engines of our vehicles which simply stopped running. The drivers took the carburettors apart and found the jets clogged with red, hard chips of red paint. The inner coating must have worked loose from a petrol can. I had to tow the radio panzer out of the danger zone; my own gun wagon also stopped twice. An awkward situation while on reconnaissance patrol close to the enemy. From now on the drivers filled the fuel tank through a gauze.

The two vehicles were up here alone with only a sparse growth of fir to shield us from the sight of fighter-bombers. The region had been abandoned by all German military posts and we observed the highway below us to Winterberg and beyond to Siedlinghausen. We heard shelling by heavy howitzers and saw big hits on Altastenberg. The whole village was soon enveloped in smoke. The shelling must have caught the village people totally unprepared and caused heavy casualties among them. There was no German military defence or troop presence. I reported the attack on Altastenberg by radio.

After quiet had returned we heard shelling close behind us. I climbed up to the top of the slope and could hardly believe my eyes: an entire American armoured column was 800 metres to our rear on a minor road to Oberkirchen and an 8.8cm battery was firing AP shells at it. I was greatly disappointed at the effect of this German shelling, mere pinpricks against the armoured column. The bombardment of Altastenberg was of a quite different calibre.

I ran back, we mounted up and drove through the woods, our only salvation. On the way we had to follow a path over a spot height in full view of the enemy tanks. My gun wagon arrived amongst the trees safely but the carburettor of the radio panzer seized up again, leaving the vehicle stopped short of the wood. The forward part of the hull was hidden by a bush but the after part could be seen by the enemy tanks which had paused at this moment. The drivers threw open the bonnet and cleaned the carburettor furiously. I watched the column of tanks through binoculars to give warning should the turret of any of the Shermans swivel towards us. Finally they got the radio panzer clear to go and after crossing a small patch of open country it made the woods successfully.

Now began the classic reconnaissance. Where was the armour spearhead going and with what forces? We had to maintain contact with it and send an hourly radio signal. As I was told later at the Battalion command post, my precise observations enabled a deep penetration by the enemy at Winterberg to be foiled. This was my last successful patrol. From now on the pocket began to contract substantially while our difficulties in obtaining fuel increased daily and fundamentally reduced our radius of action.

Towards evening next day my patrol reported back to Battalion, which had relocated in a large farmhouse on a by-road near Siedlinghausen. I reported my return to the commander, the drivers refuelled the vehicles and then we went exhausted to the big barn. Finding it full of sleeping infantry we had to locate what space there was in the darkness. An American howitzer battery was targeting the crossroads about 200 metres away in order to disrupt our retreat. Heavy shells exploded on the roads all night, and the splinters pattered on the roof of our barn. I was dog-tired, but could not sleep for the shelling and the tinkling of the splinters on the roof. I tossed and turned on the straw. The shelling offered us no danger in the barn. Whenever a salvo hit the crossroads I would wait a moment and then count the splinters hitting the roof. As opposed to the roof, the walls of the barn were so thick that they did not transmit the sound of the splinters hitting. It was driving me crazy. I put my head under the blanket and wanted to hear nothing, only sleep. On and on the shelling rumbled and the splinters tinkled. My sub-conscious started doing the counting. It was not the racket at the crossroads which drove me mad, but this tinkling. Thus the night passed and next day I was supposed to be fully operational.

A runner called out: 'Unteroffizier Henning!' searching for me amongst the sleeping infantry. I drew the blanket more firmly around my head and thought No! Not again! They want to send me on patrol again? None of my crew responded. The runner gave up and went, reappearing some time later with reinforcements. No doubt they saw our reconnaissance vehicles by the barn and guessed that was where we were. They pulled the blanket from every sleeping head to protests and shouts of annoyance. They discovered some of my crew and so only a short while later the blanket was pulled off my own head.

'Report at once to the Battalion command post!'

I received orders as follows: 'The Battalion is transferring to Meschede via Olsberg and Bastwig. Reconnoitre if the road is passable and free of the enemy for Battalion. Depart with your patrol immediately!' It was still pitch dark and we had to drive through the same crossroads 200 metres away that was being shelled by the Americans. This was not so bad. We drove up to the splinter limit, calculated the rate of fire and watched the crossroads carefully to ensure no enemy vehicles were crossing it and also checked for heaps of rubble or other obstacles. Then quickly through it, something we had done so often before.

I waited with my gun wagon on the highway for the radio panzer, whose operator had had to fetch the code book for the day. On the way to the town stood a wood rising to the right and a meadow sloping downwards to the left. The radio panzer came up and I gave the order to roll. After about 50 metres I looked back and could not see the radio panzer. I dismounted and walked back to find out where it had got to. There was a skid mark from the road to the slope and I could just make out the shadowy shape of the panzer in the meadow below. I went down and found it upside down, the commander trapped by one leg beneath it. The driver and radio operator were crouching near him, visibly distressed, and at a loss what to do next.

Dear God in Heaven, what shit situation is this and how do we get him out? The young NCO trainee's leg was trapped up to the knee but he was otherwise unhurt. By now my crew had come down and we attempted to winch the vehicle to one side but this failed because the ground was soft. I decided we should dig him out from under and two men set to the task from either side. 'The pressure on my leg is getting worse!" he complained. Finally we dragged him free. By a miracle the leg was not broken or crushed. The soft ground had been his salvation and all he suffered was a cut which bled a lot. The young man, a farmer's son from Schleswig-Holstein, had been very lucky, for the panzer had only rolled one and a half times. Another quarter-roll and the side armour would have crushed him. We all knew that an overturning panzer should not be evacuated. The other two crew obeyed the rule and were unhurt. A friend of mine from Criwitz in Mecklenburg was crushed to death by the tracks when thrown out of an overturning vehicle at Normandy. I reported the accident by radio and received instructions to await engineers with a crane. At daybreak the Battalion took off to the west, but not by the road I was supposed to have reconnoitred.

I drove my gun wagon into cover and had the radio equipment removed from the overturned panzer. All morning we watched panzers, artillery, countless lorries and AFVs, some under tow, passing us by. Around midday the sound of fighting came nearer. As a precaution I had the radio equipment stored in my gun wagon and prepared the radio panzer with demolition charges. The infantry fire from the woods above was coming ever closer. A few armoured infantry carriers drove past and some grenadiers came running out of the woods heading west, the last of them shouting: 'Get out, the Americans are already in the village!'

It was high time to blow up the radio panzer but we could not do it prematurely, for if the pioneers arrived to retrieve the machine and they found it burning there was no telling how upset they might be. I had ordered the driver to do it himself for having been so stupid. Instead of stopping at once when he saw he was slipping off the road, he had accelerated to get back. The left-hand track lost its grip and the right hand track dragged the machine down the slope. At my command he tugged on the pull cord and with an explosion the radio panzer began to burn immediately.

Now we had to flee. The crew of the radio panzer sat on the hull of my gun wagon and I drove west deeper into the pocket in search of our company. The crossroads at Meschede which we had to pass over was under heavy enemy artillery fire. It was in open country and we watched infantry vehicles and even horse-drawn wagons go across it. I did not like the idea of doing this with three men unprotected on top. Some vehicles managed it safely but others were caught in the shelling and the heap of scrap on the crossroads grew ever larger.

I consulted the map for another way but this would have involved a big detour and we were short of petrol. Others before us had attempted to get through cross-country and got bogged down in marshy ground. For more than two hours we waited behind a high stone wall observing the crossroads, waiting for the gunners to break off temporarily or run out of ammunition, this being a thin hope since they were probably accompanied by lorries loaded with shells. All agreed that we should trust to luck and run the gauntlet. We approached what we perceived to be the splinter limit and after the next salvo we would speed across. If we were forced to stop through damage the radio panzer crew would jump off and run for it.

Immediately after the next salvo we drove from the splinter limit into the cloud of smoke at the crossroads. Suddenly my drive braked sharply and the gun wagon pulled up just short of a horse-drawn supply wagon. The radio panzer crew jumped off at once and sprinted through the crossroads. 'Go! Go! Run the horses down!' I cried to the driver, but he was unable to select any of his seven forward gears and we remained immobile. One horse was lying wounded in his harness and the other stood there stubbornly, blood running from the nostrils.

'What's up?!' I urged the driver as he struggled with his gear lever. Another heavy-calibre salvo landed nearby, the splinters whizzing overhead, some of them clattering against our armour while the stinking smoke of the shells drifted over us. The driver and I removed the cover of the gearbox and he tried to put it in gear with his hands. Another salvo landed with a great crash around us and we simply had to get away from this damned crossroads. Finally he succeeded and with a jerk our armoured vehicle rattled over the horses and wagon. I was still lying down near the gearbox and did not see the effects of my order.

The three radio panzer crewmen were waiting unscathed in a ditch alongside the highway watching the fall of shells and hectic activity in the vehicle with alarm from a distance. We sought cover from the air so that both drivers could work at the gearbox. Once everything was functioning as it should we went to Battalion where I reported the loss of my radio panzer. This was accepted without comment, being just one of many loss reports. Two days later I had a replacement radio panzer and we set out on patrol again. Fuel in canisters was issued for the round trip. The pocket had shrunk alarmingly. It was quite common for us to arrive back at Battalion with a vehicle in tow which had run out of fuel.

Slowly desperation and rage at the encirclement spread through the company. Nobody wanted to do a reconnaissance any more, and a big meal was made of repairs to vehicles. At Company there was a stock of pure alcohol for the rocket industry. It was stored in water canisters, and when diluted with water was responsible for many of the reconnaissance patrols being out of action. I liked egg liqueur and was recognised at Company as a specialist mixer. The eggs were supplied by the billet hosts in the villages and thus we passed the remaining days with the local girls in a happy haze.

One evening Battalion wanted a reconnaissance patrol and, because none was operational, our commander had to report the fact in great embarrassment to the commanding officer personally. The lieutenant of one patrol was drunk and the driver of another was sleeping it off in a stupor in the gutter. Thus I had to go out again but did not return until midday and had one vehicle unserviceable. I had not reported the latter to the repair squad immediately upon my return, my intention being to remain non-operational for an extra day in the conviction that others would be available and not always just the most junior commander.

The following morning I was summoned to the commander's private rooms after his dressing down at Battalion for having no patrol available, and he took it out on me. Apart from not reporting the breakdown I did not feel responsible for the others and in the ensuing altercation pleaded for a fairer distribution of patrols. The crews should at least have a day off occasionally. The debate grew more heated and then Lieutenant Gavenat roared: 'I am court-martialling you for knowingly delaying the operational status of a fighting vehicle!' This was hot air, for then he would have to explain to the court-martial why the boozers were not operational.

'If you do that, Herr Lieutenant, will you kindly relieve me of my duties and re-install your special duties lieutenant as patrol commander. Moreover I must request clarification why the other patrols are non-operational.'

'You shut your trap – you are responsible to me personally to have your vehicles operational tomorrow morning early!' and with that I was shown the door. The house owners of the commander's billet were seated in the big living room and must have heard the commander's threat, for they all looked at me sympathetically. 'The whole theatre is just noise and smoke,' I told them with a smile.

Two days after this incident a runner arrived: 'Unteroffizier Henning, report at once to the commander!' Lieutenant Gavenat received me in front of his office. He offered me his hand. This gesture I thought very unusual. He had never done it before, and in any case shaking hands was never his forte with anybody. We entered the office together where the Spiess, Senior Warrant Officer Petschner was waiting. This looked like another bawling-out and I prepared my response.

Gavenat cleared his throat, looked me in the eyes and then said in happy tones, 'Henning, I have to inform you that with effect from today you are promoted to sergeant. My heartiest congratulations!' From Petschner's hand he took the shoulder straps with the Sergeant stars and pressed them into mine. 'Your promotion has been agreed with the Commanding Officer. He and also I are convinced that you are worthy of your post as reconnaissance patrol leader.' I was totally thunderstruck and so emotional that I could not find words. Perhaps I should have said something but nothing came to mind.

Petschner patted my shoulder and buttoned the new shoulder straps to my uniform. The Company commander cleared his throat again and got back to business. 'Henning, I have to detach two patrols directly to LIII Corps under Lieutenant General Bayerlein. Lieutenant Graf von Oberstdorf and you with your patrols are listed to go. Once you have completed your task, you will return to Company. Lieutenant Graf von Oberstdorf has already been informed. You leave at once. Your promotion will be celebrated upon your return!' With that he left. The Spiess obtained a bottle from the Duty NCO; Corporal Otto, for a quick toast. We all had a swig and as I took my leave Petschner called after me, 'It is a mission to win the Knight's Cross for yourself!' Aha, I had been promoted to sergeant and given detached duty. Was this going to be a more than usually dangerous caper?

I was a mere recruit at Stahnsdorf in 1941 when Lieutenant Graf von Oberstdorf was in the officers' training platoon there and often in competition with our platoon of volunteers. There was much ragging between our platoons in the barrack block. Von Oberstdorf reminded me of this when we met. Now as lieutenant he had overall command of our two patrols with LIII Corps, but whenever we left at night he would always let me lead, for he knew I was better at map-reading. As a result of this detached duty our last days in the Ruhr pocket were not spent at Battalion or Company. We ran a few reconnaissance patrols, mainly by day, but otherwise we felt like outsiders at LIII Corps.

The pocket was constantly contracting and now we could see general disintegration looming. This took dramatic form amongst German troops and many infantry were fighting on their own account in the woods. We also saw many Russian PoWs and so-called Hiwis (Russian volunteers in German uniform) around their camp fires. One evening we met a middle-aged captain who led a Hiwi company and complained bitterly to me that in the village below our location he had heard women crying, which without doubt was attributable to Russian PoWs being at large. I wanted to send a signal requesting the immediate presence of a German unit in the village, but what unit would respond to a cry for help from a single village while the Army was in total collapse? This captain simply could not or would not come to terms with the dramatic situation developing in the pocket, but assured me he could rely absolutely on his Hiwis.

On my trips inside the pocket I met a patrol from Battalion now and again and we exchanged views about the situation. Through signals traffic I always knew the location of the Company, which was now at Altena. My friend Hans Pischke (who lives today in Bad Friedrichshall) and I swore a pledge that we would experience the end together and remain in touch after it was all over, come what may. Thus one day I went to Company to take him to our old quarters at Hösel. He was a corporal and commander of a reconnaissance vehicle under Lieutenant Ziemke. On the way we met another radio panzer crew who attached themselves to us, and so we were now two gun wagons and two radio panzers on the road to Hösel near Heiligenhaus. At that time the pocket was 45 kilometres across. On this drive we were surprised by an American armoured spearhead. I could not understand how enemy forces were now in the centre of the pocket. I tried to get away to the north but could not. From a pre-military training camp in the final stages of breaking up we got more fuel and something to eat. Outside Hagen we had to destroy one radio panzer with engine damage.

At Altenhagen on Boeler Heath I led the three vehicles into an alder grove, righting the trees and bushes behind us so as not to be seen from the road. All of us spent the night in a restaurant on the other side of the road. From an enemy broadcast we learned that the pocket had been split into two by making a north-south scissors cut. This sealed our fate in Hagen. Perhaps we could have slipped through somewhere but things might have got very nasty and I did not want to saddle my men with it. During the night the enemy let our neighbourhood have a few desultory salvoes. There was no longer any determined German resistance.

Early on Sunday 15 April 1945 we rolled up our blankets and left the restaurant for our vehicles. The restaurant proprietors wanted to avoid any possibility of German soldiers being in their establishment should the Americans arrive. I informed the crews that we were going to be overrun here by the enemy and I gave each man the free choice to act as he saw fit – either accepting captivity or trying to make his way home. Hans Pischke and I intended to get to Hösel, anybody who wanted to do so could accompany us. The crews preferred American captivity, however. I now hammered it into the men that until the Americans came we were here on standing watch in case any field police or officers crossed our path. We remained in radio contact with LIII Corps.

At leisure we rigged our vehicles for destruction. Some of the men wanted to fit the explosives to go off when the rear door was opened. I could not allow that because children were always hanging around us and could set it off while playing. The first of them had already turned up and were at their tricks. At midday the town forester arrived with two civilians to beg me not to blow up the panzers for God's sake. Probably the children had relayed our intentions to them. 'I have express orders to destroy every panzer to prevent it falling into enemy hands,' I told them, 'If I fail to do that knowingly I could be court-martialled.' This did not satisfy them and they argued that we might set the woods on fire and probably some houses too. I should think of the women and children who would lose their homes and possessions and be left in penury. The war had already caused so much suffering and many houses had already been destroyed by the bombing. I should reflect on all that and decide against blowing up the vehicles, in the name of the women and children. In the face of all this pleading, imploring and begging I finally gave in and in their presence had the explosives removed from the vehicles.

The first American tanks and armoured infantry carriers arrived that afternoon. They came down the road without meeting any opposition between Hohenlimburg and Dortmund. There followed an endless stream of vehicles. Suddenly two middle-aged infantrymen came running out of the woods and told me they wanted to cross the road to their families. They could see their houses but dared not cross. I advised them to wait until dark and then slip across. We lost sight of them and I did not find out how they got on.

Now it was also time for me to take leave of my men. 'So, comrades, it ends here. I have no more orders for you and thank you all for your loyal fulfilment of duty. I have brought you all safe and sound through the war thus far. Be cautious and do not court danger, for able-bodied men will be needed now more than ever to rebuild our ruined homeland. Hans Pischke and I will attempt to get through to Hösel during the night. I wish you all much luck, that you get home safely and Hals und Beinbruch!'

They had got their things together and were now ready to go into captivity as a group. We watched them standing at the side of the road, but the passing Americans ignored them, and gradually we lost sight of them. Pischke and I prepared for a night march bearing in mind these columns of American troops driving by. We removed our rank insignia and decorations and secured them on the inside of our black panzer uniforms. I tied my compass by its cord so that it hung inside my trousers behind the knee. My maps I placed inside the trouser legs which were tied at the bottom and so could not fall through. With foresight we had exchanged our field boots for laced shoes at Company. I sowed my German money into the gusset of my underpants. We could not agree whether to take our pistols with us or not. Hans was in favour but I had the stronger argument. If the Americans decided we were military with a weapon and disguised as civilians they might think we were so-called 'Werewolves' and shoot us out of hand. Accordingly we wrapped our pistols in foil and buried them under a prominent tree, carving a recognition symbol into the bark. Now we waited for midnight to set out.

The greater part of my battalion and company went into captivity between Altena and Lüdenschied on 15 April 1945. My former patrol leader WO1 Otto Keichel, the only holder of the Knight's Cross in Panzer ALA 130 besides Major von Born-Fallois, fell on 14 April 1945 at Werdohl a day before the Ruhr pocket capitulated. In Berlin in 1950 Hans Suse, his driver, described how this happened. On reconnaissance patrol they were driving along a country path at the end of which they saw some German PoWs were being led away by American guards. The prisoners shouted excitedly, 'Don't shoot, don't shoot!' Keichel refrained from doing so to prevent the prisoners being endangered. The US guards, surrounded by German soldiers, then opened fire on the German vehicles and Keichel was hit in the head. He collapsed on his seat as both vehicles reversed back down the path without firing. They brought Keichel to a field hospital at Werdohl where he died of his wound shortly afterwards.

WO1 Otto Keichel had taken part in the campaigns in Poland, France and North Africa and since the invasion of Normandy had been a reconnaissance patrol leader, always at the front. He fell one single day before the capitulation in the Ruhr pocket in brave execution of his duty as a soldier. A soldier's death! (After the reunification of Germany I was able to travel with my wife in 1992 to visit his grave in the grove of honour at Werdohl, where we planted some flowering bushes in his memory.)

Towards midnight we set out on foot with rucksacks and some provisions for what we hoped would be freedom. I had committed the route to memory from the map, since we would be moving by night, avoiding those villages where we guessed the Americans would be. It started well. We followed a railway track and saw a fire ahead. We took stock then went forward. There were dark shapes around a camp fire which I assumed would be Russian PoWs or Hiwis. They seemed as unsettled as we were, and so I led the way past them without speaking. I felt naked not having a weapon to hand. Because we had made such good progress along the railway embankment we decided to follow the river Ennepe and the highway to Wuppertal. Unfortunately we did not get much farther.

At Hagen-Haspe we had to cross a small pedestrian bridge. I got across it but Hans stumbled and was heard by an American sentry who covered him with a machine-pistol. As we had sworn to stay together I went back and gave myself up voluntarily into US captivity. Three men took us away and gave us a fairly superficial pat-down for weapons during which they discovered and confiscated my maps. We then had to stand against the stone wall of a house from the first floor of which a sentry pointed his MG at us. At first we feared they might shoot us because of the maps, but then the sentry at the window sat on his chair and swung his legs on the window sill near his MG. As time went on he had a doze, from which he awoke from time to time with a jerk. Hans Pischke and I were now prisoners of war of the United States of America.

Chapter Nine

April 1945: A Prisoner of the Americans

Tired of standing we slithered gradually to a seated position. The sentry awoke with a jerk but made no objection and soon he nodded off again. Whenever he was fast asleep we would scrape a foot, and then he would come to life suddenly and grab his MG.

In the morning they took us to the highway and, with our rucksacks, Pischke and I were made to sit on the front mudguard either side of the bonnet of a captured German automobile. Wheels slipping it drew away and at the first left-hand bend I fell off. The driver braked hard and Hans fell into the mud. The three Americans in the car bawled, 'Mak' snell, let's go, let's go!' urging us to remount the mudguards. This time we grasped each other and jammed our feet against the headlights. As the car worked up to high speed we lay across the bonnet holding hands. This was deadly dangerous and no fun except for those inside the car. At Hagen they deposited us in a PoW camp with a laugh. Here we met other members of my patrol.

The camp was a wet meadow and we received nothing to eat or drink. I estimated there were about 500 prisoners and I was amazed at how well some of the infantry had prepared for captivity. Some of the older men sat on bulging rucksacks and had blankets and canvas while many of the younger soldiers and Luftwaffe auxiliaries did not even have a jacket. All the men of my patrol gathered around me and we established a community. We huddled close together on a canvas so that nobody fell into the mud while sleeping. We were all lucky to have kept our work combinations which we wore over our uniforms.

In my dejection I realised at once where I had gone wrong. We should have hidden up to ten to fourteen days in the deepest woods until all the hectic rounding-up of prisoners had abated somewhat and then sought work with a farmer or similar. Until the last I had performed my military duty loyally and never thought about what to do after the war. At age seventeen I had been sent to the German Afrika Korps and accustomed myself well to war conditions. Now I was twenty-one and though I had brought every man of my command safely through the war, at the last moment and on the threshold of peace I had failed to take a corner correctly and landed here in the shit with my men. I reproached myself bitterly at not having made better plans for them.

On the second day a column of open-back lorries rolled up and we had to parade in five ranks. We had all been doing this for years but now American camel-drivers were on hand to beat us into groups of fifty with clubs. With the usual encouragement 'Let's go, let's go' they created ten groups of fifty prisoners each. Next came the loading of each group aboard a lorry at the double. Cursing, swearing and shouting 'Bloody Heinis, snell, snell' they forced the prisoners onto the lorry, allowing their pent-up emotions full rein by aiming their clubs at our heads.

We were crammed standing sardine-fashion in the back of the lorry. In my lorry there was only room for forty-seven. GIs jumped on the tailboard and struck out at the prisoners to make room to squeeze the last three in. The lorries had obviously been purpose-built in the Unites States for fifty persons standing with arms by their sides and whoever had a rucksack or other bulky belongings had to stand on them. The drivers were mostly Afro-Americans who took no part in the beatings but had their own special delights in store for us.

After the tenth and last lorry had been loaded by the camel-drivers, the convoy set off and at the first bend our hair stood on end. The drivers took the bends in the road at such a furious speed that we thought the lorry must tip over at any moment. The prisoners immediately behind the cab had to shout which way to lean into the bend with the upper body. Along leafy avenues the drivers liked to sweep us with overhanging branches and then the most forward prisoners would shout 'Take cover!' and we would all crouch. The horrific journey supplied the Americans with good innocent fun, however, and they were very happy with this proof of their natural impishness.

At Lüdenscheid we were unloaded in the darkness under spotlights and beaten with clubs by GIs standing either side of the tailboard. I avoided being struck by working my way to the centre of the throng, but my friend Hans Pischke was hit several times. We were driven into the corner of a large prison camp and when it got light a great cry of disgust went up from the prisoners. We were in the latrine corner, the open-air shithouse, the reception point for all new arrivals. Luckily we were the last to enter and slept on the edge of the sewer and not in it.

We were, of course, all happy not to have fallen into the hands of the Soviets and many men had gone into US captivity in the expectation of receiving treatment corresponding to the terms of the Geneva Convention. No prison camp was ever a paradise, but these inhuman cruelties and beatings at the hands of simple GIs left us with many questions. To be a German prisoner of war in and after the Second World War was no less dangerous than being at the front. During my service in North Africa and during the invasion of Normandy I saw many Allied PoWs in German hands and never saw one clubbed or tortured. Of course, I know nothing of what went on in German PoW camps, my observations were made only on the front line in North Africa and the Western Front.

At Lüdenscheid we watched columns of German lorries drive into captivity, with the crews immediately made prisoners of war. With Hans I crept up on one of these convoys and from two lorries swiftly liberated a canvas sheet, two blankets, two loaves of Army bread and a box of cigars. Then the Americans discovered us and chased us away with their machine-pistols.

Water was being distributed from a tanker in the camp. Everybody ran there, helped on the way by beatings from the guards. If the prisoner had a tin, water would be poured into it, but no tin, no water. The daily rations were three biscuits, one tablespoonful of milk or egg-powder, one tablespoonful of sugar, five beans and one raw potato. No facility existed for cooking. This was a diet rich in calories by US Army standards.

The officers were separated out and went to a different camp, and we were forced to march to another camp. At a rest point on the way, many, being so weak, collapsed by the wayside. Twenty paces away was a sugar beet field already being plundered by other prisoners. I ran there and pulled up two beets. The sentries fired warning shots over our heads while the prisoners bit hungrily into the dirty beets. I had concealed a pocket knife in my first-aid pack which had eluded discovery in the search. It was strictly forbidden to have a knife, and now it served us well. If a sentry appeared I buried it in the soft earth. An American sentry saw the cut pieces and now wanted the knife. We shrugged in incomprehension. I must have looked at him the wrong way for he pulled me up by the collar and jabbed me in the back by his machine-pistol. Shouting 'Bloody Heinies – snell' he forced me to a point three metres ahead of the column where I had to sit on the ground together with two other selected 'Krauts'. This did not look good, and so when the sentry left I moved back on my bottom to the first lorry of the convoy, stood up and retired on foot to my place. Hans Pischke had meanwhile retrieved the knife. Amongst these hundreds of men the sentry would never find me again.

Now we lined up in five ranks of fifty men each to be beaten and clubbed to the lorries again. This time only forty-five men could fit into our lorry. We all had to get out, a big melee ensuing in the struggle to be in the middle and so avoid the beatings. Three men had to remount the lorry and throw out all the rucksacks and baggage. With 'let's go, let's go' we re-occupied the lorry and now there was room for fifty but all those who had planned so carefully for their captivity had now only what they stood up in.

An empty bottle was thrown out of a lorry and smashed on the road. The Americans looked horrified. This must be an attempt to sabotage their tyres. Out came the cudgels and clubs and now they went for the prisoners. Never before in my whole life had I seen such brutality as the Americans were guilty of that day, and when they got tired of it the prisoners turned on the bottle-thrower. My God, is this what our once proud Wehrmacht had come to?

Once again the black drivers took the lorries round the bends at fantastic speed and everybody had to lean left or right at the word of command. As we drove through towns and villages the women would wave to us and we saw some crying. We crossed the Rhine at Remagen over a temporary bridge and at Maria Laach-Nickenich they clubbed us out of the lorries again. Now we were in a prison camp with no shelter against cold and rain, living rough on the land in April weather.

Since Lüdenscheid, Hans and I had been contemplating escape. To get through the barbed wire seemed easy and one would be free in the homeland, but at night we always heard shooting at escaping prisoners. With jeeps and spotlights they hunted down escapers like wild prey, and when they caught one he was shot dead without mercy. To encourage us not to escape they left a few dead bodies to rot near the camp. I convinced Hans that now was not the time to make an attempt. We had come through the war and now we should not gamble our lives. In the camp there was a colleague who could actually see his parents' house but had no way of getting there.

About the end of April 1945 we made a long forced march to Andernach on the Rhine to the so-called Rheinwiesen (Rhine meadowlands). Many were so weak that comrades had to carry them, arms linked. It was the sheerest misery. At Andernach was a very large PoW camp with a broad central road and from there sprouted individual camps separated off with double-wire fences. All NCOs went into a camp of their own and thus we lost the other ranks from our patrol. The word 'camp' is a misnomer. They were just fields with no shelter. It always seemed to be raining and there was even some April snowfall. We froze day and night. Daily we looked at the sky and prayed for the sun to dry our wet clothing.

One sunny day I found a louse in the neck of my vest. The finds increased daily. We had entered captivity lice-free. American medics arrived with a long rope and stretched it across the camp. Others had a gigantic hand-spray and dusted all prisoners with a white powder at the neckband, sleeves, trouser fly and legs. Those who had been fully sprayed could climb over the rope. Thus the rope traversed the camp until all had been sprayed. Some prisoners did not want the treatment because they suspected the powder might be poisoned, but refusal meant they could not cross the rope. The powder was efficacious and from then on we were lice-free.

Near us were some young Waffen-SS men. Soon there was uproar in the camp. Everybody had to strip above the waist to be examined by an American commission whose only interest was to identify all those who had their blood group tattooed under the armpit. Colleagues who had wounds in that area of the body had to go before a medical commission to determine whether this was the result of an attempt to remove the tattoo. Waffen-SS and police with tattoos were then placed in a special camp close by. This particular camp had many imprisoned civilians who had probably been Party functionaries or denounced as committed Party members. In that camp the rations were even worse than in ours.

Early on, the latrine was a trench the width of a spade head. The prisoners had to crouch down one behind the other. Many prisoners were physically unable to crouch in this manner and now lay in the mud nearby. The stool was hardened by the nature of the rations and difficult to evacuate. Later the latrine trench was enlarged and provided with eight seats, four either side.

The daily rations were received at the gate, enough for 100 men, the fare to be split into tens and then handed out individually. Because nobody around us was prepared to volunteer for this duty it went by rank and Hans proposed me. I protested, but it was a job to benefit the community and so I gave in. With an escort of three men, I received the rations in blankets which we then shared out into tens while everybody looked on. Biscuits, bread, milk powder, egg powder, raw potatoes, prunes, raw rice, raw beans, raw peas etc. My pocket knife came in very useful and made the rounds. To allot the ten portions, each group was given a number one to ten. One man faced away while I pointed to a portion and he shouted out a number from one to ten to indicate which group should receive it. The ten portions were then distributed to each individual prisoner by the same method. Since we had no cooking facilities, everything had to be eaten raw.

The older prisoners were not happy with the portioning out and were ever critical of the system. A balance was made out of branches and now they wanted to weigh everything. The worst arguments were over bread crusts. Solidarity and comradeship amongst the older men broke down under the pressure of hunger. Hunger robs people of their humanity, but it must not be forgotten that it was more difficult for older men to adjust to living rough in these camps.

After fourteen days I had had enough of the complaining and surrendered the job to the chief moaner, but he would not accept it because it meant additional work. He was then forced to do it and with the scales it took two hours longer. I could not get out of it completely and did the dividing up for a ten-group, but I did expel the older men from my group and reintroduced the system we had started off with. While we were eating, the older men would still be sharing out. Despite hunger and thirst, the younger prisoners tolerated captivity better than the older men and recognised the value of the old adage 'All for one and one for all'.

I noticed one day that many infantrymen wore a red-white-red piece of cloth on their caps, at first just a few and then many more later. The point of this was to identify themselves as Austrians who wanted nothing more to do with us. They considered themselves 'foreigners' and removed the eagle and swastika from their uniforms because they had been 'press-ganged into German uniform against their will.' I continued to feel I was a German soldier and maintained my composure in this difficult time. Thus on 8 May 1945 when a great shout of joy ran through the camp and was repeated from camp to camp that the war was over, for me it was no day of joy to celebrate the end of a lost war and our subjugation to the arbitrary rule of the victorious Powers in these filthy and bestial conditions.

One day there was a tumult at the outer camp fence. Armed guards were throwing newspapers into the camp. What we saw in them took our breath away. There were photos of mountains of corpses, starved to a skeleton and piled high. Many of us were convinced that this was pure Hollywood, for we did not believe it could have happened in a German camp. They were pictures taken at a German death camp.

We had a German camp administration and a camp police. The latter were well-fed thugs. Colleagues told me that one of the worst of them, a WOII, came from Mecklenburg, actually quite close to my home town. I never passed the time of day with him because I cannot stomach this kind of person. Today they live amongst us pretending to be 'normal people'.

We had a long rainy period on the Rhine. The ground was churned into a morass and the wet and cold claimed many lives. The first to die were the older men who had entered captivity ill or in a weakened state. In particular, those with stomach complaints were thrown into the camp regardless of their condition. Some went mad; near me a few men in the grip of insane fantasy were digging a deep hole in the belief they would eventually strike a vein of drinkable water.

Using sods of earth which bore no grass we built a low wall in the shape of an arrowhead and secured our triangular bivouac over it. This provided shelter for three men with their legs outside. Our third man was a medical corps sergeant who had been a PoW of the Americans in North Africa and had been returned to Germany as a medic attending the wounded and sick. He always used to tell us what good PoW camps they had in the United States itself which left us incredulous. My health worsened and I became a living skeleton. I could no longer stand without seeing black before my eyes. Between that day and being put into a tub by a German Red Cross nurse at Andernach hospital I have no recall. Under the care of German and American doctors, nurses and medical corps staff I slowly regained my strength. I had a clean bed in a ward with ten other ill or wounded men. After the camp at Rheinwiesen it was a paradise. The annexe buildings were fenced off from an American hospital. American doctors allowed no food to be hoarded. Some German infantrymen had gone hungry through six years of the war and had developed the habit of storing 'bits of bread for later'. The Americans could not understand this and ruled that what was not eaten at the mealtime had to be thrown away.

An American Jewish doctor visited me. I heard him use the word 'Phimose'. It meant nothing to me. A medic explained, 'They want to circumcise you, which will mean a few more days in hospital.'

'OK, if that's the case do it. Main thing is, as long as possible here!' This operation was postponed twice and so it was some considerable time before I returned to the camp.

Chapter Ten

1945–1946: I Become a Prisoner of the French

Now under French guards, those who had recovered were returned to the camp and pushed inside. I knew nobody. There had been fundamental changes and the camp was now under French administration. Previously the Americans had released all fifteen- to seventeen-year-olds and also many others with addresses in the Western Zone. My friend Hans Pischke from Cottbus got himself discharged to my former billet hosts at Bachenau. (We remain in contact today.) The food had improved, and now we had hot cabbage soup with potato peelings once daily with bread.

The French were recruiting energetically for the Foreign Legion. Whoever volunteered went to another camp and got the same rations as French soldiers. A number of prisoners volunteered simply to get out of this starvation camp. Even if it meant dying here I would never have volunteered to fight for the French under any circumstances whatsoever.

Work parties were assembled, the intention of everybody being to find one in which he improved his lot. One day I was in a party to clean the guard barracks. Some sugar beet was piled nearby. It was a temptation to hungry prisoners, but guards brandishing machine-pistols prevented the theft. Scarcely had the guards gone than some prisoners tried it. Shots rang out and two men fell dead for a handful of roots. It happened frequently, usually at night, that French soldiers on the other side of the Rhine at Neuwied would fire random rounds into the camp. By then the war had been over for six months and PoWs were still dying because high-spirited, drunken or evil French soldiers shot at prisoners lying unprotected in large groups on the ground.

My work party of ten men had to dig by the outer fence of the

164

camp. A woman arrived carrying a small bucket with some food. The guard was indecisive and looked as though he would allow it. Up came a young French officer and kicked over the bucket of stew. We all began to curse him and at that he manhandled the old woman away.

I recalled the French prisoners in my home town in 1940. There were four of them in our joinery, Octave, Joseph, André and René. Because they lodged close to my parents' house, as a sixteen-year-old apprentice I escorted them at midday to and from their meal, and the same again in the evening. Their lodgings had a view of a lake and they occupied a lounge, bedroom and kitchen. At first a German woman cooked for them, but later they had their own cook to prepare French cuisine. They had neither fence nor guards to keep them in the buildings. I visited them often in the evening and on Sundays, and even when I came home on leave. I had a very good relationship with Octave, who came from Paris, and my parents used to invite him for coffee. Their captivity was difficult, they were married and missed home, but they were not treated inhumanly or dishonourably. One day in September 1945 we had to parade and be loaded in groups of fifty men into railway goods trucks. Without straw or any facilities we stood like cattle on the way to the abattoir. One had to urinate or defecate by the closed doors. The French told us that we were going to a transit camp for release, this to 'prevent possible unrest amongst the prisoners who had to remain'. The railwaymen informed us guardedly that the train was going to France. Naturally this gave rise to shock and dismay. When the train stopped, women would often come and throw apples to us through the hatches. At one station was a goods train which had German prisoners aboard from Denmark and Norway. It had crossed half Germany with its doors open, and there were even prisoners riding in open goods wagons. The infantry were in good heart, having been deceived into believing they were going to a camp to be released. We called over to them that all transports in this zone went to France, but most of them wouldn't believe us and so they had a rude awakening waiting for them when they got to France. Three days later the sliding doors were opened at Belfort where we were chased into a barracks and locked up in a large vehicle-hall. We had to camp on the bare concrete floor.

A petrol drum at the door served all bodily functions. We had been betrayed and sold out!

After fourteen days on very meagre rations I was put on a ten-man work party. A civilian armed with a rifle fetched us from the barracks and took us by train to a small village. Our guard had been a prisoner of the Germans. We were lodged in a small house in the village situated on a steep slope in the mountains.

Early next day our party went to the woods to familiarise itself with the new work conditions. We were to fell, de-branch and measure off the cut wood, and finally stack it. We had a daily target which was beyond us in the opening few days. After everybody had tried out the various tasks we specialised and then the work was easier. Thus I worked exclusively with the axe, made the first notch and steered the tree so as to fall free of its neighbour. I lopped off its branches while others sawed and the last one stacked the wood into fixed cubic metre sizes. The work was dangerous since none of us had ever been foresters. Mostly we worked on slopes and felled oak and beech up to 1.2 to 1.6 metres in diameter which gave us problems with the saws. In the woods we always had a spot for warming our food. We covered it over with earth in the evening and next day we would find it still glowing. Some of us had very poor footwear so the patron provided us all with Dutch clogs, and we clattered through the village to the woods morning and night. In the snow, clogs were warmer than shoes but dangerous on slopes. In the next village two prisoners died while felling trees.

One day when our patron brought our rations the guard who always kept him away from us was not present. I took the opportunity to complain to our patron that the rations were inadequate for the heavy work performed.

'In my opinion there is easily enough for the ten of you.'

'No,' I said, 'because Philippe the guard eats most of it.'

'What? Philippe eats some of the food I bring you?' And he rolled his eyes.

Philippe, who rode us spitefully, never came again and two days later we were all back at the barracks at Belfort.

Some improvements had been made to this basic camp. Split up into work parties for the French Army kitchens we got some extra food and I recovered my strength. Being able to speak some French

I got on well with some of the cooks and they would always give me something to eat whenever I was around. Unfortunately it soon ended and I was appointed interpreter to a ten-man party at a sawmill at Luxeul-les-Bains, where we were given a room in a warehouse. Previously they had ground charcoal there and our room was rather black. In time we made it habitable. We slept in five double-tiered bunks and fitted a false wooden ceiling to retain the warmth. We cooked our own food on a stove within a walled surround. Compared to Andernach and Belfort this was a paradise. The sawmill staff consisted of one manager, three French employees and ten German prisoners. The logs were cut up into planks and boards on a large saw. Our workday was ten hours, nine hours for the French, with Sunday off.

The ban on fraternisation relaxed and the flush of victory slowly ebbed away in 1946. Hate and the lust for revenge disappeared with time, and since victors and vanquished now shared the same workplace more humane dealings became normal. Nevertheless, it was a miserable feeling for us to be prisoners without rights or honour or news from our loved ones in the homeland a year after the war had ended. In the evening after the meagre meal one lay on the straw mattress, stared at the ceiling and thought of escape. Yet, although the rations were monotonous and of poor nutritional value we did not go hungry.

At the sawmill we were lodged close to a lively road junction on the outskirts of town. We could see the passers-by and they could see us. Soon we knew all the women and girls and gave them each a pet name so that everybody knew whom we meant when we talked about them. By virtue of my knowledge of French I worked in the villa of our patron René Genet. This was ten minutes' walk from the sawmill and I walked the route three times there and back daily. At the house I received my orders from 'Madame' and in the garden from 'Monsieur'.

There was a PoW camp for twenty men about eight minutes' walk from us and near the railway goods station. The inmates were all corporals and sergeants who worked as street cleaners and on other municipal jobs. There was a corporal from my company amongst them and so I spent a lot of time there. When they needed cuts of wood we prepared them for collection after dark. One manager used to put a mark on the top boards of a stack and so we removed those below them. The manager never noticed.

Over the course of time we removed the initials 'PG' (prisonier de guerre) painted on our uniforms and on Sundays would walk into town. It had a football stadium and at home games we supported the home team vociferously. We even got to know the names of the players. One day a Swiss team came and we supported them against the home team. This change of favour did not go down well with the local Luxuelers.

My work at the patron's villa involved my being house manager and maid of all work. The patron was a small but sly dog with a farmer's cunning. Madame, on the other hand, was a good head taller than her husband and made a stately, resolute impression. I stood between them. Madame ruled the roost indoors and I had to dance to her tune. My duties gave me access to all inhabited rooms, kitchen and cellar. A senior French officer lived on the first floor, rarely present on account of his duties. His wife seemed to live in purdah. I was able to greatly improve my French in conversations with Madame. She was prone to big mood swings and if it got really bad and Madame sneezed I would tell her in friendly tones, 'Bless you, house dragon!' to which she would reply, 'Merci beaucoup, Otto!'

The patron gave me errands to run for the garden and now and again I had to clean his car. While doing this I would often find a few francs inside it which I would return to him with a sly expression since it was obviously done to test my honesty. Instead I robbed the kitchen and cellar regularly without their ever saying anything. In the cellar I had a pole with a nail on the end for spearing apples through a vent when a basket was left outside after picking.

In the spring of 1946 we were given work digging the gardens of French civilians. This always gave us a problem at lunchtime, for we never knew how many courses there were going to be. Just the soup would fill us up and after the main meal, when we had to finish off with a slice of cake and a cup of coffee, our eyes would be bulging. These Sunday jobs involved just two or three of us at table with the French hosts, and besides the meal they would give us a few francs and often an item of clothing.

The relationship between ourselves and the simple Frenchman

improved enormously. It helped that there had been no fighting during the war in the vicinity. On the outskirts of town the Luftwaffe had had an airfield but I never heard the French speak of any problems between themselves and the airmen. The French did remember which of the local girls had had a German boyfriend, however, and those who had consorted with Germans were forced to continue wearing the headscarf.

One day I was asked by a man from Alsace if I could do a small job for an old lady on the Sunday. Before starting work she gave me breakfast and then I had to dig up her hen yard. The ground was hard with poultry droppings. At midday I was given a wonderful meal with many courses and wine. The old lady must have spent the whole morning preparing it. Her face was rather lined with too much smoking and she had three cats around her large hearth. She was always friendly to me and I ate heartily with her. This sudden thoughtfulness came as a strange interlude in our often so heartless captivity.

I discovered that the she owned the big house and garden with its lawn and trees, and behind that a working curtain factory. She told me that during the war Luftwaffe officers had been billeted on her upper floor and were always very courteous. From now on I spent every Sunday with Madame and she made sure I was not over-worked and did not go hungry. One day my patron turned up and forbade her to give me any more work. She was visibly depressed in telling me this and added that I could visit her at any time and she would feed me even if there was no work to be done. It was shortly before Whitsun and on the first day of the holidays she invited me to lunch. When it was dark I stole a bouquet of white flowers and presented them to Madame on Whit Sunday morning dressed in my Sunday best. The old lady was overjoyed to receive them even though she must have known they were stolen. I ate in the company of two elderly ladies at midday and had to take coffee too. Later Madame had her own personal PoW who worked only for her. I often talked to him and he told me how well she looked after him and even gave him the present of a watch.

Whenever I put on my Sunday best I lost the appearance of a PoW. In Belfort I had purloined a pair of American Army trousers. I slept with them beneath my mattress all week so as to have sharp creases for the weekend. I had a pair of gleaming shoes, a white shirt which I got from a lady billet host, whose husband had fallen at the front, and in addition a tie, a Basque beret and a dark jacket which was a gift from a French lady for the work I did for her. This get-up naturally attracted the French girls and when I wore it to the football stadium they were always anxious to collect my entrance fee on the assumption I was French. As PoWs we were exempt from paying, however. Frenchmen of the time were scruffs, but the time had not yet arrived when French girls could have a relationship with a German PoW. That would not happen for a year or so.

One Thursday, at lunchtime, I went to the sawmill to eat and the manager told me to help load planks on a horse-drawn wagon. 'OK', I said, 'but first I have things to do.' He overruled me: I must load the wagon. The reason why I could not start work at once was that I had some potatoes stolen from the patron's garden under my clothing.

My colleagues were either at the table or lying on their bunks.

'So what's up with you people?'

'We're on strike. The old man has given us no food and so we won't work.' The manager came to the door to fetch me because the French staff were at lunch. I was undecided whether I should take part in the strike when the ringleader, a veteran qualified engineer from Saxony, entered the debate in a loud voice which brooked no opposition: 'Tell this cretin that if we don't eat we don't work!'

'Ne pas manger, ne pas travailler, Monsieur,' I said in more civilized tones. This had already been made clear to the manager earlier that morning. The manager therefore had to do the loading himself with the purchaser.

The meal hour having ended, the manager appeared and called upon us to work. First he asked nicely and then threatened. The Saxon sprang up and addressed him so brutally that the man left the room trembling. I had no choice but to join the strike and could not attend Madame at the villa. That evening the patron came in his car, parked near our entrance and came in with a basket of piping hot provisions. He appeared to be in good humour and looked surprised to see so many of us lying in our beds. He left whistling, but then the manager came running up to tell him that the prisoners had not worked all day. The mood of the patron changed abruptly and he came back in a rage, with the manager. I drew my blanket over my head for I knew that I would now be the butt of his ire.

'Where is Otto? Where is Otto?' He tore away a few blankets covering men's faces and found me. He ranted and raved, waved his arms and jumped up and down on his short legs in front of my double-tiered bunk.

'Monsieur Genet,' I told him calmly, 'I have not understood, please speak more slowly.' This infuriated him even more and he threatened to send us all back to the camp, where we would certainly see how good we had things here. 'As you wish, Monsieur,' I told him, for camp life had already lost its horrors. He slammed the door and raged at the manager outside, accusing him of not doing enough to force us to work. In the future however he always brought our rations punctually himself on Saturdays and Wednesdays.

In mid-1946 I received a letter from my parents. The first letters we had written as prisoners were not delivered in the Eastern Zone. Only prisoners whose addressees were in the Western Zone received replies. I had exchanged addresses with Resi at Krefeld, and after the war she wrote to my parents asking if they knew my whereabouts, but so far they had received no news. When my first letter got to Resi she told my parents at once. Thus my first letter home as a prisoner went to my parents via Krefeld. Eventually normality returned to the postal system, even in the Russian occupied Zone, and we could correspond directly.

In the autumn of 1946 as it began to get dark earlier, I went one Saturday into town with a fellow inmate. We looked at the cinema posters and saw they were releasing a film involving German soldiers. This was something we really wanted to see and we discussed how we could get in unnoticed. The older hands advised us against it because there could be trouble inside if we were spotted. I did not want to go alone and preferred a small force. Two young colleagues volunteered to accompany me and agreed to the following plan: 'I shall buy the three tickets, go ahead into the auditorium and I shall sit in the middle seat. While the lights are on I shall speak French to you, and you will just reply, 'Oui, oui' or 'Non, non.''

On the Sunday evening clad in civilian dress I bought the tickets.

An usherette showed us to our row and I thanked her politely. Now we were sitting, three PoWs amongst pure Frenchmen and all we wanted to do was see the film. Thus we waited anxiously for the lights to go down. There were a lot of young men in the cinema. We did not know how they would react if they discovered us here. Finally the lights went out and we sank down in our seats in the darkness. The main programme began. The French underground movement took up arms when the invasion began in June 1944 and caused heavy losses to German supply troops. The film portrayed French girls luring officers into a trap where they would be liquidated. It grew noisy around us. The French jumped up and cheered when German soldiers were killed. We shrank down ever smaller. Bridges were blown up and transport trains loaded with panzers and artillery fell into a chasm. The French were out of their seats in celebration, gradually working themselves up into ecstasy. My God, if they recognise us now as German soldiers they will certainly kill us in their hate, I thought.

The men and women of the resistance movement were upstanding and harmless citizens, farmers and factory workers from cities and villages by day. Supplied with weapons and ammunition, radio transmitter/receivers and sabotage material by British aircraft, they became a danger not to be underestimated by the German supply system. I experienced them myself during the invasion but they never sought a confrontation with our reconnaissance vehicles.

In the film, lots of Germans were annihilated by 'The Maquis' to great jubilation and shouts of Bravo! The German officers were too gullible and fell for it in every situation. All these local boys, worked up into a frenzy by the film, needed only a couple of stupid Germans like ourselves, voluntarily watching this garbage, upon whom to work out their hate and rage. We might have Gott mit uns! on our belt buckles, but faith in God never helped us.

Finally it came to an end and we joined the crowd heading for the side exits. A young girl recognised me and said to her mother: 'There's a German in the cinema!' The mother turned round in horror and searched left and right over my shoulders calling 'Where is the German? Where is the German?' The daughter apparently did not like to point out that her mother was facing him directly and we slunk out with the crowd. Probably the daughter did not like her mother's attitude. A number of other persons had taken up the search; perhaps the mother expected us to be in uniform. Once in the open air we took to our heels, and when we could see no cinema-goers we returned slowly to our lodging. We described the film and the reaction of the mob to our colleagues, and decided this would be our first and last visit to a cinema in France.

Chapter Eleven

Thoughts of Escape

In mid-1946 it was rumoured that prisoners of war in the older age groups were to be released. These promises proved false. Frenchmen who had been in German prison camps for five years prophesied: 'We did five years, you do five years.'

Most German soldiers at work in France were prisoners of the Americans and working as slaves 'to repair the ruined French economy and agriculture'. We saw this as the work of years. After work I often used to lie on my sack of straw and contemplate escape. Escape to distant Mecklenburg. Escape from French captivity had to be carefully prepared, for to be caught escaping usually meant a bullet. If not, the punishment would be the day shift in a coal mine or even worse, mine clearing. Untrained men clearing landmines amounted to a death sentence, for any false step meant death or mutilation.

I have to be honest and say that, apart from hunger and thirst, I personally had not suffered actual beatings and torture in captivity. Now, almost two years after the end of the war, nostalgia and homesickness for Mecklenburg became ever stronger and flooded my brain with thoughts of escape. Even today I consider captivity to have been something far worse than performing endless dangerous front line patrols with an armoured reconnaissance unit. At least in the latter one had contact with the homeland, comradeship, and friends. In captivity all that was missing, one was a nobody, felt lost and helpless, and the only person close to oneself was oneself. When old comrades were no longer around, comradeship no longer existed. If somebody spoke the word 'comrade', the chorus would come back: 'The last comrade fell at Stalingrad!' In the military hospital at Andernach I looked after a blind panzer comrade who had lost his sight when his panzer was knocked out. The Americans had put this helpless man in the PoW camp and no comrade bothered about him. He was pushed from pillar to post and who could or would give the man a bit extra from his own starvation rations?

In our work party there was no comradeship or friendship. We were picked out from a big mass of prisoners, formed up into a party and had to adjust to each other's peculiarities of character and age differences. The young men preferred to stick together, while the older men, most with families, found it more difficult to get on with anyone. We had an older colleague from Berlin, father of two, who wanted to distinguish himself through high work output. All the others did not a stroke more than was absolutely necessary to survive captivity with their health intact. One day passers-by drew our attention to a comrade of ours who had fallen between the woodpiles. He was taken away in an ambulance and we never saw him again. It illustrates our indifference to one another.

In the NCOs' camp at the railway goods yard I had become friendly with a colleague and we spent almost every Sunday together. I felt more kindly towards this man than to those in my work party – we were on the same wavelength and had lively discussions about our escape plans.

The first of these would have involved walking through the Vosges. I still had my compass which would have been useful. My friend had relations in Alsace whom he would visit and perhaps they would help us. I do not remember the name of the place where they lived. Then we were warned by other prisoners that Alsace was a no-go for escaping German prisoners of war, even the children there knew the bounty on offer for turning in an escaped German. This bounty had to be paid by the person from whose custody the escape had occurred.

We received a lot of valuable information from escapers who spent a day or two resting at the goods station before moving on. In the big camp nobody noticed a few extra prisoners. Some of these men had made their way right across France, thus providing many details for consideration. At the goods yard there were many opportunities to obtain food and assist comrades on the run with provisions. A lot of wine flowed in the camp and social evenings were common there. The wine was procured by boring through the bottom of the big wine vats on the goods wagons, sealing the hole afterwards with a wooden bung. I also considered stealing the patron's car if it had enough petrol in it, but we had to guarantee ourselves an eight-hour start if we did that. The main problem was getting the car off his property without him noticing.

Our second plan involved getting to Switzerland. We would take the local train to the Swiss border as civilians and then cross on foot. I would buy the tickets and my friend who spoke no French would have to remain mute throughout the journey. Then we were informed by escapers that the Swiss handed German PoWs back to the French.

Our third plan involved a train journey to Strasbourg and crossing the Rhine at Kehl. My friend was not keen on this, and everybody with whom I discussed it considered it too bold. Personally I thought this one had the best chance, but I had to have enough money for a ticket to Strasbourg. Secretly I occupied myself for days with this plan. At the station I tried to study the timetables and remember departure times, where I had to change trains and the price of a ticket. None of my colleagues had any enthusiasm for the idea and I came gradually to the conclusion that a second man would be dead weight and an additional risk.

At the end of November 1946, together with two other prisoners, I had to load railway sleepers at a remote small station. The patron drove us there in his car, no lunch provided, and would collect us that evening. Before leaving he had not told us what the job would be in order to avoid protests. We were no longer so docile as we had been at the beginning of our captivity in France, but would now demand that he returned us to the camp if the work conditions were too demanding or excessive, or the rations inadequate. We also knew he would then get no new prisoners as cheap labour, whom he desperately needed for his business.

In our work party we had a capable young electrician who knew his job. He would often take the patron and manager to task when the work he had to do fell short of the safety regulations. One day the thing got out of hand and our colleague refused to do the job, resulting in two gendarmes being summoned. We feared the worst, but after three days he was back. At the police station he was on a soft number, chopping wood with good food and a clean bed in return. This naturally strengthened our self-confidence and we upped our demands little by little to improve our lot.

But back to my loading railway sleepers; we had to carry the very heavy and wet oak sleepers to two open railway wagons. This work was very demanding and our rations, low in calories, inadequate. Accordingly, we had not finished by evening and our patron cursed us and called us lazy bastards as now he also had to come tomorrow. I had strong words for Monsieur René Genet in his car and pointed out that we wanted additional rations for heavy labour and we also had no lunch. He said he would send us all back to the main camp. I retorted, 'You can try, but we won't be getting out of your car!' Cursing and swearing he set us down at our quarters.

Annoyed at the heavy labour, hunger and the attitude of the patron, I declared to my fellow prisoners, 'I have had enough of it and am leaving.' With looks of disbelief they said 'Don't talk big' and 'How, when and with what will you be going?'

'Tomorrow evening I shall buy a ticket and take a train to freedom!'

'They will collar you before you can blink!'

'Well then, this skinflint of a patron will have to pay out the bounty for me, won't he?' I told them.

Next day we loaded the remaining sleepers and came back a little earlier, which gave me more time to prepare my escape. I advised my colleagues to hide all personal objects, for afterwards there would certainly be a body search and an investigation. Into a cardboard box I packed my black panzer uniform, thermal underwear, singlet, a round loaf and a song book which I would keep to read in the bunker should I be caught. In the crotch of my underpants I sowed my German money, which was still legal tender. I attached my compass by its cord to the waistband of my trousers so that it hung behind my right knee. I looked like a Frenchman in my civilian attire, American trousers with creases, dark lounge jacket, polished shoes, white shirt with black tie and Basque beret, and naturally black hair.

The electrician gave me valuable advice. If I crossed the Rhine at Strasbourg-Kehl, I had to be careful at Appenweier, for there were other lines to Offenburg and also Karlsruhe-Mannheim. Also, if I went to Appenweier I should visit his parents at Schutterwald near Offenburg. Most of my fellow inmates told me: 'They will catch you at Luxeul station and we shall all meet again!' On the far side of the well-lit station was a slope from where they wanted to see how I got on in the dark. I agreed on the condition that not everybody came, and they should keep silent so as not to jeopardise my escape.

Just after seven that evening my train pulled in. I had taken leave of all my party individually beforehand. My departure into an uncertain adventure lay more heavily upon me than I thought it would. But there was no going back, I had to hold firm to my decision and promise.

With a confident stride I walked to the station and bought a ticket to Strasbourg without difficulty and soon I was standing on the platform with a few French people waiting for the next arrival. In the darkness I felt my comrades' eyes on me. Finally the lights of the train approached and I had my first shock. My God, only two coaches! There was nothing for it but to carry on, and I boarded by the first door, finding a place with my back to the driver's communicating door, my box in my arms, the object of interested stares from all the passengers facing me. I felt like a neon sign. Finally, 20 kilometres later, I alighted at Lure.

At Lure there was only a short wait for the express to Belfort, and on the same platform. This train had few passengers and I found an unlit compartment which was not occupied. I entered and sat by the window. Whenever the train stopped all boarding passengers went past, preferring not to share a blacked-out compartment with a lone stranger. My confidence was slowly growing. The only upset was that I had to change again at Belfort.

I alighted and looked for the platform from which the Strasbourg train departed. Here I had another shock, for the wait was three and a half hours. How to pass the time? It was a big station and I joined a crowd waiting for a train. Once it pulled out, the platform emptied and I had to join passengers waiting for another one. This was not a good idea for eventually my presence, wandering from platform to platform, was bound to be noticed. I did not like the idea of a waiting room and selected a toilet cubicle to sit out the time. There were many voices, probably railway workers, in the attendant's room and so I went on to the far end of the Strasbourg platform which was unlit. I found a small signal box in disrepair and got down under a sloping corrugated iron roof. It was cold and drizzling. I had no watch, but could hear the clock on a distant church tower chime every quarter-hour. I worked out the number of chimes I had to count off before the time came to move down the platform. When that moment arrived I strolled to the illuminated section of the platform and joined a quickly swelling crowd of waiting passengers.

When the train pulled in I saw on the destination plate affixed to each carriage 'Berne–Strasbourg–Brussels'. This was an international run from Switzerland to Belgium and my heart fell. Did my ticket allow me to travel on this train? I had paid no express supplement as was usual in Germany. I weighed up the pros and cons feverishly, then decided to chance it and boarded.

The train was packed. All compartments were occupied by many passengers and French military filling the corridors, probably more military than civilians. Some of the passengers were sitting on their bags in the corridor and I found a spot at the end of it to do the same. I pretended to sleep with my head in my hands but remained fully alert, wound up like a clock. The train stopped at Mulhouse and I had to stand to allow passengers to enter or alight. When the train moved off I resumed my seat on my cardboard box of clothing.

After the stop at Colmar the conductor came to check the tickets, looked at mine and returned it, mentioning the time of arrival at Strasbourg. We got there long after midnight and, after passing through the ticket barrier, stood in the station courtyard. My problem was now to get from here to Kehl. I followed some passengers a short way until spotting a French military patrol, one officer and two men, at which I turned away and spent the hours until light sitting on my cardboard box in a derelict house.

Frozen to the core, when day broke I returned to the station courtyard where I would be less conspicuous amongst all the comings and goings. At the tram terminus I discovered which line ran to the river bank opposite Kehl, the departure times and a plan of the tram routes. I could have taken a tram there for I had enough francs, but considered it less dangerous to follow the tram rails. Once I set out I found that the route plan had been torn off at every tram stop, and at the major interchange point the tracks branched. I chose to follow the stretch leading east. I was befriended by a homeless dog, which I thought was good camouflage, and passed a group of twelve to fourteen German prisoners marching in two ranks.

At the terminus of the tram line I had chosen the houses and the street ended at a field. There was nothing to be seen either of the Rhine or Kehl. This meant I had to return to Strasbourg. I could not ask anybody the way because my poor command of French could betray me. The dog abandoned me, and when I got to the inter-change point again I passed another group of about twenty German prisoners. In a narrow street of businesses near Strasbourg cathedral I noticed a large street plan of the city hung as a decoration on a shop wall. I could not stand long before it, and passed the shop on several occasions attempting to commit the eastern track to memory. Apparently Schwarzwalder-Strasse led directly to the bridge for Kehl, and I set off again.

At the tram interchange point I could not find Schwarzwalder-Strasse because the French had renamed all the streets and so I had to go back to the street map in the shop. On the way I rested on a park bench and ate half of my round loaf. This was difficult because I had nothing to drink, not even water. Continuing to the cathedral I found the shop with the street plan again and now I saw what street I should take to reach the Rhine opposite Kehl.

In the afternoon I reached the terminus for Kehl, and hid my parcel in bushes because it was dangerous to be seen with it so close to the Rhine. I surveyed the area. There was a railway bridge and a footbridge over the Rhine to Kehl. Civilians crossed the bridge without passing a control point. I saw some German prisoners walking near the wooden bridge but under guard. Walking back to the houses a lone PoW overtook me.

'Tell me, is the bridge watched?' I asked.

'Are you a prisoner?' In response I nodded.

'On the Kehl side. Take care, only yesterday they brought back two men in chains.'

'Enough,' I said, and left him. He went into a tobacco shop and I decided to make myself scarce.

I took a closer look at the railway bridge which crossed to Kehl a bit further down the Rhine. The rails ran along a high embankment. I saw two French sentries armed with rifles. Presumably there would be more on the German side. Therefore I could not cross the railway bridge on foot. Returning to the wooden bridge all was quiet and I assumed that PoW with whom I had spoken had not reported me. Men and women crossed the wooden bridge in groups without producing their papers. I attached myself to a large group and had almost got across unnoticed when I saw the checkpoint on the Kehl side and had to turn back, mingling with a returning group. I did consider crossing the wooden bridge hand over hand below the supports, but finally favoured concealing myself on a goods train. Unfortunately during all the time I had been here I had not seen any goods trains pass in either direction.

Upon reflection I saw that my escape had been impulsive and not properly planned beforehand. The principal complications were my lack of food – I had one round loaf which I had portioned off into rations – and my failure to consider my need for water. I should also have obtained much better information about Strasbourg and Kehl beyond ascertaining where they were on the map.

It was the beginning of December 1946 and it got dark early. In the bushes where I had hidden my parcel I put on my black panzer uniform over my civilian suit, ate some bread and tried to sleep. I woke up freezing, wrapped the remains of my bread in a towel and, leaving the parcel and its contents behind, headed for the embankment. The permanent way was brightly lit and so I hid in the shadows in my black uniform. After what seemed like an age I heard a train coming up from Strasbourg. I secured my bread in a sling over my upper arm so as not to lose it when I jumped on the train. It was a goods train, and once the locomotive had passed I got over the signal wires but found it was going too fast to attempt a jump. I gave up and went quickly back into the darkness for fear of the two sentries 200 metres down the line.

A locomotive came from the Kehl side and stopped close by me. I crawled to the upper edge of the embankment and watched it blowing off steam. The driver and fireman were in conversation but I could not make out in what language. After about two hours the locomotive went back over the bridge to Kehl. Long after midnight I heard the whistle of an approaching train. The locomotive passed me, I jumped over the signal wires, ran a few steps in its direction of travel and caught the grab-handles of the brake-van. The nearest wagon had a tarpaulin cover, I got over the buffers and slipped below it, working my way across pipes and iron bars to some wooden crates, where I hid myself facing forwards. After a while the train slowed and appeared to enter a station yard. The wagon had got colder during the short journey over the Rhine and I was trembling with the cold. I also had a pain in my left hip after colliding with some of the load while jumping aboard the wagon.

I heard footsteps on the gravel and voices. The tarpaulin was opened on one side and a light shone inside. The footsteps went away only to re-appear on the other side of the wagon to repeat the operation. In my crate I escaped detection. Finally, after a long wait the train set off again. I was in Germany, limbs trembling with cold and the bitter wind of the transit. But what was that compared to the feeling of being back in one's native land after so long as a prisoner? After a while the goods train came to a stop. Frozen as I was I crept forward and surveyed the situation from beneath the tarpaulin. Because of the numerous cross-tracks it seemed we must be in a large marshalling yard. I got out and walked across the rails to a street where men were cycling to work. A street sign told me that I was in Appenweier. I stopped a cyclist and asked the best way to Schutterwald. 'Take the train to Offenburg and from there it is not far,' he told me. Off the street and in darkness I took off my panzer uniform, dropped my American trousers and underpants down and retrieved my German money, still legal tender, from the crotch.

At Appenweiler station I bought a ticket to Offenburg. In the train I heard some girls in the next compartment singing *Wenn auf Capri die rote Sonne im Meer versinkt* (When the red sun sinks into the sea at Capri). I knew all the wartime hits, as well as those from pre-war, but this one was new to me. It was a wonderful experience to hear those girls' voices in the homeland. Whenever I heard this song sung in the future it always reminded me of the railway journey from Appenweiler to Offenburg.

At Offenburg I asked the way to Schutterwald and was given a very warm welcome by the parents of my PoW electrician friend. They had a small farm and so I had my first good meal since my escape. I got a clean bed and at the weekend everything went into the washtub. On the Sunday I went along to a baptism. This meant going to Offenburg and from there to a village in the Black Forest. I was given an endless supply of food and wine as a soldier returning home. On the way back to Schutterwald the parents walked ahead and I followed with the daughter. I was very worried about being stopped by a military patrol in Offenburg and having no papers but the daughter reassured me: 'We will explain that we are a courting couple following our parents.'

I spent a good week there and with plentiful rations set out for Appenweiler to jump a goods train into the American zone. The parents of my PoW friend told me to come back should I not be able to get away from Appenweiler. I spent the night freezing in the brake compartment of a railway wagon in a snowdrift in a siding. Two railwaymen were working there. At daybreak one left and, having deposited my pack on the low wall, I went down the steps and opened the door. The other man was seated at the far end of the narrow room and I asked him politely when the next train left for Karlsruhe or Mannheim.

'Are you a prisoner of war?' he asked. 'Yes,' I replied. At that he jumped up and shouted: 'A prisoner of war! Get him! Get him!' In shock I slammed the door from the outside, ran up the steps, grabbed my pack and sprinted over the rails to the street. My God, what sort of country had this been turned into, where one could not trust a fellow German not to turn you in? I had been told at the baptism that many escaped prisoners of war were betrayed to the French and shipped back to France. Now I had to be doubly cautious and avoid the marshalling yard in particular.

I decided to go back to Offenburg to pass the day and return to Appenweiler when it got dark in the hope of jumping a goods train. Otherwise I had no plan. I saw a three-man French military patrol approaching and crossed the road to avoid it. Then I saw another one and realised I had to get off the streets. I went to the nearest barber shop. It was fairly full and I spent a long time there wasting time in the warm. I had concluded I should speak only to young men of my own age who were also soldiers. The door opened and two youths fitting the bill entered and occupied two vacant chairs. I eavesdropped their conversation and heard them discussing a refugee camp. I plucked up courage and asked the youth closer to me how I could get to the American Zone.

'Where have you come from?' he asked softly.

'From France.'

'Prisoner of war?' I nodded and he spoke with his companion before telling me, 'We are in a refugee camp as refugees, when we've all had a haircut you can come with us.' We left the barber's shop together and now they wanted to know about my military service and captivity, then where I wanted to go.

'To Krefeld in the British zone and from there to Hamburg and onwards into the Eastern Zone,' I replied. They took me into the refugee camp and in their room told me that they had been Waffen-SS and I need have no more worries, they would give me full instructions on what had to be done to be transferred to the British zone as a refugee.

First, I saw their camp director and told him my whole story. He could do nothing for me but sent me to the camp manager. This involved queuing. Seats were provided in queue order and one moved forward from seat to seat. I had informed the female secretary of my situation and she put me last of those to be seen. I repeated half my life story to the camp manager, where I had come from and where I wanted to go. Finally, he asked if I had a photo of myself in civilian dress. I produced one taken in France. 'Good, this will do! Now listen to me carefully. Take this photo to the ID office, but you will have to hurry because they close at one. They will give you a transfer form as a refugee to Krefeld.' He told me how to get there and added, 'Do not get caught by a patrol under any circumstances. If you do, you do not know us and have never seen us.' He added that German citizens who helped PoWs escaping from France were taken off for forced labour in the mines. I swore myself to silence. I arrived at the ID office through the back streets. The lady clerk there seemed to know all about me. I got an ID document (a sheet of A4 paper with my name and attached photo). It had a nice stamp at the bottom and I was now a refugee in process of transfer from Offenburg to Krefeld. I did not have much faith in this document which seemed very flimsy on information.

I returned to the refugee camp where my two ex-SS friends had arranged lunch for me.

'Are you Protestant or Catholic?' I was asked.

'Protestant.'

'Then go to a vicar and collect five marks for the journey. Catholics get ten marks.'

I collected the five marks handout and so now officially I was no longer a soldier or PoW but simply a refugee with a document and stamp. I spent the night at the camp and left at midday, thanking my friends and heading for the station. In the big waiting room there was a crowd of German prisoners of war in their dark-dyed uniforms, returning from the United States, all waiting for a connection. I sat amongst them and we were soon discussing American PoW camps. Suddenly the door opened and a French military patrol appeared. Two of them guarded the door to prevent anybody leaving while the officer checked the discharge papers of all the former American prisoners. As a civilian he ignored me. They were heading for Karlsruhe and Mannheim. The train stopped at Mannheim and we all had to alight. We went down a tunnel under the tracks at the end of which were American soldiers with rifles. The tunnel was cordoned with ropes and everybody had to pass through two barriers. Many women were there with bags and rucksacks. They had tried to slip through with contraband and been sent back by the MPs at the second barrier. Some travellers turned around on seeing this and tried to go back up the steps, fearing for their contraband. I also wanted to avoid the control for I had no knowledge how the Americans would view my document. There was no way to avoid it, however, and after tarrying in the hope that they would lift the barriers and leave, I decided I had to go through with it. The MP inspected my refugee paper, looked me in the eyes and then spent a long time flicking through a thick Wanted Persons file. Then he said, 'OK'.

I wasted a few hours on Mannheim station before the Krefeld train arrived. It was already dark and so I went to a tavern. Over a beer I got into conversation with two repatriated crewmen from the 'pocket battleship' *Admiral Graf Spee*, scuttled in the River Plate in December 1939. They described how good it was in Argentina and they wanted to emigrate there now that they had seen the ruins of the homeland. [The Argentine Government encouraged *Admiral Graf Spee* men to apply for immigration into Argentina, and from 1947 onwards about half the crew accepted and returned. Tr.]

On Saturday 7 December 1946 I alighted at Krefeld and at midday arrived at the Holterhöfte home of my female pen friend Resi, who had maintained the correspondence with my parents while I was a

PoW. She was sitting with a young man on the veranda and was surprised to see me appear suddenly without forewarning. The family received me with open arms. Later I learned that the young man was Resi's boyfriend, a student whose father was a director at a steelworks. I saw that as a returnee with no prospects there was no chance for me.

I wanted to leave for Hamburg next day but Resi's mother insisted I recover fully first in the bosom of that large, hospitable family. The father was then in Holland, the eldest daughter a nurse at Krefeld – she had been engaged to a Luftwaffe officer who fell in Russia. A son of the family had been a prisoner of the British but was now home. Two other daughters were at a convent: I never knew them. Another son was training to be a businessman in Krefeld and the youngest daughter was not yet out of school. (I describe this family in detail because in the immediate post-war period, despite their worries and needs, they were still prepared to help out and put me up for several days at their house.)

I got on well with the ex-PoW brother and he took me to the Residents' Office at Willich with my refugee papers to exchange them for a proper ID. This was achieved without serious complications and thus I lost my refugee status and became a citizen of West Germany with an officially recognised document. I sent my parents a telegram: 'Am with Resi – arrival shortly.' Resi took me to see an ice-hockey game and I also saw my first political demonstration in the streets. It was a silent protest but what it was for I no longer remember.

On the day before I intended to depart Resi's mother said I should cycle to the farm at Fellerhöfe where I had once had quarters. Perhaps the lady of the house would give me something for my journey. I went unwillingly, for it seemed to me like begging. The farmer's wife recognised me, but had little to spare. In life it does happen unfortunately that those who have are loath to give. Perhaps there I am being unjust, for after the war many came begging to the farms.

On Friday 13 December 1945 Resi took me to the station for my next stage to Hamburg. I had much for which to thank her and her family, for she restored the contacts to my parents and also to myself in France. We kept in touch for a long time but unfortunately the division of Germany into two parts sundered the contact with this kind family.

Late that evening I left Hamburg main station for Norderstedt where my uncle Ewald lived. He had also been a soldier. His family had been bombed out in Hamburg and now lived in a summer house. I arrived at Norderstedt very late in the evening. It was bitterly cold. After asking many people the way, a girl who knew the street and lived nearby accompanied me there. It was quite a walk and we fell into conversation. I told her my story and where I was heading. She suggested that I could look to see in the morning if my uncle lived at that address; her parents would give me a bed for the night. This was a good idea, but I did not want to be a burden to strangers so close to my goal. After another fifteen minutes' walk I saw the garden number and the name 'Ewald Henning' on the name plate. The summer house, built in the style of a bungalow, was in darkness. I knocked on a window, my uncle awoke and engaged in a question and answer session until he realised who I was. At ten-thirty that night he let me in. My aunt and her small niece were with relations in Hamburg. We fetched them next day and on the Sunday I met the family of another aunt who had also been bombed out. The families were very opposed to my going to the Russian Zone because many former soldiers were sent off to Siberia from there. My uncle contacted a friend so that I could resume the trade in which I had been apprenticed. I sent my parents a second telegram: 'Am with Ewald. Coming as soon as possible'.

The family council could not dissuade me from my plan to go to the Eastern Zone. I had got to Hamburg, now I wanted to finish the last stage and get home. If it was intolerable in the Russian Zone I could always come back. On Saturday 21 December 1946 I set out for Lübeck on the last stage of my odyssey. I could not find a way to cross the frontier between the two zones without danger, and after a night in a cold air raid bunker I set out next day to discover how the Russians guarded the frontier. To be a prisoner of the Russians was every German soldier's nightmare and I had no wish to continue my captivity in Siberia.

In Lübeck I got to know a group who had come from the East and were returning that night. Because of the cold I wore my panzer uniform over my civilian clothing, put the remainder of my bread in my trouser pockets and was now the owner of only what I stood up in. The group was aiming to cross the Wakenitz over a bridge at St Hubertus or Gross Grönau south of Lübeck. There were sentries on the far side. It was very cold and my whole body shivered. Suddenly figures came running over the bridge shouting 'The sentries have gone!' At that they all ran off, I followed but caught my foot in a gap on the bridge planking. Once I got free I limped on, but the group had moved up a gear to a sprint to get clear of the immediate vicinity of the border zone. Once on land I kept going east, happy to be alone again since it seemed better than 'safety in numbers'.

Lacking a map or local knowledge I was quite lost and so hoped to find a haystack or barn to spend the night. Following a path, I found a primitive signpost at a fork. In the darkness I had to climb the post and light a match to read the characters. They were Russian. Therefore the way to which it pointed was not for me and I kept on the path to the north, but more cautiously and with an uneasy feeling. After a while I came to some houses and, after assuring myself that no Russians were billeted there I spoke to three civilians talking in the street. I asked how to get to the Lübeck–Bad Kleinen railway line and they showed me the way.

It was a three-kilometre walk. I mounted the embankment to find only a single track when there should have been two. I knew the line since childhood, and it had always had traffic in both directions, as it did when I travelled it as a soldier. Thinking I must have gone astray somewhere I walked back, but finding the civilians gone I tapped on a window pane. A voice asked what I wanted.

'There is only one track on the embankment and there should be two.'

'Man, where have you come from? The Russians took the second track away.'

I returned to the embankment thinking the situation must be catastrophic if the Russians needed to take up half the railway lines. Now I saw clearly on the embankment the sleepers with missing track. I set out towards the east walking along the sleepers, but this was difficult because they were laid shorter than a comfortable stride. Some dark figures came towards me and asked if I had come from the west and where I crossed the border. I told them what I knew but could not be precise about which bridge I had used to cross the Wakenitz.

Shortly before Schönberg station I detoured off railway property to avoid the possibility of awkward questions, then continued along the tracks to my home town of Grevesmühlen. There were many infantry trenches near the railway line and I continued through the bushes at one side of the embankment. I followed a country path to my parents' house where early on the morning of 23 December 1946 I tapped on the window. They threw open the door and exclaimed 'We were expecting you every day!' Thus did my military service and captivity come to a happy end. I had begun in the desert of North Africa at the age of seventeen and finished the war at age twenty-two, and I was never wounded.

Next day my father retrieved my watch from the lampshade where he had secreted it against possible looting by the Russians. Once 1947 dawned I went to the town hall to obtain my personal ID for the Eastern Zone. I met a school friend there and we discussed our time in the military. In passing he asked if I had been in a quarantine camp. I had never heard of such a thing and he explained that all persons arriving in the Soviet zone had first of all to go into quarantine. Ah, now I remembered being in a quarantine camp. This resolved all difficult questions and I received my ID for the Eastern Zone. Now I possessed an official ID issued by both the Western and Eastern Powers and had to decide which side offered me the better prospects. In my heart I leaned more to West Germany but my family and its property were decisive, and I opted for East Germany where I had my roots.